A gift for: [9-8 2012]
윤성오빠.

From: Grace

윤섭 오빠를 만나게 해주신 하나님께 감사드려요.
Everyday에 꾸준히 나아가는 삶에
전공이나다 도움이 되길 기도합니다.

P.S : 영어공부도 될껌~ ^^

RIGHT
from the
HEART

Turning Your Day Toward God

Bryant Wright

A Division of Thomas Nelson Publishers
Since 1798

Published in Nashville, Tennessee, by Thomas Nelson. Thomas Nelson is a trademark of Thomas Nelson, Inc.

Thomas Nelson, Inc., titles may be purchased in bulk for educational, business, fund-raising, or sales promotional use. For information, please e-mail SpecialMarkets@ThomasNelson.com.

Grateful acknowledgment is made to the following for permission to reprint previously published material: The quote from Norman L. Geisler on page 179 was taken from *Decision* magazine, July/August; ©2006 Billy Graham Evangelistic Association; used by permission, all rights reserved. The quote from Ronald Reagan on page 182 was taken from *Dutch: A Memoir of Ronald Reagan*, ©1999 by Edmund Morris (New York: Random House, 1999), used by permission, all rights reserved.

Unless otherwise indicated, Scripture quotations are taken from the *New American Standard Bible* , © The Lockman Foundation 1960, 1962, 1963, 1968, 1971, 1972, 1973, 1975, 1977, 1995. Used by permission.

Other Scripture references are taken from the following sources: *The English Standard Version* (esv). © 2001 by Crossway Bibles, a division of Good News Publishers; *God's Word* (gw), © 1995 God's Word to the Nations. Used by permission of Baker Publishing Group; *King James Version* (kjv); *The Message* (msg) by Eugene H. Peterson. © 1993, 1994, 1995, 1996, 2000. Used by permission of NavPress Publishing Group. All rights reserved; *New Century Version* (ncv). © 2005 by Thomas Nelson, Inc. Used by permission. All rights reserved; *Holy Bible: New International Version* (niv). © 1973, 1978, 1984 by International Bible Society. Used by permission of Zondervan Publishing House. All rights reserved; *The New King James Version* (nkjv). © 1982 by Thomas Nelson, Inc. Used by permission. All rights reserved; *Holy Bible, New Living Translation* (nlt). © 1996. Used by permission of Tyndale House Publishers, Inc., Wheaton, Illinois 60189. All rights reserved.

Designed by Lori Lynch

Library of Congress Cataloging-in-Publication Data

Wright, Bryant.
 Right from the heart : turning your day toward God / Bryant Wright.
   p. cm.
 ISBN 978-1-4041-9002-3 (hardcover)
 1. Devotional calendars. I. Title.
 BV4811.W683 2011
 242'.2—dc22   2011005860

Printed in China
11 12 13 14 RRD 5 4 3 2 1

To the staff and supporters of Right from the Heart Ministries and those who take part through radio, television, and the Internet. It's for you that the ministry exists.

Introduction

Fitness is a big part of my life. However, the longer I live, the more I realize that exercise doesn't go well without warming up. The muscles need to stretch. The blood needs to flow. Warming up is the key to having a quality workout.

And fitness has to be regular—a discipline to do something our bodies need us to do but we never really have time to do. We have to make time regularly, especially on those days when we are not in the mood, our energy is sagging, and we just don't want to work out. Those are the days when discipline is most important and most necessary to stay fit.

One of the key aspects of spiritual fitness is regular time alone with God. Like physical fitness, it's something we never have time for, can always put off, and seem to find most difficult when we are not in the mood. But regular time alone with God is essential in getting to know Him.

And like a fitness workout, I need a spiritual warm-up. For me, that spiritual warm-up is found in devotional books that get my spiritual thoughts flowing and help me focus on God and be ready to talk to Him and listen to Him through His Word.

I hope these daily devotionals will be your spiritual warm-ups over the next year. I hope and pray they will be used by the Lord to draw you to Him and give you a hunger to know Him, to trust

Him, to worship Him, and to follow Him. Most of all, I hope they will help you connect with God through His Son, Jesus.

I wrote these devotionals with two groups of people in mind:

1. *Those who are not connected to God.* Hopefully these daily readings will help you begin a relationship with Him and see that faith in God really makes sense and that Jesus is who He says He is. I hope these thoughts give you a desire to know Him. I really think you'll like Him.
2. *Those who already know God and His Son.* These words are food for thought that can strengthen your faith and enlighten your thinking.

For both groups, I hope these thoughts will help you understand the world we live in through a biblical lens—to see things from God's perspective.

I'd like to make a couple of requests:

1. Read just one a day. They are short and easy to understand. You may be tempted to read ahead. Don't do it. Just one a day so you'll have some fresh food for thought to get your spiritual juices flowing each day.
2. Nothing in this book is a substitute for talking with God and listening to Him through His Word. I hope these thoughts will draw you to the Lord. But remember, God is the One you will need to hear from. His Word has all the wisdom and enlightenment you need. And most of all, God's Word reveals to us the way to salvation and abundant, eternal life, to make our journey meaningful as we walk down the road of life.

January

Do not call to mind the former things, or ponder things of the past. Behold, I will do something new, now it will spring forth; will you not be aware of it?

Isaiah 43:18–19

The New Year

*Therefore if anyone is in Christ, he is a
new creature; the old things passed
away; behold, new things have come.*

2 CORINTHIANS 5:17

So what is so special about a new year? Maybe it is this: Once a Wednesday is gone, another pops up seven days later. We'll see a December every year, and as much as we'll miss the spring, we can take comfort in the fact that we'll see another one the next year, and the next, and the one after that. But it doesn't work that way with years. Once this calendar year expires, it's gone. Days, months, seasons, and holidays will all eventually return, but once this year is over, it's over.

Maybe that is why we tend to schedule our resolutions for change at the beginning of each new year. The year is gone—maybe bad habits will be too. Yet real change requires so much more than a New Year's resolution.

It's tough to break established habits, but remember that there is hope for the person who sincerely desires change. The power for real change is in admitting that we are helpless to do it on our own. Lasting change requires the help of the Lord.

The Bible says that if anyone is in Christ, he or she is a new creation. Christ transforms us when we give our lives to Him. He changes us from the inside out. He gives us an "inner want-to" to please Him. Now that's a change for the better. And it's a change that can truly last.

The Path You Choose

You have made known to me the path of life; you will fill me with joy in your presence, with eternal pleasures at your right hand.

The story is told of two teenagers living in a small village where most made their livings either as shepherds or in other occupations related to sheep. One day they decided to steal a few sheep and sell them—but they got caught! To make an example of the wayward boys, the village elders branded their foreheads with the letters *ST*. This visible reminder of their shame would forever warn others what happens to "Sheep Thieves."

One boy became bitter. His life spiraled progressively downward until the day he fell to his death during a drunken rage. But the other young man confessed his sin, got right with the Lord, and built a life of integrity and service that eventually brought him great respect throughout that little village.

Many years later, the now-elderly man passed a father and his son along the road. The boy asked his dad why the old man had the letters *ST* on his forehead. The father thought for a moment, then replied, "Something happened years ago, but I just can't remember what it was. But knowing the man that he is, I guess it just stands for *Saint!*"

That's what the power of Jesus can do in an individual life— supernaturally transform a sinner into a saint. No matter what your past, Jesus can cleanse you and put you on a path of great value to Him and to others.

What Lurks in the Dark?

*You light my lamp; the L*ORD *my God
illumines my darkness.*

PSALM 18:28

She had been driven crazy by her energetic children and just needed to get away, if even for only a moment. She ran upstairs to her daughter's bedroom and closed the closet door behind her. And there, in the solitude of the dark closet, she cleansed her mind by letting out a long, loud scream. She immediately felt better and opened the door to leave. But blocking her exit, with eyes the size of saucers, were her three children. Her four-year-old daughter spoke first: "Mommy, I told you there were monsters in there."

The truth is, both children *and* adults fear the "dark"—the unknown—and our fears are intensified when we cannot see what is really before us. Listen to these words from the psalmist: "Where can I go from your Spirit? Where can I flee from your presence? If I go up to the heavens, you are there; if I make my bed in the depths, you are there. If I rise on the wings of the dawn, if I settle on the far side of the sea, even there your hand will guide me, your right hand will hold me fast" (Psalm 139:7–10 NIV).

Like a loving father, God promises us He'll *always* be with us. He's there to offer us His hand in life's darkest hours. He'll carry us through the darkness and lead us where we need to go. And He'll be with us forever.

First, Your Sword

Submit yourselves, then, to God. Resist the devil, and he will flee from you. Come near to God and he will come near to you. Wash your hands, you sinners, and purify your hearts, you double-minded.

Britain claims no greater naval hero than Lord Horatio Nelson, the British admiral from the eighteenth century. Although best known for his brilliance and dedication to his duties, Lord Nelson was also noted for his courtesy and kindness toward those he defeated. On one occasion, a defeated admiral strode across the deck to meet Lord Nelson. With a sword at his side, the bested admiral put his hand out in surrender. Lord Nelson looked at him but did not immediately shake his hand. Instead he nodded and said, "Your sword first, then your hand."

What our heavenly Father does is greater. He wants to give us the gift of grace and provision, and He wants us to enjoy the love of Jesus Christ. So first He extends His hand. Then He demands that we submit our swords and any area of self-reliance in our lives to Him. We are to give Him our hearts and our wills first. Accept the hand of the Lord by submitting to the lordship of Jesus and you will immediately be blessed with all that He has to offer—like kindness that knows no bounds.

Involved Versus Committed

*They gave themselves first to the Lord and then
to us in keeping with God's will.*

2 CORINTHIANS 8:5 NIV

A pig and a chicken took an afternoon stroll that led them near their neighborhood Waffle House. They looked up at a sign in the window that advertised the daily special—Ham and Eggs for only $3.99.

"Look at that!" said the chicken. "I am involved!"

"You may be involved," replied the pig, "but for me, it's total commitment."

Lou Holtz, the famous football coach for several great schools, said of one of his teams, "They remind me of a kamikaze pilot who flew fifty missions. He was involved but not committed!"[1] On a team, in the office, there are lots of folks who are involved but not many who are totally committed to the success of the team.

In church, to just be involved and not committed is a testimony of a lack of commitment to Jesus Christ. As people drift away from church in record numbers and still claim commitment to Christ, they are simply delusional. We don't love Jesus if we don't love His bride, the church. Now more than ever, Jesus longs for His followers not just to be involved but also to be committed to Him by being committed to His church.

Get into a Routine of Prayer

In the early morning, while it was still dark, Jesus got up, left the house, and went away to a secluded place, and was praying there.

The new year is young, and if you've never been consistent in spending time in conversation with God, there's no time like the present to start.

1. *Pick a regular place to pray.* You may have a quiet spot in your home where you could meet with God each day, or perhaps it would work better to get to the office early and close the door. If you travel a lot, you may have more trouble finding a routine place. But what could be more private than a hotel room? Each person has a different place that feels right, but the important thing is to find one that works for you.

2. *Pick a plan.* It's good to set a routine so you can flow right into it and not have to reinvent the wheel each time. Perhaps you can start with a devotional reading that whets your spiritual appetite. Then read from the Bible, reflect on the words, and think about God. Finally, begin to pray. If you're not sure what to say, look at Jesus' model prayer, not to recite but to remind you what to include in your prayers. And then just listen for the voice and inspiration of the Holy Spirit.

You can use different places and routines to develop a healthy prayer life. Find what works for you, and begin enjoying the blessing you will receive by being alone with God.

Overwhelmingly Conquer!

What then shall we say to these things?
If God is for us, who is against us?

ROMANS 8:31

I have always been inspired by people who have faced great setbacks in their lives, yet fought hard and achieved amazing comebacks. There is a long list of people who have done this: both real and fictional, secular as well as biblical, from centuries past to recent days.

I have tremendous news for you. Comebacks are not just for people you read about in the history books or the latest edition of a weekly periodical. The power to bounce back is available to all. God is in the business of turning *your* setbacks into comebacks! Note what God's Word promises the Christian in Romans 8:37: "But in all these things we overwhelmingly conquer through Him who loved us."

Realize that God doesn't say, "Well, I'll arrange things so you can just squeak by!" Neither does He say, "I'll arrange your life so you can just barely endure." No! He says, "In *all* things, you will overwhelmingly conquer!" We don't just *conquer*; we *overwhelmingly* conquer, through the power of our Lord and Savior Jesus Christ. And it is this amazing power—the power of the Creator of the universe—that will help you not to give up but instead to keep on keeping on so you can turn your setback into an overwhelming victory. May that victory be for the glory of God!

Making the Most of Your Time

Be careful how you walk, not as unwise men but as wise, making the most of your time.

EPHESIANS 5:15–16

Do you ever struggle with making the most of your time? Do you feel as though there's just not *enough* time in each day? Well, we have to remember that we all have the same amount of time: 168 hours a week, 24 hours a day. The key is *making the most* of our time. This is a spiritual as well as practical issue.

Today's scripture says, "Be careful how you walk, not as unwise men but as wise, making the most of your time." So how do you do that?

List the top three to five priorities in your life. This list will help you plan your activities so you can spend your time wisely. Concentrate on what's most important, and major on the majors.

Now, as you approach each day, make a list of things you need to accomplish, and prioritize what is on that list. Begin by writing down the most important thing you need to do, and commit to doing it. Then go to the second most important thing, and do it. It sure feels good to have checked off completion of those tasks at the end of each day.

Effective time management is an important discipline to have to live a successful life. So get with it—before you run out of time.

The Best Way to Be a Good Parent

However, each one of you also must love his wife as he loves himself, and the wife must respect her husband.

EPHESIANS 5:33 NIV

Mom and Dad, the best way to be good parents is for the two of you to love and respect *each other*. Nothing gives a child greater security. When love and respect are modeled in front of the child on a daily basis, he or she grows to understand how God wants family members to relate to one another. The child feels secure in the home and is emotionally able to receive instruction, wisdom, and discipline from his or her parents.

If you are divorced, you may be thinking, *Well, that leaves me out of the process.* Actually, there is an even greater message for divorced parents. Seek to *never* tear down your ex in front of your child. You may feel that the comments are fully justified, but your criticism crushes the spirit of that child. That's because a child's identity is wrapped up in both Mom and Dad. Remember, when you criticize your ex-spouse in front of your child, you are actually criticizing half of your child.

The best thing Mom and Dad can do is to love and respect each other. But if love is gone, then it's even more important that the child witness Mom and Dad demonstrating respect for each other. Nothing is more important in being a good parent.

Where Is Your Strength?

The LORD is my strength and my shield; my heart
trusts in him, and I am helped.

PSALM 28:7 NIV

He had not spoken with her since high school and was enjoying their impromptu reunion. She had been his favorite teacher, and her impact went far beyond the facts and information she had taught. It was also in the character she had role-modeled.

He proudly told her of the things he had accomplished and of his family. "How's Millie?" he then asked, referring to her energetic, always-smiling eight-year-old daughter, whom he had often seen playing in the classroom after school. The teacher's eyes suddenly became sad and misty as she told him that Millie had died a few years earlier. "She had an unexpected and unexplained heart attack when she was twenty-three."

"I don't know how it is possible to handle that," the man responded. "I could never have the strength to handle the death of my child."

Then his former teacher presented him with one more bit of wisdom. "I've discovered that sometimes God does not give us the strength we need until we need it," she said. "But then, when you do need it, you can always count on His providing it."

Do you believe that? Will you choose to believe that? When the need comes, God will meet the need. Not before it comes, but when it comes. God doesn't promise to meet tomorrow's need today. He promises to meet today's need today.

Just How Big Was That Cross?

He Himself bore our sins in His body on the cross,
so that we might die to sin and live to righteousness;
for by His wounds you were healed.

1 PETER 2:24

We Christians have a pretty good track record of condemning sins, particularly those in which we are not currently participating. But condemnation is not our real mission. In fact, God demands that we embrace the spirit of Jesus. Although we are to hate sin, we are to love the sinner.

Anyone who is a sinner (which is all of us) can take great comfort in this fact: the gospel clearly states that Christ paid the penalty for your sins. Anyone who confesses and repents of his or her sins will receive forgiveness and salvation. Recognize that Christ did not die just for certain sins, or "little" sins, as we sometimes like to say, but for all sins. Never fear that your life has been so sinful or that your sins are so very horrid that you are beyond the power of the cross. And certainly never declare that other people are so sinful that they are beyond forgiveness. The cross of Jesus Christ is stronger than any sin!

Yes, we Christians must take a firm stand against sin. But we completely fail in our duties if we do not pair this condemnation of sin with the proclamation that the cross of Christ is big enough to forgive any sin.

Praying for Daily Needs

"Give us today our daily bread."

MATTHEW 6:11 NIV

A man was late for a job interview because he couldn't find any place to park. As he circled the block one more time, he cried out, "Please, God. This interview is so important. If you will provide a parking space, I'll be on the front row at church every week!" Just as he spoke those words, a space opened up, right in front of him. "Oh, never mind," he said. "I found one."

Perhaps this man exemplifies the extent of many of our prayer lives. Yet doesn't the Lord's Prayer tell us to pray for our *daily* needs? Yes, but one of the ways prayer can disappoint us is when we confuse needs and wants. We get so wrapped up in praying for our *wants* that we tend to see God as somebody we can use to get what we want! And that's a terrible misunderstanding of prayer and of God.

Is God going to give us everything we ask for? Absolutely not! Loving parents don't give their children everything they see in a toy store, and likewise God is not some genie saying, "Your wish is My command." God wants us to seek His will—not ours. Then we begin to learn our needs versus our wants. When we do, we can knock on the door of heaven and see God pour forth blessings to meet the daily needs of our lives.

Where to Start

*Be diligent to present yourself approved to God as
a workman who does not need to be ashamed,
accurately handling the word of truth.*

2 TIMOTHY 2:15

If you're new to Bible study, begin studying in the New Testament. The Bible is a unique book. It's best not to begin at the beginning, but in the middle, with the story of Jesus. We can't really understand the Old Testament until we first understand Him.

Jesus initiated the new covenant (New Testament) when He observed the Lord's Supper the night before His crucifixion. But the old covenant (Old Testament) all points to Him. It has thirty-nine books; the first five are called the Torah (books of Mosaic law and the origins of the human race and the nation of Israel). The next twelve are called the Historical Books, telling about the history of ancient Israel. After that, you come to five books that are called the Poetic Books. Then you come to the seventeen Prophets. When you read the old covenant, think *BC*—before Christ.

But with the new covenant—think *AC*—after Christ. It introduces the life of Jesus in the four Gospels and the beginning of the church in Acts. Then come letters to early churches on what we believe as Christians and how we should live. And it ends with Revelation and the events around Jesus' second coming and the end of this age.

The Bible begins in a garden and ends in a city—and what a great city! Here's the key—start with Jesus, and when you read it, ask God to speak to you. After all, it is His Word.

How to Study the Bible

The law of the LORD is perfect, restoring the soul; the testimony of the LORD is sure, making wise the simple.

PSALM 19:7

Yesterday we focused on where to begin in reading the Bible. Today we'll focus on how to study the Bible.

1. Find a modern translation of Scripture. The message is un-changed, but the language is like people talk today. The King James Version is beautifully written and was a great "modern" translation in the early 1600s. But language has changed. People don't talk like that today.
2. Start with Jesus—read one of the Gospels. Ask God to help you see and know Jesus. Mark is like a newspaper account; Matthew and Luke like a weekly periodical. John is like an authoritative biography.
3. Read a few verses a day and reflect—*what is God saying to me?*
4. Study Scripture in light of Scripture: one verse in light of the chapter; the chapter in light of the book; and the Old Testament in light of the New Testament.
5. Seek to join others in Bible study with a knowledgeable Christ-centered and Spirit-led teacher.

Why study the Bible? It's not for spiritual knowledge. It's to get to know God and have a closer relationship with Him. Any other reason is missing the point.

Miracle on the Hudson

*For the wages of sin is death, but the gift of God is
eternal life in Christ Jesus our Lord.*

ROMANS 6:23 NIV

On January 15, 2009, when the world was in the dumps over bad economic news, we were all inspired as we heard that US Airways Flight 1549 had ditched safely on the Hudson River. We were especially thrilled because every single passenger was saved. The man most responsible for saving the lives of all those people was the pilot, Captain Chesley "Sully" Sullenberger. Without his heroism, all the people on board would have been doomed. In fact, the story is often referred to as the "Miracle on the Hudson."

But as miraculous as it was, the people on that US Airways flight were only saved from physical death. An even greater miracle is that because of the extraordinary work and life of Jesus Christ, we can have victory over physical death *for eternity*! The bad news: because of our sin, we are all doomed to die and spend eternity separated from God. The good news: Jesus Christ came to give us life—forever!

The key: entrust your life to Him as you do when you board an airplane, entrusting your whole life and future to the pilot. Jesus will save you from death and get you where you need to be. The "Miracle on the Hudson" inspired us all, but the miracle of salvation in Jesus is the greatest miracle of all!

What Makes a Woman Beautiful?

*Your adornment must not be merely external—braiding
the hair, and wearing gold jewelry, or putting on
dresses; but let it be the hidden person of the heart, with
the imperishable quality of a gentle and quiet spirit,
which is precious in the sight of God.*

1 PETER 3:3–4

Have you ever wondered why Anna Kournikova was at one time the most popular women's tennis player even though she had never won a tournament? Easy answer. She is beautiful, and from a worldly perspective, a woman's glory is primarily in her beauty. I realize this makes many successful women resentful and feminists gag, but look at the women who get all the press! Ladies, if this superficial evaluation of women within our world frustrates you, you might want to consider Christianity and what God's Word says about beauty in a woman. In Christ, a woman can have a growing inner beauty, one that becomes more and more radiant with every passing year.

Think about a Hollywood starlet as an elderly woman. A few decades earlier, the starlet might have been an absolute head turner. But when she is in her eighties, the world sees only age spots and wrinkles. In contrast, think about a godly woman who has really grown in Christ. She has an inner beauty, and that's the beauty that gets greater with age. Yes, the wrinkles and age spots are there, but the spirit—the sparkle in her eyes, her countenance—grows more beautiful over time. From God's perspective, that makes a woman beautiful.

True Success

*Train up a child in the way he should go, even when
he is old he will not depart from it.*

PROVERBS 22:6

Our culture is obsessed with success. Not only do we obsess over our own personal achievement, but we may also become even more fixated on providing our children with the tools they need to become successful. We all want to do our best, but a lot of times there's confusion about what real success is. There's a nebulous belief that success means that our children will one day get good educations, have high-paying jobs, raise good families, and be upstanding citizens.

That is a very shortsighted view. We have not been very successful if our children grow up to have worldly success for fifty years but then spend eternity in hell. That's a temporary success but an eternal failure.

In God's eyes, success means discovering and fulfilling His will for our lives. It is about fulfilling that purpose for the glory of God, not for the glory of self. We must see that big picture to help our children become truly successful. When a child is taught and grows to understand the real meaning of success, he or she has a far greater chance of experiencing real, lasting success.

Let's help our children be successful in God's eyes. That is true success.

Prayer and the Healthy Church

*These all with one mind were continually
devoting themselves to prayer.*

ACTS 1:14

To grow in your relationship with Christ, you need to associate with a solid, healthy church. How can you identify a healthy church? First, it needs to be centered in Christ, grounded in God's Word, and empowered by prayer as it is fulfilling His mission. Let's talk about the "empowered by prayer" part as central to a healthy church. The Christian church actually began through a prayer meeting. After Christ's resurrection, He spent forty days with His disciples, explaining what the mission of the church should be. Before He ascended to heaven, Jesus told them to go to Jerusalem and wait in the Upper Room. They were there for ten days—in a prayer meeting—asking for God's guidance and waiting for Him to lead them. God responded powerfully with the coming of the Holy Spirit at pentecost. Thus began the church.

During Jesus' ministry, He was quite clear that His house was to be a house of prayer. Throughout His mission on earth, Jesus regularly immersed Himself in prayer, setting the example for His followers. He taught us how to pray. And His church was founded on prayer.

So when you are searching for a healthy church, be sure it is centered on Christ and fulfills His mission. That only occurs when it is grounded in the written Word of God. Then look for a church that follows Jesus' example of prayer.

Christ, God's Word, and prayer—the right starting points in looking for a healthy church.

Is Jesus the *Only* Way to God?

"I am the way, and the truth, and the life; no one comes to the Father but through Me."

JOHN 14:6

There are many adherents to a new spiritual movement that combines many religions. They may wrap their arms around Christianity, Judaism, Islam, Buddhism, Hinduism, and any other belief they stumble upon. I guess they are playing the odds, figuring that if they embrace many religions, they'll stumble their way into heaven! These people are working hard to create a connection to God when one is already laid out for them.

Let me ask you this question: If someone says, "I am the way to God; I am the truth and the life; no one comes to the Father but through Me," would He be lying or telling the truth? An arrogant megalomaniac or really God? None of the other so-called gods claimed this. Only Jesus did. So was He right or wrong? A liar or a truth teller? Delusional or clearly sane? If He's a deluded liar, you don't want to follow Him. But if Christ is telling the truth, He really is the Son of God. His resurrection proves it.

We have to make a decision. We're either going to accept Him as the Truth or follow many who didn't even claim to be the Way. You can't embrace them all; you've got to make a choice.

What do you choose?

The Dangerous Game of Comparison

*I have learned to be content
whatever the circumstances.*

PHILIPPIANS 4:11 NIV

An armchair philosopher once declared, "Don't try to keep up with the Joneses. Drag them down to your level. It's cheaper." We can applaud his creative solution to this age-old problem, but I prefer God's advice on the subject. He tells us just not to play that game at all.

We fall into a destructive trap when we compare ourselves to others, because the fact is, there will always be someone who has more than we do. On Monday we are so proud of our shiny new car, but on Tuesday a newer one is parked in the driveway next door. And that 48-inch plasma TV will soon pale in comparison to your brother-in-law's 60-inch model with surround sound. Here's a guarantee in life: no matter what you acquire, somebody, somewhere, is going to have something newer, shinier, and better.

So what's the harm in comparing ourselves to others? Comparison takes our eyes off of the blessings God put into our lives. When we compare our things with those of others, we feel superior if we have more and inferior if we have less. Comparison cheapens our appreciation for what God has done in our lives, and we can easily shift from gratitude to "attitude." God wants us to be content with how He has blessed us in life. The sooner you learn this, the happier you'll be.

Life's Storms

They cried to the LORD in their trouble, and he
delivered them from their distress. He made the
storm be still, and the waves of the sea were hushed.

PSALM 107:28–29 ESV

By this time, you have probably figured out that life is not free of challenges. Difficulties and even tragedies are to be expected. As a matter of fact, Jesus told His disciples, "In this world you will have trouble. But take heart! I have overcome the world" (John 16:33 NIV).

Whenever you face a storm, your first urge may be to scream, "Why?" Certain storms do come into our lives because of our own sin, but many occur when we're right in the middle of God's will. We're not doing anything wrong. We're doing what God wants us to do. Certainly that was the case for the disciples. Jesus told them to get into the boat and row across the Sea of Galilee. They were obeying Jesus when they suddenly found themselves in a horrific storm. It was so bad they thought they would not survive. But they did. With Jesus' help, they made it to shore.

Are you going through a difficult storm? Worried you are not going to make it? Jesus said to expect these storms. But there is good news—Jesus helps us through the storms. If we'll trust Him, we *will* survive.

Fleeting Wealth

어느래바다 떠오르기 쉬운 곧없는 transient

*Instruct those who are rich in this present world
not to be conceited or to fix their hope on the
uncertainty of riches, but on God, who richly
supplies us with all things to enjoy.*

1 TIMOTHY 6:17

If you are reading this, you are wealthy. In fact, if you can afford this book, then compared with the majority of the world, you are rich. But there is a great hazard that often occurs when we are wealthy: we become prideful, thinking we're a little smarter or a little better than others. We may even begin to feel we're entitled to our wealth because of the wonderful people we are.

God's Word warns us, "For the love of money is a root of all sorts of evil" (1 Timothy 6:10). Don't make the mistake of fixing your hope on the uncertainty of riches. Remember the economic madness of the 1990s? Think about all the extraordinary wealth generated by dot-com companies that soon became "dot-bomb" companies. Some of those who were megamillionaires lost it all in the new millennium. The next decade brought us the real estate boom, but before it was over, the wealth it created transferred into the worst economic recession in our lives.

God's Word reminds us over and over that wealth can come and go. There's no certainty in wealth. Here today, gone tomorrow. So don't bank on it. Instead, fix your hope on God. Find your security in Him. It's a hope that will not disappoint. You may lose your money, but you'll never lose Him, and in the process, He'll teach you to be content whether you have much or little.

Prayer Calls for Praise

[Jesus] said to them, "When you pray, say: 'Father, hallowed be your name, your kingdom come.'"

LUKE 11:2 NIV

The Bible tells us that when we pray, it is important that we praise God. What is praise? First, what it's not: praise is not flattery. *Flattery* is when we say something good about another person just because we want him to do something for us. It may or may not be true. But praise is very different. It simply acknowledges, with no self-serving desires, the good qualities in another.

Jesus teaches us to praise God. We want to acknowledge the fact that there is a difference between God's character and our sinfulness. Praise simply affirms who He is and reminds us what we're not.

But there's also a wonderful by-product of praising God. Praise helps us focus on the greatness of God. This lifts us above our troubles. You see, when we begin to focus on how great God really is, we realize that no matter what trial, what difficulty, what hardship we are facing, God is bigger than all of that. When we remember that God is big, our troubles begin to seem small.

Give Me a Sign!

*Now faith is the assurance of things hoped for, the
conviction of things not seen.*

HEBREWS 11:1 ESV

I chuckled as I read the words posted on a sign at a local church: "'Well, you have been asking Me for a sign!'—God." Now, be honest. Are you one of those folks who has said at different times in your life, "If I could just see a sign, if I could just see a miracle, I'd believe in God."

That simply is not true! Look at all those plagues in Egypt. How did Pharaoh and the Egyptians respond? Their hearts just got harder. And look at what happened with the miracles of Jesus. People witnessed Him raise a man from the dead, and all the religious leaders could think about was how to get rid of Him. They didn't change; their hearts just got harder and harder. Throughout history, people's hearts didn't change just because they saw or experienced a miracle. Miracles simply reveal if people are hardhearted toward God or if they have any <u>inkling</u> of faith.

Are you waiting for some sign to give you the proof you've been looking for to believe in God? Remember, "Faith is the assurance of things *hoped for*." The evidence for God's existence is everywhere. What you have to decide is if you'll be open-minded enough to acknowledge it, change your mind, and believe.

inkling - 어렴풋이 감지함, 희미한 지식

Facing Family Rejection

So it came about, when Joseph reached his brothers, that they stripped Joseph of his tunic, the varicolored tunic that was on him; and they took him and threw him into the pit.

GENESIS 37:23–24

Although we all experience rejection in life, nothing cuts more deeply than rejection from your family. Maybe your siblings have turned their backs on you. Perhaps your spouse has divorced you. Or maybe you feel rejected by your adult children or a parent.

Joseph experienced the ultimate rejection when his own brothers sold him into slavery. And Jesus knew painful rejection as He heard the very people He had been sent to redeem screaming, "Crucify Him!"

It is so easy to give up when rejected by those who know us best. But a horrible tragedy occurs when we do. We miss out on the incredible plans God has for us upon overcoming that family rejection.

No matter how much the rejection hurts, no matter how deep your pain, never give up. No matter what kind of hatred and rejection you have faced, God can overrule all of that to fulfill His plan for your life—just as He did with Joseph and Jesus. That's the message of the story of Joseph (Genesis 50:20). It's the message of the story of Jesus (Romans 5:8). Trust in God can help us overcome any family rejection.

It's All About Me!

Be subject to one another in the fear of Christ.

EPHESIANS 5:21

Americans love to watch television reality shows. This has been true ever since the debut of the first reality hit, *Survivor*. We enjoy watching the contestants scheme and backstab their way to the million-dollar prize. They all hope to avoid being voted off the show by looking out for number one. The winner of this reality show is usually the person who best adopts the all-about-me attitude!

Although that may be a successful strategy for playing a TV game, the all-about-me philosophy is devastating to the family. Today, more marriages end by divorce than by the death of a spouse. Thirty-five percent of our nation's children live apart from their biological fathers. That is the real reality of the all-about-me strategy.

Christianity rejects the self-centered attitude and teaches that the winning strategy is really all about submission. We are to first trust in Jesus Christ as Savior and Lord, and then we are called to submit to Him. As part of that, we are called to submit to our government officials, employers, and spiritual leaders. Christian husbands are called to love their wives as Christ loves the church. Yet wives are called to submit to their husbands, and children are called to submit to their parents. It's all about seeking what is best for others before ourselves.

When our outlook changes from *It's all about me* to *It's all about God and others*, there is peace with God and a better chance for peace within our families and with our fellow man. When that becomes reality, we don't just survive—we soar!

Sexual Temptation

Flee immorality. Every other sin that a man commits is outside the body, but the immoral man sins against his own body.

1 CORINTHIANS 6:18

How can we successfully deal with sexual temptation? Perhaps the best way is to avoid it in the first place. Here are some ideas to help you do that.

1. *Stay out of vulnerable situations.* When Jesus taught us to pray, "Lead us not into temptation, but deliver us from evil" (Matthew 6:13 KJV), He was really teaching us to ask God to help us make decisions that will give us a better chance of avoiding temptations. What are vulnerable situations? A teenage boyfriend and girlfriend in the home when the parents are not. Having no blocks on your computer or keeping that computer in a private place where no one can see it but you. Or staying late at the office alone with a person of the opposite sex. Avoid temptations by avoiding vulnerable situations whenever possible.

2. *Don't see people as objects of sexual desire.* See them as made in the image of God. Show them respect. Don't confuse lust with love. Remember, garbage in and garbage out—and porn is pure garbage. How we view others has a great impact on how we think and what we do.

3. *Use the foolproof strategy.* Here is the ultimate key: when it comes to temptations, ask yourself, "Would I be embarrassed if Jesus saw me doing this or thinking this?" I assure you—He does.

Why It Matters

In the beginning God created the
heavens and the earth.

GENESIS 1:1 NIV

The debate continues over evolution versus creation versus combinations of all sorts of theories in between. Many see this as a simple philosophical conflict; others see it as a matter of science and proclaim that science wins. Does it really matter what we believe about the origin of humankind? Yes, it does. And here's why: If God is completely left out of your theory of origins, life is meaningless. If God is not involved, then we are nothing but a bunch of molecules that just magically came together over billions of years. Without God's involvement, ethics and morality become nothing but a loose collection of beliefs enforced by whoever happens to have the most power at the moment.

If you leave God out, there is nothing left except each person looking out for number one, the survival of the fittest: *I'm going to get all I can while I'm here because I'm just an accidental mass of molecules accountable to no one.* There's nothing more.

But if God put life into motion, then we have a reason for living. We have a purpose. Only then does life begin to make sense. Because then we have Someone to answer to. And that gives us a healthy appreciation of life itself.

Most of all, it is a matter of faith—faith in God or faith in scientific theory. Faith in God, where science explains how He did it, or faith in science that doesn't acknowledge God. I'll put my faith in a never-changing God versus ever-changing scientific theory.

To Cleave

Therefore shall a man leave his father and
his mother, and shall cleave unto his wife:
and they shall be one flesh.

GENESIS 2:24 KJV

The eight-year-old girl was cuddling on the sofa with her parents, munching on a big bowl of popcorn and watching the video of their wedding. She found the whole process fascinating! Full of observations and questions, she contributed her own play-by-play analysis during the "show." Her unique perspective was particularly displayed during the exchange of vows. When the preacher asked, "Will you take this man for richer or poorer?" the little girl looked up at her mom and commented, "So I guess you chose 'poorer,' huh?"

Contrary to the thoughts and practices of many people today, wedding vows really aren't multiple-choice questions. They are actually a description of the commitment God expects us to make when we join with our mates. The King James translation uses the word *cleave*. What a wonderful term to describe this commitment! *Cleave* forms a picture of being bonded together, being so tight that nothing can separate the relationship. And that is why many wedding ceremonies go into such detail describing the inseparability of a God-made marriage. Through those vows, we commit to always cleave and promise to stick together no matter what the challenge, in a manner and for a union that was designed by God Himself.

A Wonderful Opportunity

*It was at this time that He went off to the mountain to
pray, and He spent the whole night in prayer to God.*

LUKE 6:12

Sometimes the demands of my ministry are overwhelming.
I wake up in the night, greatly burdened. Whenever I fight
the restlessness, just tossing and turning and trying to go back
to sleep, I find myself exhausted the next day. But sometimes I
have enough sense to recognize that perhaps it's the Lord who
has awakened me. I will get up and start pouring out my heart to
God. Here's what is amazing: those impromptu sessions in the
middle of the night are some of my most rewarding times. Those
moments create an opportunity to have unrushed time alone with
God. I'm able to hear His voice and understand His guidance. It's
as if He speaks in a special way that shows me I haven't really been
hearing Him. I treasure those times (even though I am sometimes
slow to recognize that I need to get up and get out of my warm
bed). And there is a miraculous bonus. I wake up refreshed even
though I've been up half the night.

It encourages me that Jesus needed these times with His
Father as well, even though He is God with no sin. Knowing how
weak and sinful I am, I certainly need special time alone with God.
So when you wake up in the night overwhelmed, be surprised by
the joy that comes from getting up and being alone with God.

Statistics 101

"The thief comes only to steal and kill and destroy; I have come that they may have life, and have it to the full."

How are you at statistical analysis? If you're like me, you might not be very good. But I have a copy of the results of a survey conducted by LifeWay Research. They polled 1,402 unchurched adults (defined as people not going to church in the last six months) and found some interesting responses:

+ 71 percent think believing in Jesus makes a positive difference in a person's life
+ 72 percent believe that God actually exists
+ 72 percent say the church is full of hypocrites
+ 78 percent say, "I would be willing to listen to somebody tell me about Christianity"
+ 79 percent say Christianity today is more about organized religion than about loving people
+ 86 percent say, "I believe I can have a good relationship with God without belonging to a church"[2]

What conclusions do you draw from these responses?

Arthur Farnsley, administrator of the Society for the Scientific Study of Religion, interprets it this way: "Is there a workshop for churches in being less annoying, less hypocritical?"[3]

Key thought: if Jesus is so attractive to the majority of the unchurched, couldn't the church become more attractive by becoming more and more like Jesus? Hint: it begins with you and me.

February

*We have come to know and have believed
the love which God has for us. God is love,
and the one who abides in love abides in
God, and God abides in him.*

1 JOHN 4:16

The Truth About Suicide

*Do you not know that your body is a temple of the
Holy Spirit, who is in you, whom you have received
from God? You are not your own.*

1 CORINTHIANS 6:19 NIV

Perhaps no issue is more painful and complex than suicide. Some of us cannot understand the despair felt by people who have taken their own lives. And most of us cannot begin to measure the horrors faced by families left behind.

First, a word for the family of someone who has committed suicide. You may be struggling with the fear that your loved one has committed the unforgivable sin and is not in heaven. Let me make this absolutely clear: Christ forgives all sin. Although suicide is clearly outside the will of God, it is a sin for which Christ paid the penalty on the cross. If your loved one ever trusted Christ as Lord and Savior, be assured that he or she is in heaven right now.

If you are thinking about suicide, recognize that these thoughts come directly from the devil. Here is the lie he is putting in your head: *If I'm gone, I'll no longer be a problem for my family. They won't have to worry about me anymore.* This is a delusion. The fact is, your family will suffer with your death forever. It will haunt them, devastate them—possibly even destroy them. That's why suicide is such a selfish sin.

If Satan is putting these thoughts in your head, please tell a friend or seek help from a pastor or a Christian counselor. God has great plans for your life. Don't let the devil convince you to destroy what God has created for a purpose. Tell him, "Go back to hell. Jesus has great and meaningful plans for me, and I'm going to trust Him."

When Bad Things Happen

No temptation [trial] has overtaken you but such as is
common to man; and God is faithful, who will not allow
you to be tempted beyond what you are able.

1 CORINTHIANS 10:13

Rabbi Harold Kushner said this: "There is only one question which really matters: Why do bad things happen to good people?"[4] This question became the title of his best-selling book *When Bad Things Happen to Good People.* Sadly, Kushner's book paints a picture of a very small God, although his book did help a lot of people going through tough times.

There is a wonderful Bible story that describes a much greater God. Three Hebrew boys refused to worship the idol of the Babylonian king Nebuchadnezzar. Even though they were threatened with being thrown in a fiery furnace, their response was, "God can spare us from the fiery furnace; He has that power. But even if He does not spare us, we'll never serve your gods or bow down to your statue" (Daniel 3:17–18, paraphrase). They chose to trust God even when it made no earthly sense to do so. And God repaid that faith by seeing that they were not harmed by the fires in the furnace.

God will never take us through a difficult time that is too tough for us to deal with. No matter how difficult your trials, you can bank on His promise in 1 Corinthians 10:13. He will give you a way to get through it.

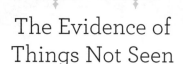

The Evidence of
Things Not Seen

*For his invisible attributes, namely, his eternal power
and divine nature, have been clearly perceived, ever
since the creation of the world, in the things that have
been made. So [you] are without excuse.*

ROMANS 1:20 ESV

We pride ourselves on being logical creatures who demand
proof before believing most things. Yet a professor can tell us
that there are 100 trillion stars in the sky, and we accept it without
question. We accept as absolute fact that an atom has neutrons
and electrons spinning around a nucleus even though we have
never seen any of them. We know that light travels 186,000 miles
a second even though we've personally never measured it. And
that E does, in fact, equal mc2. We accept all these things as facts
without ever demanding proof of their authenticity.

Yet so many of us reject Jesus, risking our eternal souls even
when presented with solid evidence. What evidence? The order of
creation, from the basic cell to the complexity of all life. The witness of the Gospel writings from those who saw the miracles of
Jesus. Testimonies from dozens who witnessed His death then saw
Him alive after His resurrection. And what about the fulfillment
of prophecies concerning Jesus? The historical documentation of
Jesus' life, death, and resurrection is far greater than the historical
writings about Julius Caesar and other ancient figures.

"Now faith is the substance of things hoped for, the evidence
of things not seen," says Hebrews 11:1 (KJV).

Heavenly Justice

He will judge the world in righteousness;
he will govern the peoples with justice.

PSALM 9:8 NIV

It's been said that General Robert E. Lee returned to his camp-site late one evening to see a handcuffed soldier being held for a hearing on an alleged misconduct. The soldier was shaking and obviously terrified of the trial, as well as the judgment he was facing from the general. "Relax, Corporal," General Lee said. "You'll get justice here." The trembling soldier replied, "That's exactly what I'm a-feared of, General!"

The judgment of man is very different from the judgment of God. Whereas man focuses on guilt or innocence, God's judgment is so much more. That's because God already knows our guilt from sin. He needs no evidence of that. What He wants is for us to acknowledge our sin and offer a willingness to change. He wants us to recognize that our sin has separated us from Him and to express a mourning that cries out for His mercy through faith in what Jesus did on the cross—dying to pay the penalty for our sin.

Unlike human justice, God's justice is always righteous, always perfect. But if we want His justice to be merciful, then we *must* confess and forsake our sins. Have you?

If You Are a Victim of Adultery

Be kind and compassionate to one another, forgiving each other, just as in Christ God forgave you.

EPHESIANS 4:32 NIV

Nothing devastates a home like adultery. If you are a victim of that sin, you know the deep personal hurt it causes. The consequences are so severe that God has even said that you may choose to end your marriage if you are the victim. He does give you that right. But please know this: what God really desires is reconciliation in your marriage.

Reconciliation is difficult, requiring repentance on the adulterer's part, as well as a supernatural forgiveness from the one who has been sinned against. Forgiving your spouse may be the most difficult thing you will ever do in your life. And it is almost impossible without the power of Jesus Christ.

Yes, divorce is allowed. But know that the desire of the Lord is for marriages to be reconciled. It will take superhuman effort on your part, and it may take years to build trust again. But in the long run, for your marriage, for your children, and for *you*, it can be the right decision to make.

Who Said Miracles Don't Happen Anymore?

*Be astonished! Wonder! Because I am
doing something in your days—you would
not believe if you were told.*

HABAKKUK 1:5

Let me tell you of a miraculous moment in our church's history. It was a critical time for our congregation. We were meeting in a suite of offices and bursting at the seams—we needed to build a facility. We were approaching our first annual payment on land for which we had made a down payment a year earlier. As the payment day approached, we still needed more than fifty thousand dollars. We asked our small membership, just about fifty families, to pray about what they could give. We then gave each child a dollar, told the children the parable of the talents, and urged them to take the dollar (God's money), multiply it, and return what they made.

There was a lot of anticipation as the congregation gathered to present their special gifts on the Sunday before the payment was due. All the checks and bills and coins were gathered; the church family waited nervously as the money was counted. I will never forget the stunned gasps and then the prolonged, dumbfounded silence when the finance chairman announced that the church had given to the *exact dollar* what was needed. That included the hundreds of dollars those beautiful children had made and given. What a miracle!

Since that time, our church has experienced hundreds and hundreds of miracles. If you doubt whether God still performs miracles, doubt no more. He's still in the miracle business!

The Lions Never Retired

*Then the king gave orders, and Daniel was brought
in and cast into the lions' den. The king spoke and
said to Daniel, "Your God whom you constantly
serve will Himself deliver you."*

DANIEL 6:16

When publicizing a mission conference at our church some
time back, we couldn't print the last names of some of the
missionaries or even mention the location where they were serving.
The reason was that if it became known they were missionaries,
they could be expelled, imprisoned, or even killed in the country
they serve.

Paul was keenly aware of the dangers of sharing Christ. Today,
missionaries still face very real persecution—a fact that has hit
close to home over the past few years. In 2002, several of our medical missionaries in Yemen were brutally murdered by a pack of
Islamic terrorists in the hospital where the missionaries had served
the people of Yemen for years.

And there was the case of Graham Staines, a missionary to
India. He ran a leper clinic, caring for the most outcast of Indian
society. Yet he was martyred for his faith, killed along with his two
young sons by Hindu nationalists.

No, persecution of Christian missionaries didn't end with the
lions in Rome. It continues today, throughout the world, led by a
legion of groups that are anti-Christ and hate those who spread
His Word. We need to pray for our missionaries, support them,
honor them. And pray that we who call ourselves Christians will be
willing to pay the price they pay daily to follow Jesus.

What We Treasure

So whether you eat or drink or whatever you do,
do it all for the glory of God.

1 CORINTHIANS 10:31 NIV

I chuckled when I read a magazine cartoon that showed a news conference called by a United States senator who announced he was divorcing his family so he could spend more time with politics.

We may scoff at the folly of his announcement, but the truth is that many people make that same statement every day, maybe not with words but with their actions. So many more, in fact, that if a politician retires from his work to spend more time with his family, it becomes the lead story, met with cynicism on the evening news, whereas the one who announces he's rejecting his family to advance his career would be noticed with an "At least he's honest."

God tells us we should work heartily and do everything to the glory of God. But to do that, we must have priorities. Pleasing God and meeting the needs of the family must come before career.

Think about your priorities and the things you cherish in your life. It's good to focus on the things that matter most. Start with God and then family. Everything else tends to fall in place.

God: The Answer for Temptation

"Lead us not into temptation, but deliver us from evil."

MATTHEW 6:13 KJV

Have you ever given much thought to the wording of the Lord's Prayer? The most puzzling part is the phrase "Lead us not into temptation." It's confusing. It just doesn't seem to make sense. After all, the Bible is clear that God does not tempt us: "Let no one say when he is tempted, 'I am being tempted by God'; for God cannot be tempted by evil, and He Himself does not tempt anyone" (James 1:13).

So why would Jesus teach us to pray, "Lead us not into temptation, but deliver us from evil"?

1. He was reminding us that in the face of temptation, it is God we need to call to for help. We need God's help to gain the strength to resist temptation and make it through life's trials.
2. We also need God to help us make wise decisions that *keep us out* of vulnerable situations where we are more prone to give in to temptation.
3. "Evil" in this verse actually means "the evil one." Satan is both smarter and stronger than we are—not smarter and stronger than God, but smarter and stronger than you and I. Only God can deliver us from the evil one.

The devil wants to destroy our lives, but God wants us to live life to the fullest. It just makes sense to call on God to help us resist temptation and to believe that He will deliver us from evil. Otherwise life can become hell.

Was Jesus Silent About Homosexuality?

And He answered and said, "Have you not read that He who created them from the beginning made them male and female, and said, 'For this reason a man shall leave his father and mother and be joined to his wife, and the two shall become one flesh'?"

MATTHEW 19:4–5

Some liberal theologians justify the gay lifestyle by saying, "Look, Jesus is our ultimate authority, and He never spoke about homosexuality, so there must be a freedom to decide on that issue!" Nice try, but let me explain why there are no direct words from Jesus on the subject. This is because Jesus' ministry was primarily directed to the Jews, and in the first century, homosexuality was just not an issue for them. Sure, it occurred, but it was seen as evil perversion. It was not a part of Jewish contemporary debate.

But Jesus did discuss the many issues related to homosexuality as He taught us our most basic Christian principles. And He was quite clear that marriage is only for a man and a woman in Matthew 19:4–5.

When we study the biblical teachings concerning marriage, we see that sex is a wonderful gift that God has created for a husband and wife to enjoy. But sex outside of marriage is always wrong in God's eyes, be it premarital sex, adultery, or homosexuality. Although Jesus never specifically spoke about homosexuality, His Word certainly does. Jesus said, "Thy Word is truth." And the Word is absolutely clear: sexual intimacy is God's gift for a man and woman to enjoy in the context of marriage only.

A Stunning Revelation

"Then they will see the Son of Man coming in
clouds with great power and glory."

MARK 13:26

I learned about the second coming of Christ as a child. One thing that puzzled me was hearing that everybody would see Jesus as He arrived. This just didn't seem possible because I knew the world was round. And there's no way those of us in America would be able to see Him if He came again somewhere in the Middle East. The earth would block our view!

Well, that was before CNN and the Internet! Before we were able to witness live, breaking international news events anywhere in the world. With the development of worldwide news, my question about how all could see Jesus is now irrelevant. Now, I understand.

But my question about seeing His return is not nearly as important as this one: will you be ready for His return? The next time you see Jesus—be it upon your death or upon His return—will it be a joyous reunion or a moment of stunned realization that you missed your chance and are now facing the judgment of God? You can be sure of a joyous reunion if you know Jesus as Savior and Lord.

Please, if you haven't already trusted Jesus as the Lord and Savior of your life, do it before it's too late, when all the world will see Him "coming in clouds with great power and glory."

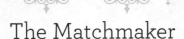

The Matchmaker

The LORD God said, "It is not good for the man to be alone. I will make a helper suitable for him."

GENESIS 2:18 NIV

Choosing the right mate isn't easy. In a poll conducted several years ago by a Christian evangelical magazine, people were asked, "If you had it to do it all over again, would you choose the same mate?" If I recall correctly, about one-third said they wouldn't—and remember, these were Christians who responded.

Part of the problem is that so often our decision is based only on physical attraction, and we neglect the need for shared beliefs and values. In another time, and in some customs still, parents and matchmakers arranged marriages—a practice that actually resulted in far lower divorce rates than we have today! Divorces were fewer because the match was made on the basis of compatibility—similar values and shared beliefs. The modern-day matchmaker is the computer. More and more are meeting their mates over the Internet. But this modern matchmaker has the same goal as the days of old—compatibility.

Wouldn't it be great if there were a matchmaker who could select a perfect match? A mate for whom you'd have romantic love and with whom you'd be compatible? Well, I've got good news for you. *God* is the ultimate matchmaker, and He wants to serve in that role for those of you who are single. He knows you and your future spouse better than anyone. So if you hope to be married, let God be your matchmaker. He knows the perfect match.

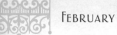

Agape Love

*May the Lord direct your hearts into God's
love and Christ's perseverance.*

2 Thessalonians 3:5 NIV

You may have heard the term *agape love* but may not be real clear on what it means. What is agape love? How is it any different from the dozens of other ways we use the word *love*? First, let's understand what it is not. It is not romantic love, because people of all faiths (and no faiths) experience romantic love. It is not brotherly love, where you have a natural chemistry with another person. Terrorists and members of the Mafia experience brotherly love. There's certainly nothing uniquely Christian about that!

Agape love is unconditional love. It is a *choice* we make to love another person whether he or she loves us back or not. It means that you choose to love someone even if he is your enemy! Agape love is not based on emotion at all. In fact, it may be contrary to every emotion you have. It is an act of the will.

Agape love presents a real challenge for us. It is tough to live out because it's hard to love someone who doesn't respond to you in the way you would desire. And all of us are going to have certain individuals—even within the body of Christ—whom we struggle to love. And yet God's Word is very clear: "Love your neighbor as yourself" (Mark 12:31 NIV). Our "neighbor" is anyone. Now, you couldn't find a clearer command about what we're called to do as followers of Jesus Christ. Jesus "agape loves" us and commands us to "agape love" others as well.

A Beautiful Mind

And now these three remain: faith, hope and love.
But the greatest of these is love.

In 2001, the Oscar for Best Picture was awarded to *A Beautiful Mind*. The movie tells the story of John Nash and his being awarded the Nobel Prize in economics. But as inspiring as the story is in showing his fight against schizophrenia, the movie was even more impactful as a beautiful love story.

Alicia Nash stuck by the often-deranged genius, loving him, caring for him, and steadying him despite the fact that Nash brought nothing to the marriage but strain and heartache. Although he was totally incapacitated at times because of his mental illness, his wife stood by him, even when her own life was endangered. As the film concludes, John Nash stands before an admiring audience of the world's greatest intellectuals, accepting the prize that recognized his monumental achievement. Nash uses the moment—the apex of his life—to declare that there was really only one thing that mattered in his life, and that was the love of his wife, who had stayed with him all those years.

No matter what else was discovered in his life, Nash learned that the most beautiful mind is possessed by the one who demonstrates devoted love—especially if that love is from a spouse. God's Word calls this kind of love the greatest character trait of all.

Tolerance

Who is wise? He will realize these things. Who is discerning? He will understand them. The ways of the Lᴏʀᴅ are right; the righteous walk in them, but the rebellious stumble in them.

HOSEA 14:9 NIV

We hear it often today that we should all become more tolerant and less judgmental. Tolerance, taken in its intended form, is indeed a virtue. It means the acceptance of others who approach life in a different way.

But in its current state, tolerance has become the supreme virtue for the politically correct gestapo. It has been redefined as an obligation to *affirm* all sorts of immoral behavior. Everything is to be accepted, and to feel otherwise makes you—*gasp!*—judgmental. Americans are so afraid of being labeled as intolerant or judgmental that we have warped into a society with few boundaries.

William Bennett addressed this misuse of the word *judgmental* when he said, "Without being judgmental, America would never have put an end to slavery, outlawed child labor, emancipated women, or ushered in the civil rights movement. Nor would we have prevailed against Nazism and Soviet communism, or known how to explain our opposition."[5]

Do not let the "PC police" define your core ethical standards. Tolerance is about showing respect and fairness to all people with whom we disagree while affirming what God says is evil and not calling it good. When in doubt, go to the Word, focus on Jesus' life and teachings, and ask the Holy Spirit to show you how to be tolerant of people you disagree with while never affirming evil.

Fall on Your Knees

*That at the name of Jesus every knee should bow, of
things in heaven, and things in earth, and things under
the earth; and that every tongue should confess that
Jesus Christ is Lord, to the glory of God the Father.*

PHILIPPIANS 2:10–11 KJV

The Bible tells of the interesting reactions many had upon first seeing Jesus. For instance, when the wise men first laid eyes on Jesus, they fell down and worshipped Him. And do you recall the woman in the crowd who touched the hem of Jesus' garment? Jesus turned around and said, "Who is the one who touched Me?" (Luke 8:45). I love the sensitivity of Jesus; He felt her touch, and He healed her—and the woman just fell down to the ground in worship and thankfulness! Then there was Peter, who couldn't catch any fish until Jesus showed up. When the catch was great, what did he do? He fell down and worshipped Jesus. And my favorite, Thomas, another disciple, when hearing from the other disciples that Jesus had risen from the dead, vowed, "I won't believe it unless I see the nail wounds in His hands." And then Jesus appeared and said to Tom, "Put your hand into the wound in my side." And an awed Thomas responded, "My Lord and my God!" All he could do was worship Him (John 20:25–28 NLT).

That is what the heavenly Father wants us to do even today. Though we may not always do this physically, He wants our hearts and minds and souls to fall down and worship Jesus. If you have not yet accepted the good news of Jesus Christ, I pray you will. When you really see Him, you will fall down to worship Him and commit your life to Him!

Pass It On

*Do not conform any longer to the pattern of this world,
but be transformed by the renewing of your mind. Then
you will be able to test and approve what God's will
is—his good, pleasing and perfect will.*

ROMANS 12:2 NIV

What does it mean to "pass it on"? How can a person with humble, possibly evil beginnings "pass on" the amazing powers of God? Here is an example of how God can use *anyone* as an example of His powers of transformation.

As a dedicated member of the Ku Klux Klan, Bob Terrance was involved in more than thirty bombings of homes, churches, and synagogues. He was sentenced to a thirty-year prison term in Mississippi. While serving his sentence, Bob began to read the Bible, discover the love of God in Jesus Christ, and become convicted of what a sinner he was. He renounced racism and hatred. And then he cried out for the mercy of God in Jesus Christ and received salvation and forgiveness. Paroled a few years later, Bob attended college and then seminary. Eventually he became an ordained pastor because he wanted to share what Christ can do in a transformed life. Later, the most unlikely candidate of all became president of the C. S. Lewis Institute in Washington, D.C., where he reminded people of the amazing power of Jesus to transform a life.

Through the testimony of Bob Terrance we get to see the embodiment of God's love in the flesh, in the body of Christ, as someone once filled with hate is now filled with love. That is receiving the blessing, and that is passing it on.

What Do Women Want?

Husbands, love your wives, just as Christ loved the church and gave himself up for her.

The famous psychiatrist Sigmund Freud once said, "The great question that has never been answered, which I have not been able to answer, despite my thirty years of research into the feminine soul is, 'What does a woman want?'" The *Marietta Daily Journal* finally gave him the answer a few years ago: "What women really want, put simply, is chocolate."[6]

I'm going to let Sigmund and the *Journal* fight that one out, but the Bible actually answered that question centuries ago. The number one thing for all husbands to know is that our wives' greatest need is to feel loved. What is meant by "loved"? The word used in Scripture is *agape*, which means "unconditional love." It's not speaking of romantic love. Agape love means loving people in a way that meets their needs. Yes, most women have a need for romance, and there's no doubt that romantic love is important. But over the long haul, what is needed most of all is a mature, unconditional, committed love.

Scripture mentions other traits a woman seeks from her husband, such as patience, kindness, and understanding. These are certainly important, but all of these traits keep coming back to the core need to be loved unconditionally. In fact, if you love her unconditionally, the other traits she needs will usually follow. So although it is certainly okay for you to keep on buying your wife chocolates, never let material gifts be a substitute for your clear responsibility to provide her with pure unconditional love.

Two Perspectives

*Now when the Pharisee who had invited Him saw this,
he said to himself, "If this man were a prophet He would
know who and what sort of person this woman is who is
touching Him, that she is a sinner."*

LUKE 7:39

Picture the scene: Jesus had been invited to dinner by some of the religious leaders in town. It wasn't really a social courtesy—they were checking Him out! And then, just after the salad was served, a beautiful young woman entered and dropped to the ground beside Jesus. She was weeping so hard that she actually used her tears to wash His feet, wiping them with her hair.

I can just picture the Pharisees, jaws dropped to the floor, eyes the size of saucers. What do you think was going through their minds? The woman was of questionable reputation. *Men of good reputation would never allow this!* But those Pharisees, they're like a lot of good, longtime church folks—quick to judge known sinners but blind to their own sin. Sound familiar?

This woman appreciated Jesus because she was keenly aware of the immoral life she had lived. She was overcome by the forgiveness Christ offered her. Washing His feet with her tears was pure worship and gratitude.

Two very different responses to Jesus. With whom do you most identify? The religious moralists who self-righteously judged the woman? Or the sinful woman who knew she deserved God's judgment and was surprised by His grace? Two different perspectives on Jesus—which is most like yours?

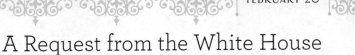

A Request from the White House

*God . . . has called you into fellowship with
his Son Jesus Christ our Lord.*

1 CORINTHIANS 1:9 NIV

God pleads with us to regularly spend time with Him. He wants us to talk to Him about our needs and seek His guidance. Yet even though we are offered this remarkable privilege, we are reluctant to make that commitment or to carve out any meaningful time with Him. We treat this offer with complete nonchalance. It doesn't make sense.

But suppose there is a voice mail on your phone when you get home from work today. It's a call from the assistant to your favorite president, who says, "The president would like to spend some one-on-one time with you this week. He wants to get to know you to see how he can help you." Your first thought would be, *This must be a joke. Who is messing with me?* But what if you found out the call was real, and the president really did want to spend time with you? My guess is you'd be excited and feel pretty special!

Think about how quickly you'd jump to go spend time with the president you most admired. Yet *any* president of the United States is small in importance and power when compared to the King of the universe. Now think about the awesome privilege the God of the universe continually gives us to spend one-on-one time with Him! No greater privilege indeed.

The Toughest Temptation

His wife said to him, "Are you still holding on to your integrity? Curse God and die!" He replied, "You are talking like a foolish woman. Shall we accept good from God, and not trouble?" In all this, Job did not sin in what he said.

JOB 2:9-10 NIV

One of Satan's great tools is discouragement, for if the devil can get us discouraged, we will often turn from God. We can see this happening in the book of Job; the devil attacked Job with catastrophe after catastrophe. There seemed to be no hope of any relief. So what advice did he get from his wife? She said, "Curse God and die!"

Never forget, the toughest temptations we face will often come through people who love us the most. That's because these people don't want us hurt. So they will urge us to take the easy way out. The devil knows this and enjoys using those who love us. That's how he got to Adam. Jesus experienced this when Peter urged Him not to talk about going to the cross. But He knew the source of Peter's thinking and responded angrily, "Get out of here, Satan" (Matthew 4:10 NLT).

That's why Christian spouses and friends have an incredibly important responsibility. Don't be an unwitting pawn of the evil one. Become your loved one's encourager in his or her difficult struggle. Patiently encourage the one you love to do things the Lord's way—even when it's the hard way—because His way is always best.

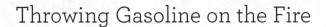
Throwing Gasoline on the Fire

*But when you are tempted, he will also provide a way
out so that you can stand up under it.*

1 CORINTHIANS 10:13 NIV

You can't avoid it, no matter how hard you try. Television commercials, the Internet, billboards on the road, window displays in the mall, even magazines in the supermarket checkout line—we are constantly assaulted with sexual images everywhere we turn. These media and cultural assaults are like throwing gasoline on the fire. They make it even more challenging to live a life that is pleasing to God.

Notice that I said these things *add* gasoline to the fire—the "fire" is already there. Even if we lived alone on a desert island with no TV, no computer, no magazines, nobody else there, we would still struggle with the lusts of the flesh. We would still wrestle with our thought lives. We will always struggle with attitudes and drives that are displeasing to God! Avoiding outside temptations is certainly important in avoiding sin, but recognize that the real problem begins—and ends—with how we deal with temptation inside our own minds. We can't stop being tempted, and temptation is not sin. Jesus was tempted in every way we are. But don't flirt with it. Show real courage and run from it. Ask the Lord to help you turn your thoughts over to Him, and you will be able to have the power to resist temptation.

Good from Evil

And we know that in all things God works for the
good of those who love him, who have been called
according to his purpose.

ROMANS 8:28 NIV

Could there possibly be a more vivid example of evil than
Adolf Hitler and his effort to exterminate the Jews? And yet,
incredibly, God was able to bring good even from Hitler's horrific
evil. Because of the world's reaction to this horror, the nation of
Israel was reborn after not existing for almost nineteen hundred
years. Once again, the Jews claimed the permanent homeland
God had promised their forefathers thousands of years before.

But there is actually an even greater example of God taking
evil and using it as a means of great good. It is the story of the
cross. Each one of us—through our sinful natures—is responsible for murdering the innocent Son of God. *This* was truly the
most evil act in all of history. Yet God took our evil and turned it
into the greatest act of good. He did this by offering us salvation
and forgiveness of sin. He used this great evil to offer us a relationship, oneness, and reconciliation with God.

The cross gives us hope that no matter what evil we have
done, or what evil others have done to us, God has the ability to
turn evil into a means for good and to accomplish His intended
purposes.

Good Fear

The LORD is the one who goes ahead of you;
He will be with you. He will not fail you or forsake
you. Do not fear or be dismayed.

DEUTERONOMY 31:8

I'm afraid of snakes—all snakes, poisonous and harmless. I'm scared of big snakes, little snakes, live snakes, and dead snakes. Once I was jogging and almost stepped on a smashed, dead, six-inch garter snake; I jumped three feet in the air. This is a fear I've always lived with and I intend to always keep. That garter snake may have been harmless, but the next snake I come upon just might not be! Some fear is good.

I've also struggled with the fear of failure. For a few years after college, I worked in sales on straight commission. When you work for straight commission, you have no idea how much money you're going to make each week, if any at all. So every week I would get the "Monday morning sweats," wondering if I'd make any income that week. Believe me, that type of fear gets you out of bed and serves as a motivator! That's a healthy fear.

God doesn't take away all our fears. In fact, He sometimes gives us fears in order to help us. The good news is that sometimes He uses our fears to get our attention, protect us from danger, and motivate us to get out and do what we need to do. More good news is that He gives us courage to face those fears. But the best news is that He gives us victory over one of life's great fears—death—through faith in His risen Son. Jesus conquered death, and we can too when we put our trust in Him. He makes the fear of death disappear.

Love Thy Neighbor

*"But a Samaritan, as he traveled, came where the man
was; and when he saw him, he took pity on him."*

LUKE 10:33 NIV

The reason we are commanded to love our neighbors *and* to love
our enemies is that they are often the same people. We can see
how this bit of philosophy was developed if we closely examine
the story of the good Samaritan.

Notice that the Samaritan was from an ethnic group that
the Jews positively despised. Yet, although the assaulted man
was repeatedly ignored by his own people, the hated Samaritan
willingly gave aid to the injured Jewish man. Now, if Jesus were
telling the story in Israel today, He might change "Samaritan" to
"Palestinian." Or if He were speaking to Palestinians, He might
say it was an "Israeli soldier" who helped. If He were speaking to
liberal Democrats, He might change "Samaritan" to "conservative
Republican." If He were speaking to conservative Republicans,
He might change it to a "liberal secularist Democrat." Whomever
Jesus addressed, He would probably replace "Samaritan" with that
group's current enemy. That's how Jesus expects us to define the
term *neighbor*.

One reason Christianity is so unique is that we are called to
love our enemies. We're called to be fair with them and compassionate toward them and to demonstrate love—even if they hate
us. God's Word is clear. You can't claim to love God and not love
your neighbor. Jesus told the story of the good Samaritan so we
would be clear who our neighbor is and so we would go and do
likewise.

If He Parted the Red Sea . . .

Then Moses stretched out his hand over the sea;
and the LORD swept the sea back by a strong east
wind all night and turned the sea into dry land, so
the waters were divided.

EXODUS 14:21

We all have times when we feel we have no options. Maybe we're in a job crisis and we feel there is just no way out. Maybe we don't even have a job, money is rapidly running out, and we're beginning to feel despair. Sometimes it's a marriage that seems hopeless. There are many possible scenarios, but they all have this in common: it seems as though we've run out of options, and we don't know what to do. We feel trapped in a hopeless situation with no possible way out.

We can learn how to face these crises by remembering the children of Israel. They faced a stormy sea to the front and Egyptian soldiers to the rear. Talk about no options—they truly had no way out! But if you'll remember, God led them from desperation to complete victory. Realize that the same God who parted the Red Sea is standing beside you whenever you think you're out of alternatives. There is no lasting defeat for children of God; He always gives us the option of allowing Him to lead us, teach us, and build our faith. If He parted the Red Sea for the people of faith, then through faith no situation is hopeless—for you or for me.

The Unpardonable Sin

"Him that cometh to me I will in no wise cast out."

JOHN 6:37 KJV

After committing adultery and then having the woman's husband murdered, King David wondered if he had committed the unpardonable sin. "Don't cast me away from Thy presence, God!" he begged, fearful that his act was so heinous that he was beyond God's redemption (Psalm 51:11, paraphrase).

Christians have long debated what the unpardonable sin is. Some Christians live in fear, terrified that they may have committed it. They wonder if God will forgive them.

I have good news. If you worry that you have committed the unpardonable sin, it's one of the clearest signs that you have not. The very fact that you are bothered by your sinfulness shows that the Holy Spirit has not abandoned you!

The only unpardonable sin is *total rejection* of Jesus Christ. The one thing God can't forgive is when we reject His Son all our lives. God will not forgive our rejecting what His Son did for us, paying the penalty for our sins so they could be washed away when we have repentant faith in Him.

Whatever evil you have done and however bad you feel you are, God offers His forgiveness in Christ. So come to God, and confess your sins to Him. Then claim your forgiveness today.

A Word from Andy on Parenting

A truthful witness gives honest testimony,
but a false witness tells lies.

PROVERBS 12:17 NIV

Television isn't always a waste of time. Notice this little gem of wisdom from *The Andy Griffith Show*. As Andy, Aunt Bea, and Barney sat around the dinner table, eight-year-old Opie amused them with stories about a new friend, a magical man by the name of Mr. McBeevee. He had a shiny metal hat and made a jingling sound as he walked in the treetops. At first they laughed at Opie's imaginary friend, but his pa became concerned as the stories grew a bit too outlandish. After yet another evening of Mr. McBeevee stories, Andy decided it was time to put an end to the nonsense. Andy demanded that Opie admit he had been making up the adventures. But even under the threat of a whippin', the boy would not recant. "I ain't lyin', Pa. Promise," Opie told his father. Andy retreated downstairs and stared into space.

"Did you punish him?" Aunt Bea asked.

"No," Andy said quietly.

Barney was shocked at Andy's failure to act. "Don't tell me you believe in Mr. McBeevee!"

"No," Andy replied, "but I do believe in Opie."[7]

Andy's trust in Opie was rewarded the next day when he met Mr. McBeevee, who turned out to be a hard-hatted telephone lineman with a belt full of jingling tools. Sometimes when you deal with your children, it's a good idea to check things out rather than rejecting them for what appears to be a childhood fantasy. Often it is, but what if it's not?

Pride

*Pride goes before destruction, and a haughty spirit
before stumbling.*

PROVERBS 16:18

It was a spring day, and it seemed that all of South Hampton, England, had gathered in one place to celebrate one of the pinnacle accomplishments of man. About 2,200 people had the privilege of a firsthand view, among them some of the wealthiest people in the world. It seemed the whole world was marveling at this awesome accomplishment: eleven stories high, 900 feet long, 46,000 tons. Yet just five days later, it was all gone—disappeared—a massive wreckage at the bottom of the sea. The name *Titanic* was always preceded by the word *unsinkable*. On board, many joked, "Even God couldn't sink the *Titanic*," but it will forever serve as the twentieth-century example of the foolishness of pride.

God's Word says, "Pride goes before destruction, and a haughty spirit before stumbling." Prideful *Titanics* sink into destruction, but a good life that is humble before God and man has a better chance to withstand the storms of life.

March

Trust in the L<small>ORD</small> with all your heart and do not lean on your own understanding.

P<small>ROVERBS</small> 3:5

Love God with All Your Heart

Jesus answered him, "The first of all the
commandments is: 'Hear, O Israel, the LORD our
God, the LORD is one. And you shall love the LORD
your God with all your heart, with all your soul,
with all your mind, and with all your strength.'
This is the first commandment."

MARK 12:29–30 NKJV

To love God with all your heart means to love Him with all your feelings, all your emotions, and all your passion. Now, passion is a very hot term in contemporary culture. People ask, "What's your passion?" What they're asking you is: what is it that really gets your juices flowing? It could be a certain ideology, social cause, or politics. Perhaps it's theater, movies, or music. Or it could be making money, physical fitness, or watching college football. You can be passionate about a lot of things, but the number one passion of your life should be your relationship with God.

Think about your relationship with God this way. When you first came to Christ, there was no problem in feeling passionate about God. You had a hunger for the Word, longed to be in worship, and itched to tell others about Christ. You were excited about God, and there was a very real passion there! But then as time went by and life presented its many challenges and opportunities, it became easy for other things to become higher in priority. And if we're more passionate about anything else than our relationship with God, our priorities are simply out of whack. Jesus reminds us that when we give our hearts to God, we need to maintain that passion and love Him with *all* of our heart.

Love God with All Your Soul

*Jesus answered him, "The first of all the
commandments is: 'Hear, O Israel, the LORD our
God, the LORD is one. And you shall love the LORD
your God with all your heart, with all your soul,
with all your mind, and with all your strength.'
This is the first commandment."*

MARK 12:29–30 NKJV

What is the *soul?* One's soul is his life and the seat of his being. Confusing? Think about it this way. When a man and woman fall in love, their hearts knit together. Although passion may have drawn them together, it is a decision of the will and the mind that keeps them together in a committed relationship. Sinful human nature often causes us to be tempted to be unfaithful to our spouses. And if we went by our feelings, we would follow the temptation! It's during those times that we have to completely ignore temporary feelings and be strong in our commitment to stay faithful. We express our love through our hearts, our minds, and our strength. This is how we love our spouses with our souls—our very lives.

It's the same with God. When we give our hearts to God, we begin a relationship with Him. Then we decide (with our minds, our wills) to follow Him. Along the way, we're tempted to fall into sin. If we simply follow our feelings, we will give in to the temptation. But if we're really going to love God, we will choose to be strong and faithful to Him, thus loving God with all our souls.

So do you? I hope you will.

Love God with All Your Mind

*Jesus answered him, "The first of all the commandments
is: 'Hear, O Israel, the LORD our God, the LORD is one. And
you shall love the LORD your God with all your heart, with
all your soul, with all your mind, and with all your
strength.' This is the first commandment."*

MARK 12:29–30 NKJV

All around us, every day, there is a constant battle for our minds.
That is why we need to study the Word of God so we can
know the mind of God. We need to know what He expects of
us and how He wants us to live. You're not going to learn that by
reading the daily newspaper, listening to talk radio, or vegging out
in front of the TV.

One of my favorite passages of Scripture is Isaiah 55:8–9:
"'For my thoughts are not your thoughts, neither are your ways
my ways,' declares the LORD. 'As the heavens are higher than the
earth, so are my ways higher than your ways and my thoughts than
your thoughts'" (NIV). This is a beautiful passage that describes
why the Word of God is so unique. So many things we read and
hear in this life tend to be contrary to what God's Word is saying.
We need to immerse ourselves in the Word of God so we can get
to know Him. It's the only way we can love God with our minds.

Love God with All Your Strength

Jesus answered him, "The first of all the commandments is: 'Hear, O Israel, the LORD our God, the LORD is one. And you shall love the LORD your God with all your heart, with all your soul, with all your mind, and with all your strength.' This is the first commandment."

MARK 12:29–30 NKJV

We need to love God with all of our strength. That means all of our energy. It's interesting that the word the gospel of Mark uses for "strength" also means "ability." I love that. But what does that tell us about loving God?

God has given all of us talents and abilities. And when we use those talents and abilities in church, or in vocation, or in relationships with others, we can approach it one of two ways—we can seek glory for ourselves, or we can look to glorify God.

You see, to love God with all of our energy, with all of our abilities, with all of our spiritual gifts, means to serve the Lord in ministry. It's a way of expressing our love to Him. It means holding nothing back when it comes to our energy level in showing our love for God. It means that when we're using all that energy in our vocations or in school, we're doing it because it is pleasing to God to make the most of our abilities for Him. We are loving God with all of our strength, with all of our being.

So, are you strong in your love for God?

Consider: Seventy Times Seven

Then Peter came and said to Him, "Lord, how often shall my brother sin against me and I forgive him? Up to seven times?" Jesus said to him, "I do not say to you, up to seven times, but up to seventy times seven."

MATTHEW 18:21-22

Chuck Colson tells about an amazing event that occurred at one of his prison ministries. In this program, prisoners who come to Christ go through an eighteen-month discipleship period and then have a graduation. When one of the prisoners came forward for recognition, a very stately woman rose in his support. She was the mother of the young woman the prisoner had killed fifteen years before. The man had denied his crime for many years. And then he came to Christ and, while going through this discipleship program, became convicted of his need to come clean with both God and those he had hurt. He confessed the crime and then asked forgiveness from the victim's mother.

But that's not the amazing part. Before that woman received his letter, she had called on the Lord to help her forgive the man who had murdered her daughter. So in that graduation ceremony, this woman stood beside the man who had killed her child and announced, "This is my adopted son."

My friends, that's true Christianity. When we are reconciled with God through faith in Jesus Christ and confess our sins, the Holy Spirit blesses us with a supernatural power. That power causes us to seek forgiveness from those we have wronged and forgive those who have horribly wronged us—even up to seventy times seven.

What We Have in Common

But know this first of all, that no prophecy of Scripture is a matter of one's own interpretation, for no prophecy was ever made by an act of human will, but men moved by the Holy Spirit spoke from God.

2 PETER 1:20–21

Currently, Christianity has more than two billion adherents divided into three great traditions: Catholic, Orthodox, and Protestant. And the Protestants are divided into more than six hundred separate denominations. With that kind of diversity, it's inevitable that there will be disagreement over many doctrines within the whole of Christianity.

But when it comes to the big issues, when it comes to what we believe about Jesus, most are in solid agreement. True Christians—regardless of denomination, language, and nationality—believe alike concerning the most basic principles of our shared faith. We believe Jesus was born of a virgin; He is both fully God and fully man. Christ paid the penalty for our sins when He died on the cross. He rose from the dead and ascended to heaven and is reigning at the right hand of the Father. We know that He will come again one day, and when He comes, it will be judgment on the final Antichrist and all of his followers, as well as the moment of ultimate salvation for those who follow Jesus!

Although there may be differences on secondary doctrinal issues, most Christians, regardless of denomination, share these core convictions. And when you look at the power of these common beliefs, they give us great unity in our diversity.

Social Networking

"Therefore go and make disciples of all nations, baptizing them in the name of the Father and of the Son and of the Holy Spirit, and teaching them to obey everything I have commanded you. And surely I am with you always, to the very end of the age."

MATTHEW 28:19–20 NIV

When Jesus left His disciples with the command to go and make disciples of all nations, the task was not an easy one. They had to walk everywhere. They had the ability to write letters, but the time and distance made letter-writing a slow process, so word of mouth was pretty much it for hearing about the goings-on outside of their general area. Not particularly conducive to having an easy time of spreading the Word.

Compare that with today's high-speed technology, making it possible to send information in the blink of an eye to anywhere on the planet. These fast-delivery services are available on home and office computers, in Internet cafés, and on phones, to name a few.

The fastest growing Internet phenomena in the world today is the rise of "social networking." Even a technical airhead like me knows about Facebook and Twitter. They're surely not perfect, but they're great conduits for spreading information, as well as your faith.

Technology is amoral. It is simply a tool for information, entertainment, and communication. Some is evil. Some is good. Had the disciples had access to today's technology, they would surely be using it to talk about Jesus. How about you? If not, realize that technology is a way to share the Word about Jesus.

You Are Somebody

"Indeed, the very hairs of your head are all numbered."

LUKE 12:7 NIV

A young girl confidently introduced herself to her new second-grade classmates. "My name is Martha Bowers Taft," she began. "My great-grandfather was president of the United States. My grandfather was a United States senator. My father is the ambassador to Ireland." She then puffed out her chest and proudly declared, "And I am a Brownie!"

We all enjoy having status. Unfortunately, many of us think we are not significant enough to be used by God for great things. We might say, "Oh, I'm *only* a janitor," or "I'm *just* a repairman," or "I'm *only* a housewife." We think that if only we had a more prestigious title—such as doctor, professional athlete, or reverend—God could use us to do mighty things.

Perhaps the prophet Amos thought that way when God called him to serve. "After all," he could have said, "I am *only* a shepherd. Who will listen to me?" But instead of questioning his status, he obeyed and became a powerful voice for God.

Remember, with God there are no "if onlys." No matter what you perceive about yourself, God has numbered the very hairs on your head, and He sees you as having potential for great things. Those "great things" will always be about service to Him and to the people He created. They will be about using your gifts and talents for His glory.

From Adversity to Greatness

*[Be] confident of this, that he who began a
good work in you will carry it on to completion
until the day of Christ Jesus.*

PHILIPPIANS 1:6 NIV

In Genesis 37, when Joseph was seventeen, he had a dream prophesying that he would someday rule over his brothers. This peek into his destiny filled him with self-confidence; he was a young man who was riding high. But the fact is, he wasn't ready to rule over his brothers right then. He needed to go through some character-shaping times. And indeed, he did just that, spending thirteen years facing setbacks, challenges, and even prison. Although Joseph was forgotten by man during those times, he was never forgotten by God. Through adversity, God molded his character so that when Pharaoh appointed him prime minister of Egypt, he was ready to fulfill his God-chosen destiny.

Think about Joseph when you go through tough times in your own life. Sometimes God breaks us and allows us to hit rock bottom so He can shape us into the people He is calling us to be. Maybe the adversity is God's way of strengthening you, teaching you, molding you, and preparing you for the great plans He has for your life.

When Does a Baby Become a Baby?

I will give thanks to You, for I am fearfully and wonderfully made; wonderful are Your works, and my soul knows it very well. My frame was not hidden from You, when I was made in secret, and skillfully wrought in the depths of the earth.

PSALM 139:14–15

About half the people in the United States say they are pro-life, and about half say they are pro-choice. How is this affiliation determined? For the most part, if you consider a fetus nothing but a blob of tissue that is part of a woman's body, you become pro-choice. If you believe that fetus is a human being, you are pro-life. Who is right? Let's see what God says.

The psalmist wrote, "For You formed my inward parts; You wove me in my mother's womb" (Psalm 139:13). And then he went on to say, "Your eyes have seen my unformed substance; and in Your book were written all the days that were ordained for me, when as yet there was not one of them" (v. 16). God is the Creator of life, and life is formed within a mother's womb. Scripture is clear: God declares that a fetus is most certainly a human life from the moment of conception (Jeremiah 1:5).

Some say that a fetus is nothing but a blob of tissue. God says a fetus is a person. Who do you think is right?

The Real Lesson at the Well

A woman from Samaria came to draw water.
Jesus said to her, "Give me a drink."

JOHN 4:7 ESV

Jesus broke a lot of taboos while He walked this earth. One huge cultural faux pas was when He spoke with the woman at the well. In this single act, Jesus actually broke *three* taboo rules that good Jewish men did not break: He traveled into Samaritan territory, He spoke to a woman in public, and He interacted with a woman who had a "reputation." But the fact is, Jesus was always more concerned with reaching out to those in need than in dodging man-made social taboos.

Let me ask you a question. Are you willing to reach out to those who are different from you, culturally, socially, and morally? Students, are you willing to reach out to that person who's often left out, maybe a classmate who's on the fringe? Adults, are you willing to reach out to those folks at the office who are different, maybe the office rabble-rouser or the known homosexual, or—heaven forbid—the conservative Republican or liberal Democrat? Or is observing cultural taboos more important to you?

Are *you* willing to reach out? Jesus certainly did. He broke one social taboo after another so that He could reach out to people in need. If you call yourself a Christian, are you willing to be like Jesus?

Connecting with Jewish Friends

*All of us like sheep have gone astray, each of us
has turned to his own way; but the LORD has caused
the iniquity of us all to fall on Him.*

ISAIAH 53:6

One reason Christians are hesitant to witness to Jewish friends is that we just don't know how to approach the subject. Here are some ideas:

+ Be a friend first. Show the love you have for that person and that you care what happens to them. Within the relationship, you might ask some questions like, "What do you think about what's going on in the Middle East today?" Or, "What does your family do at Passover?"

+ Show love to a Jewish friend by saying, "Would you be willing to let me visit synagogue with you so I can learn more about the Jewish faith?" Often we Christians don't take the time to show interest in their beliefs.

+ When the timing is right, read Isaiah 53 to them and ask, "Who do you think this passage is talking about?" Most will respond, "That's talking about Jesus." And then say, "Do you know where that is?" And they will usually respond, "It's obviously in the Christian Bible." But then show them, "No, it's the Jewish prophet Isaiah, more than seven hundred years before Christ came, prophesying of Christ's death." That's a biblical connection that might create some openness to look further at Jesus.

So, build the relationship; then build *on* the relationship.

Why God Hates Divorce

"I hate divorce," says the LORD God of Israel.

MALACHI 2:16 NIV

God could not be clearer—He hates divorce. Scripture actually lists three specific reasons why He feels this way.

First, divorce so often springs from adultery—a complete violation of the marital bonds. God calls this "deal[ing] treacherously" with one's wife (Malachi 2:14–16). Second, it treats the sacred institution of marriage with contempt, as the couple has disregarded the covenant commitment they made before God (v. 15).

But perhaps God's greatest reason for hating divorce is because of the harm it brings to children. Scripture refers to "godly offspring," but it is difficult to have godly offspring with the children of divorce. Why is this? Because these children have seen the most sacred human relationship trivialized and destroyed. They have been disillusioned. And what do children do when they are disillusioned? They become confused and angry and often blame God, and saddest of all, they sometimes blame themselves.

God hates divorce for all the unnecessary pain it causes. But God loves the divorcee and offers His forgiveness and love. God hates divorce for the same reason divorcees and children of divorce hate divorce. He wants to spare us the pain and wants us to know the joy of marriage.

The Trinity

*The mystery of godliness is great: He appeared in a
body, [and] was vindicated by the Spirit.*

1 TIMOTHY 3:16 NIV

The *Trinity* is a theological term used to describe God as three persons in one. Although this is a sound theological belief, it is a concept most of us have a tough time putting our arms around. That's because there are some things the human mind just can't fully comprehend.

Here's an analogy that might be helpful. Imagine the ocean. It consists of a great body of water at its base, but the surface churns into constantly moving waves, as well as an enveloping mist. These are three distinct features, but it is not possible to know where one ends and another begins. Although the deep waters (God the Father), the waves (God the Son), and the mist (God the Spirit) are certainly all the same ocean, each is also a separate manifestation of that one body of water.

But here's where any analogy on the Trinity breaks down. How do you explain Jesus, the Son, praying to God, the Father? Try getting your arms around that. The Trinity is Truth—yet it's a concept that is difficult for our finite human minds to grasp. But the Trinity—God as three-in-one—fills us with wonder at the unexplainable greatness of God.

Righteous Anger

In your anger do not sin.

EPHESIANS 4:26 NIV

All of us struggle with anger; it's a part of life. Do you ever feel your anger is justified? Have you ever used the term *righteous anger?* The phrase is often used when someone has wronged us; we say, "I have every right to be angry." And then to justify our anger, we'll add, "Jesus showed righteous anger, didn't He?"

Well, yes, He did. But it is important to note what triggered His righteous anger. When Jesus entered the temple and found it had been turned into a place of greed and materialism for taking advantage of the poor, He was furious. Why? Because God was not being respected, and people were being taken advantage of.

Jesus became indignant when the disciples would not allow children to visit with Him. The disciples didn't consider the children as important. They felt that Jesus was "too busy" for them. It made Him furious.

But understand this: Jesus never got angry when *He* was treated unjustly. So how did He react when He was the target of injustice? Look at what Jesus did when He was unfairly sentenced to death, the ultimate act of personal injustice. He prayed, "Father, forgive them" (Luke 23:34).

Look to Jesus for how to deal with personal attacks. And save your righteous anger for situations where God is not respected and other people are mistreated. God's Word teaches us that this is the time to be angry—but not to sin.

Victimless Crime?

*"But I say to you that everyone who looks at a
woman with lust for her has already committed
adultery with her in his heart."*

MATTHEW 5:28

Here is a lie you often hear: pornography is a victimless sin. The fact is that looking at porn is an incredibly addictive behavior. It has even been called the crack cocaine of sexual addiction; dabbling in porn carries the same dangers as dabbling in cocaine or heroin. It has the same kind of addictive draw, especially in a man's life. And this addiction can have a devastating effect on both the men who engage in it and their families.

Pornography cheapens what God created as a beautiful pleasure to be enjoyed between a husband and wife. It creates a mind-set where a woman is seen as an object to be used, like a bottle of booze. When it's used up, throw it away; discard it. Find another one!

Porn creates a fantasy world—totally out of touch with reality—that can cause a sense of dissatisfaction within a man's marriage. There's just no way a wife can compete with this fantasy world. And the effect of the divorces caused by porn addiction is catastrophic—to men, their wives and children, their extended families, and society as a whole.

Victimless crime? Not on your life. Our communities are saturated with the tears of devastated victims.

Prayer

Pray without ceasing.

1 THESSALONIANS 5:17

It was said that President Lyndon Johnson invited one of his aides, Bill Moyers, to a family dinner at the White House. Since Moyers was an ordained minister, the president called upon him to say grace before the meal. Moyers began his prayer, quietly asking the Lord's blessing. Johnson, on the other end of the table, soon bellowed, "Speak up, Bill! I can't hear you," to which Moyers replied, "I wasn't speaking to you, Mr. President."

Many of us have some trouble when it comes to praying. We search for all the right words, or we worry about touching on all the right points. Sometimes the process is so distorted that some people believe only an ordained minister should even take a stab at it.

But think about this: what is one of the most-mentioned commands in the Bible? It's to pray. In fact, God not only commands us to pray, but He also says to pray *without ceasing*. Now, would God tell us to constantly do something that was beyond our capabilities? Don't worry about choosing beautiful words, or using correct tenses in Old English, or producing deep theological truths. Just speak to the Lord from your heart, and tell Him what's on your mind. It's as simple as that. And relax. You are talking to Someone who loves you and wants the best for you.

Justice

Do not take revenge, my friends, but leave room for God's wrath, for it is written: "It is mine to avenge; I will repay," says the Lord.

ROMANS 12:19 NIV

King David knew what it was like to be treated unjustly. His predecessor, King Saul, tried to kill him. Then, later in life, he was betrayed by his son Absalom, who took away the throne that rightfully belonged to him. David protested and cried out to God for justice but recognized that vengeance is a matter for God. It wasn't long before Absalom—who was very proud of his beautiful head of long, flowing hair—had his gorgeous locks caught in a tree as he was riding by. He couldn't untangle himself, and one of David's men killed him. God brought about justice in a rather colorful manner, and David, who wept for his son, was restored to the throne.

God delivers justice in different ways. Sometimes it's through routine personal (and peaceful) interaction. Other times normal office procedures result in a just solution. Some actions require the involvement of the police or the courts. And sometimes justice will not be revealed until after our deaths, but recognize that God sees an eternal picture that we cannot comprehend while wrapped up in our temporal, earthly matters.

In every case, know this: God *will* bring about justice. Maybe it won't be as dramatic as a vain man getting his hair stuck in a tree. But in the end, God's justice will most certainly be done.

You've Been Replaced

*For this reason a man shall leave his father and
mother and shall be joined to his wife.*

EPHESIANS 5:31

There is a moment in the marriage ceremony when a father may shed a tear. It is when Dad escorts his daughter down the aisle and places her hand into the hand of her new husband. This is symbolic of God's declaration that a man shall leave his father and mother and be joined to his wife. From the very beginning, God laid down this most basic principle of human relationships. No matter how much you love your parents, a sibling, or a good friend, no one is to be closer than your mate.

Parents, you need to know that this moment in the ceremony is not just for the newlyweds. It is also for you. Understand that the relationship with your child has changed. God has now joined your child together with his or her spouse, and their prime earthly relationship is no longer with you. It is with each other. But relax. This is how God designed it. From here forward, no relationship with Mom or Dad can come close to matching the relationship of a husband and wife. So with God's help, let your child go, and allow him or her to build a new family in His image. It's one of the greatest ways you can bless your child.

Preparing to Be a Witness

*But in your hearts set apart Christ as Lord. Always
be prepared to give an answer to everyone who asks
you to give the reason for the hope that you have. But
do this with gentleness and respect.*

1 PETER 3:15 NIV

Christian, sometimes you will have an opportunity to share your faith, but you may have only thirty seconds to do so. Be prepared to make good use of these moments so that you can open the door to future conversations. Prepare a brief story (about a hundred words) of your Christian experience, made up of three parts:

1. your life before you met Christ,
2. how you met Christ, and
3. the difference Christ has made in your life.

Let me share my story. I grew up in a Christian home. Into my teenage years, I would have told you I was a Christian. Then I went to a Christian camp where the focus was on God's love and all that Christ had done for me on the cross. I became convicted that I had been using God to call on before a big test, an important ball game, or a special date—otherwise I kept Him at arm's length. In realizing God's love on a deeper, personal level, I committed my heart and life to follow Christ wherever He wanted me to go. And ever since, I've had purpose and meaning to my life. I have been sure of salvation and eternal life. What is your story in one hundred words?

The Need to Need More Than You Need

"Beware, and be on your guard against every form of greed; for not even when one has an abundance does his life consist of his possessions."

LUKE 12:15

The desire to acquire more stuff than we need is called *greed*. This is a huge issue in our society just as it was when Christ walked the earth. Jesus told the parable of a rich fool who had had such a good year that he had run out of places to store his crops. He decided to solve this "problem" by building bigger and bigger barns so he could have a place for all his stuff. With all these riches, he reassured himself that he could now take it easy and enjoy early retirement.

Doesn't this sound great? It's the American dream! He had everything he needed and much, much more. Only he didn't expect God to say, "You fool! This very night your life will be demanded from you" (Luke 12:20 NIV). This man never gave a thought to the fact that it was God who had blessed him and entrusted him with all his stuff. He was rich in his own eyes but poor in God's eyes, for he never realized that God had blessed him with much so he could give more to the Lord's work and others in need. He greedily hoarded all he had and died in spiritual poverty.

The need to need more than you need equals greed. Eternal wealth lasts forever. Earthly wealth can be gone tonight.

Blind from Birth

By what a man is overcome, by this he is enslaved.

2 PETER 2:19

When I read the story in the *New York Times*, I couldn't believe it—a blind receiver in football?

He played for Wofford College during the 2002 season. He said he ran his patterns carefully and looked for a dark, fuzzy spot coming toward him. Talk about overcoming adversity—that was amazing!

In an age of self-indulgence and a victim mind-set, this player stood out as an example of hard work and perseverance. He accepted and overcame his adversity and used it as a motivation rather than an excuse. By doing so, this young man challenged each of us not to be defeated by our limitations.

Wouldn't all of our lives be more fulfilled and effective if we followed his example? It can happen with God's help. With God as our strength, we won't see ourselves as victims, but as overcomers. Jesus Christ said, "In this world you'll have problems, but take heart. I have overcome the world" (John 16:33, paraphrased).

Making the Best out of a Bad Situation

"These things I have spoken to you, so that in Me you may have peace. In the world you have tribulation, but take courage; I have overcome the world."

Winston Churchill inspired the free world as he defiantly declared, "We shall never surrender!" during England's darkest days. History has shown that he, more than any other person, can be credited with saving Britain from an almost certain enslavement by the Nazis. Yet as World War II ended, his beloved country unceremoniously dumped him as its prime minister. Attempting to comfort him, his wife declared that this rejection might actually be a blessing in disguise. "If it is," he replied, "then it is certainly very well disguised."[8]

Despite this humbling rejection, Churchill went on with his life. In fact, the following year he made the "Iron Curtain" speech upon which the free world based its policy during the Cold War. He also won a Pulitzer Prize for his six-volume history of World War II and served another term as prime minister and many years as the elder statesman of the free world.

Jesus warned that "in [this] world, you will have tribulation." You will face many rejections, roadblocks, and even landmines in your life. Sometimes God allows us to face these challenges to teach, test, or even redirect us. Learn to view these hardships as opportunities to make yourself stronger. You just might discover that Mrs. Churchill was right! It could be a blessing in disguise.

Saved Forever

*Whoever has the Son has life; whoever does not
have the Son of God does not have life.*

1 JOHN 5:12 ESV

There is a theological term called *eternal security*. What this means is that once you are saved, you are always saved; you can never lose your salvation.

How can we be so certain of this? You are saved by the grace of God, not by your deeds or actions. You cannot be religious enough; you cannot help enough people; you cannot donate enough money—there is absolutely *nothing* you can do to earn your way into heaven. And because there is nothing you can do to earn salvation, there is nothing you can do to lose it. Once saved, always saved.

So, you may ask, "If I'm always saved, does that mean I can go out and live a rebellious life without having to worry about being shut out of heaven?" Well, yes, you could. But if you were genuine in accepting Christ, you will not want to live this selfishly. You will have such gratitude to Jesus for His remarkable gift that you will seek to live your life in a manner that pleases Him. He loved you enough to save you, and you'll want to love Him back.

Perhaps some of you are worried that maybe you weren't really saved years ago. Perhaps your decision to come to Christ was done on a whim or without the proper analysis. If you're still unsure, you can always ask Him to save you for sure. Read Revelation 3:20 and John 3:36. Believe those wonderful words of God, and you can know *for sure* that you have eternal life.

The Right Values

You shall have no other gods before Me.

EXODUS 20:3

Modern man is in a continual search for values. Every person has values—even the Mafia and drug lords; even Hitler, Stalin, Mao, and Saddam Hussein had values. Confusion about values comes because man starts at the wrong place—with himself. Our culture is filled with people who are seeking to do what is "right in their own eyes," and it's led to chaos—morally, spiritually, emotionally, and relationally. I urge you to start with God's number one commandment: "You shall have no other gods before Me."

Some argue that what is most important to you is really your god. So what's most important to you? Is it family, success, money, power, possessions, happiness, or self? What is your most important value? When it's anyone or anything besides God, it's still a "god," and our value orientation gets out of whack.

When we start from the wrong place, we always wind up lost and confused, following false gods. But the one true God says, *Start with Me; put Me first, and all other values have a way of falling into place.* It's the key to right values.

No Going Back

*For I do not want you to be unaware, brethren,
that our fathers were all under the cloud, and all
passed through the sea.*

1 CORINTHIANS 10:1

The book of Exodus comments on the actions of the Israelites after Passover. It says that after the Passover Lamb, God saved their lives and led them to freedom. Then they demonstrated their faith by walking through the sea. In a way, their obedience was similar to a baptism, just like the baptism of a new believer in Jesus Christ. God was saying to Israel—just as He was saying to the early church—*Look, once you take that first step, there's no going back!* Once God brought the waters of the sea together again, there was no going back to slavery in Egypt. The Israelites had to walk forward on their journey of faith.

The same is true when we accept Christ. Once we are saved, we are to be baptized as a testimony of our faith in Christ. When we enter those waters, there's no going back! There's no going back to the pre-Christian days. Sure, we can try, but it will never be the same. We're now on an irreversible journey that follows Jesus to the ultimate Promised Land! So don't look back—keep looking forward to follow Jesus.

The Supernatural Power of God

*And [Peter] went out and continued to follow, and he
did not know that what was being done by the angel
was real, but thought he was seeing a vision.*

ACTS 12:9

Dayna Curry and Heather Mercer, former aid workers in
Afghanistan, have spoken about Qalzai, a man their ministry brought to Christ. As with many Muslims who convert, he
was arrested, tossed into a prison cell, beaten daily, and left to
await his almost-certain execution.

One night, their new brother in Christ dreamed that a large,
strong-looking man surrounded by a glowing light suddenly
appeared in his cell. The man led him out of the cell, into the
prison courtyard, and out the front gates. When Qalzai awoke,
he immediately realized that it had all been just a dream and was
understandably depressed. But then, as he sat up, he noticed that
his cell door was open. He didn't see a guard anywhere, so he
began to think, *Hey, maybe God is up to something here!* He walked
out of his cell, into the courtyard, and right through the unlocked
front gate of the prison. Qalzai had experienced a miracle exactly
like the one Peter did two thousand years earlier. They had both
witnessed the supernatural power of God.

Miracles didn't just happen in the Bible; they happen every
day in the twenty-first century, but they most often happen when
man is powerless. So when you are powerless, don't worry. God's
power will get the job done.

How Great Thou Art!

He is your praise; he is your God, who performed
for you those great and awesome wonders you
saw with your own eyes.

DEUTERONOMY 10:21 NIV

Swedish pastor Carl Boberg was enjoying a nice walk through the woods when, suddenly, a thunderstorm struck. He sought shelter underneath an ancient oak tree and braced himself against the cold rain and wind. Then, as suddenly as it had appeared, the storm subsided, leaving a clear blue sky and the gentle scene of nature at its most glorious. Boberg heard the ring of a church bell in the distance, and a feeling of peace enveloped him as the words to one of Christianity's greatest hymns, "How Great Thou Art," formed in his heart. Take a moment and read his words:

O Lord my God, when I in awesome wonder,
Consider all the worlds Thy hands have made.
I see the stars, I hear the rolling thunder,
Thy power throughout the universe displayed.
And when I think that God, His Son not sparing,
Sent Him to die, I scarce can take it in.
That on the cross, my burden gladly bearing,
He bled and died to take away my sin.
Then sings my soul, My Savior God, to Thee,
How great Thou art, How great Thou art.
Then sings my soul, My Savior God, to Thee,
How great Thou art, How great Thou art!

May you sing it all day!

Listened to Song Lyrics Lately?

*Whatever is true, whatever is noble, whatever is right,
whatever is pure, whatever is lovely, whatever is
admirable . . . think about such things.*

PHILIPPIANS 4:8 NIV

A while back, I overheard some "tweenage" girls say that their favorite song was "Soldier Boy." I chuckled, thinking it quite nostalgic that a 1962 rock-and-roll hit was being recycled for yet another generation. Later I discovered that I had misunderstood the girls—they actually said that their favorite song was *by* Soulja Boy. And then I saw some of this rapper's lyrics, which are too profane to print in this book!

Parents, three things:

+ First, listen to the music. Sometimes this isn't easy—the pounding music often doesn't sound like music at all, but be assured that after constant exposure, the attitude and mood projected are being firmly planted in your child's brain.
+ Pay close attention to the lyrics. What is their message? Put simply, much of today's popular music tragically devalues women. Girls listening to such songs become programmed to think of themselves as far less than the treasures they are in Christ.
+ Beware if your daughter is dating or hanging out with a boy who listens to such music. How do you think he perceives women? How will this training cause him to treat your daughter?

God's Word teaches us that how we think, so we are.

Trusting God

*I will say of the Lord, "He is my refuge and my
fortress, my God, in whom I trust."*

PSALM 91:2 NIV

Think about all the different people to whom we entrust our
lives. We trust pharmacists to give us the right pills from a
prescription we can't read. We trust pilots we don't know to take
us to the right destination, believing that they know how to fly
that metal tube exactly where we need to go. As we soar down
the interstate, we trust other drivers to stay alert and follow the
road. We trust our lives to engineers and road construction crews,
believing the bridges will hold. We make countless decisions to
trust people we don't even know every single day.

Yet people have trouble trusting God. They often say, "I can't
see Him." Do we see the engineers who designed the bridge? Do
we know the pilots? Not usually. Yet God, our Creator, who loves
us more than anyone, who even sacrificed His Son for us to have
forgiveness of sin and eternal life, is difficult to trust. It's amazing.
It just doesn't make sense to trust imperfect men and women and
not to trust a perfect God. From the love He shows us through
His Son, it just makes sense to trust Him.

Heading to Jerusalem

While [Jesus] was on the way to Jerusalem, He was passing between Samaria and Galilee.

LUKE 17:11

If you study the New Testament, I hope you'll begin to note that time and again it says something like, "While Jesus was on the way to Jerusalem . . ." Don't ever forget that. Christ came to teach. Christ came to preach. Christ came to heal. He came to perform miracles. But the main mission of Christ, always, was to head to Jerusalem. Why? Because at Jerusalem was the cross, and there He would pay the penalty for our sins. And why was that important? Because the main reason Jesus Christ came was to be our Savior, to die in our place so He could save us from sin and death and hell. All through His ministry, amid all the great things He was doing, there was one central focus. He was headed to Jerusalem. He was headed to the cross. *This* is why He came.

April

For as the earth brings forth its sprouts, and as a garden causes the things sown in it to spring up, so the Lord God will cause righteousness and praise to spring up before all the nations.

<small>Isaiah 61:11</small>

Fool

In all your ways acknowledge Him, and He
will make your paths straight.

PROVERBS 3:6

You make a fool of yourself when you argue with a donkey. In Numbers 22, the Bible tells of a man named Balaam who was headed in the wrong direction. He wanted to please himself and was ignoring God, so God spoke to him through his donkey. Balaam was furiously mad at the animal! He argued with it and almost beat it to death until he realized that God was seeking to speak to him and to help him get on the right path.

Sometimes God goes to extraordinary means to get our attention when we are set on going our own self-destructive ways. It could come through a financial jolt or through a rebellious child. When those times come, getting angry may be foolish, but taking time to listen may be the key to seeking God's guidance about the right way to go.

Is God trying to get your attention to keep you from making a fool of yourself? Take time to listen, and He'll change your course and get you where you need to go.

Real Marriage, Real Friends

"They are no longer two, but one flesh. What therefore God has joined together, let no man separate."

MATTHEW 19:6

Jesus taught that marriage is not just about the husband-and-wife relationship. A Christian marriage is really a symbolic reminder of Christ's relationship with the people of faith. That is why Jesus added a most important aspect to loving our mates: exclusive loyalty in the marriage relationship.

We could look at many aspects when learning how to love our mates with the exclusive loyalty of committed love: the importance of the husband's need for respect from his wife, and the wife's need for romantic love from her husband; the importance of listening, time, forgiveness, compassion, kindness; the importance of controlling our tongues and not saying those hurtful things we're so prone to say. You see, there are all kind of things we could talk about in loving our mates, but behind Jesus' basic explanation of what it means to love our spouses is this insight: your spouse is to be your best friend. Not Mom or Dad, sibling or friend, even a child—no one should be closer to you than your spouse! With a real friend in our spouse, we have a sense of commitment that truly says in our hearts and our actions, till death do us part.

Forgiveness

"For if you forgive men when they sin against you,
your heavenly Father will also forgive you."

MATTHEW 6:14 NIV

Have you ever noticed the presence of a little two-letter word in the Lord's Prayer? It says, "And forgive us our sins, *as* we have forgiven those who sin against us" (Matthew 6:12 NLT). Did you catch that? The word *as* implies that we cannot be forgiven until we offer forgiveness to others. In case we miss the *as*, Jesus makes it very clear a couple of verses later: "But if you do not forgive men their sins, your Father will not forgive your sins" (v. 15 NIV).

Forgiving someone who has treated you poorly, said evil things about you, even broken up your family, is a very difficult thing to do. But God commands us to do so, and He never commands us to do anything that He wouldn't provide the ability to do.

Right now, pray for God to give you the strength to forgive those who have hurt you. Not only will God give you the power to do so, but He will also empower you supernaturally to love them, even though you hate what they did. Remember, bitterness is the poison we swallow while hoping the other person dies. Enjoy the release of this terrible burden by experiencing the cleansing power of forgiveness.

Our Greatest Generation

*Do nothing from selfishness or empty conceit, but
with humility of mind, regard one another as more
important than yourselves.*

PHILIPPIANS 2:3

If you visit the mall in Washington, D.C., you will see our new-
est national monument, the National World War II Memorial.
It's a grand celebration of the greatest generation America has ever
produced.

Some important symbolism is often missed with this memorial.
Although the Second World War occurred first, the monuments for
the veterans of Korea and Vietnam were actually built first.

How appropriate. This greatest generation was raised during
the Depression, when neighbors personally sacrificed to keep friends
from starving. Just as that crisis was ending, the men left to fight evil
on foreign soil, while the women laced up their boots and worked
in this country's industries. After the war, they brought America to
historic levels of prosperity while saving the economies of the very
people they had just defeated. They lived their lives well and stayed
quiet about the price they paid to do such great things.

Even though many of its honorees never lived to see its completion, how appropriate that it was the last war memorial to be built.
This amazing generation had a way of putting others first and themselves last.

Jesus taught His followers, "The last shall be first" (Matthew
20:16). The greatest generation often lived that way, and that's why
they are the "greatest."

The Heart of Worship

I hate, I reject your festivals, nor do I delight in your solemn assemblies. Even though you offer up to Me burnt offerings and your grain offerings, I will not accept them.

AMOS 5:21–22

Wow. That's pretty strong condemnation from God! Obviously, this was a time when the children of Israel were engaging in all kinds of evil. They were worshipping idols, committing adultery, divorcing, and giving God only their leftovers. They had turned their hearts against God.

And now they wanted God's help. The economy had gone south; their crops were not fruitful. They couldn't understand why God wasn't coming through. "God, we're worshipping with passion. We're weeping on the altar. We're bringing You our offerings. What in the world is going on?"

Sound familiar? The economy has gone south. Jobs have been lost. Marriages ruined. Do you ever find yourself asking the same question? "Hey, God, I'm going to church; I'm singing Your praises. So why haven't things turned around for me?" *(Never mind that I'm cheating on my income taxes. Or that I'm feasting on pornography. Or that I'm mistreating my children . . .)*

We cannot buy God's favor with our offerings. We do not impress Him with an emotional, weeping, passionate worship if our lifestyle doesn't show a heart for God. He is far more concerned with our obedience. In fact, He won't even *accept* our offerings or our songs of worship unless our hearts are truly repentant and our lives are following Jesus.

Where is your heart?

But Wasn't It Simply His Destiny?

"The Son of Man goes as it is written of him, but woe to that man by whom the Son of Man is betrayed! It would have been better for that man if he had not been born." Judas, who would betray him, answered, "Is it I, Rabbi?" He said to him, "You have said so."

MATTHEW 26:24–25 ESV

Here is a question I'm asked every Easter. Since Christ had to go to the cross in order to fulfill His mission on earth, wasn't Judas simply fulfilling the will of God? Wasn't God using him as a tool to get Jesus to the cross?

Well, no and no. Even though God had His predetermined plan and knew what Judas was going to do, He did not force him to do it! Judas still had a choice, and he chose to betray Jesus. And though it's sometimes difficult to reconcile the theology, understand this: *all of us have a choice.* Yes, God does have a predestined plan for our lives. But realize that there is no sin in that plan. We choose whether to accept or reject His plan by inviting sin into the equation. And although God does know what our choices will be, that does not mean He forces us to make them.

The best thing we can do is constantly seek God's will in our lives, asking Him to show us what His perfect plan is for us each and every day.

A Secret Christian

After these things Joseph of Arimathea, being a disciple of
Jesus, but a secret one for fear of the Jews, asked Pilate
that he might take away the body of Jesus; and Pilate
granted permission. So he came and took away His body.

JOHN 19:38

Crucifixion is the most horrible form of execution man has ever devised. It was so degrading that those crucified were not supposed to be buried in a cemetery. Very often their bodies were cast on the garbage dump outside the city. Because He was crucified, Jesus would have been considered unclean and denied burial in a Jewish cemetery. But for some reason, a rich man intervened.

Joseph of Arimathea was that man. He was a member of the ruling council. But he was also afraid of what his fellow Jews would think if they knew he were a follower of Jesus. What would it do to his wealth, prominence, and influence? So to protect himself, he kept his love for Christ a secret. Yet there was something in Jesus' death that caused him to go public. In fact, he went so public that he went before Pilate and asked for permission to bury Jesus in a tomb that had been reserved for his own family.

Let me ask: In your daily life, are you one of those secret Christians? Would people at the office know that you're a follower of Christ? Would your neighbors? This Easter, use Joseph's example to move from being a secret follower to a public follower of Christ. Jesus said, "But whoever denies Me before men, I will also deny him before My Father who is in heaven" (Matthew 10:33).

He Is Risen!

"Why do you look for the living among the dead?
He is not here; he has risen!"

What is the one single act that defined Christianity? The virgin birth? The revolutionary philosophies of Jesus Christ? The great miracles—feeding five thousand men, turning water into wine, healing the sick? Although all of these acts of Christ certainly set Him above any other person who has ever walked the earth, nothing compares to His death and resurrection from the dead. Through His death, Jesus gave His life to pay the penalty of our sin. Through His resurrection, He conquered sin and death, and He gives us that power as well. On Easter we celebrate this wonderful moment and the joyous consequences that stemmed from it. When I contemplate the amazing grace that exploded from His resurrection, I find myself humming, then singing, some of the words to the classic hymn "He Lives!" We do indeed serve a risen Savior, and He lives within all our hearts![9]

Celebrate Resurrection Day! Because He lives!

Writing Your Legacy

*An inheritance quickly gained at the beginning
will not be blessed at the end.*

PROVERBS 20:21 NIV

The mortality rate for humans is 100 percent. The fact is, someday you are going to die. People will say nice things about you, watch your casket roll out, then go back in your house and eat fried chicken and green bean casseroles. And then they are *really* going to talk about you!

What will they say? Will they talk about your business accomplishments and awards? Will the conversation read like a résumé, listing titles you have been given and degrees earned? Or will people talk about the good things you have done for others, how well you led your family, and how you loved the Lord? Will the stories be about outrageous public actions or examples of your integrity?

Your legacy is up to you. Wouldn't it be better for your heirs to be left with a legacy they are proud of? When they talk about you after you die, what will they say? Will they speak of a life well lived and a person they were thankful to know?

Fearing God

My son, do not reject the discipline of the LORD or loathe
His reproof, for whom the LORD loves He reproves, even
as a father corrects the son in whom he delights.

PROVERBS 3:11–12

My father is one of the great blessings in my life. When I was growing up, he never hesitated to give me his approval and express his happiness with me. I never doubted my father's love, and I always wanted to please him. But I still had a healthy fear of him because I knew that if I did wrong, I would face discipline. So I learned early on that it was a good idea to obey him because it eliminated a lot of punishment. This understanding of my father served as protection for me, as well as motivation to do the right thing.

This is similar to our relationship with our heavenly Father. Just as discipline from our parents is a sign that they love us, God's discipline is a sign that He loves us. We want to have a healthy fear of God, knowing that if we do something wrong and displeasing to Him, we will face negative consequences for it.

"Fearing God" does not mean having a cowering anxiety about the Lord; it means having a healthy respect for the loving discipline we receive from an affectionate heavenly Father. And in the world in which we live, it surely would be wonderful if more people had a healthy fear of God.

Corporate Integrity

*He who walks in integrity walks securely, but he who
perverts his ways will be found out.*

PROVERBS 10:9

Enron was once the darling of Wall Street. In early 2000, it was the seventh-largest Fortune 500 company and the sixth-largest energy company in the world. And then, in just a little more than eighteen months, Enron was gone. It was one of the largest and swiftest falls in corporate history.

What was the problem at Enron? The company, with the support of their accountants at Arthur Andersen (another corporate giant that also collapsed in the debacle), would report profits from the purchase of a company—except they wouldn't be actual profits; they would be speculative or anticipated profits. Eventually people started asking some tough questions, and Enron was exposed for "speculative" record keeping. The truth was exposed, and the whole house of cards came crumbling down. And along the way, hundreds of thousands of innocent people were brought down with it. Leadership's greed and deception brought about this self-destruction.

The Enron debacle is a reminder of how important character is, especially at the top. The world is longing for leaders of integrity, godly men and women who are trustworthy and who will keep their word. What happens when leadership lacks this basic character? Proverbs 10:9 answers clearly: "The man of integrity walks securely, but he who takes crooked paths will be found out" (NIV). The hundreds of thousands of employees and stockholders at Enron and Arthur Andersen sure "found out" what "crooked paths" their leaders had taken.

The Cure for Worry

"Look at the birds of the air, that they do not sow, nor reap
nor gather into barns, and yet your heavenly Father feeds
them. Are you not worth much more than they?"

MATTHEW 6:26

One morning I walked outside of our house as the light was just beginning to show on the horizon. The birds around our yard were chirping and singing. They were pumped about another day, getting ready to go to work, finding twigs for their nests and luscious worms for their stomachs. Those birds didn't have a worry in the world! They lived a lifestyle that showed a trust in their Creator, going about gathering the resources He made available to them.

What's the lesson?

Although the birds trust God day by day, they also work hard from dawn to dusk. St. Augustine once said, "Pray as if everything depends on God, and then work as if everything depends on you." Pray to the Lord; share your worries and concerns. And then work hard like the birds. They just don't have time to worry. Neither do we if we'll work hard and trust our Creator.

Bouncing Back from Indiscretion

*The sacrifices of God are a broken spirit; a broken and
contrite heart, O God, you will not despise.*

PSALM 51:17 NIV

Are you struggling with a life crisis caused by a personal character flaw, indiscretion, or misstep? Consider the mess Moses got himself into. At age thirty-nine, Moses was at the apex of society, status, wealth, and educational pedigree as the adopted son of Pharaoh's daughter. And then he murdered an Egyptian he saw beating a Hebrew slave. He buried the body and thought he had gotten away with it, but the next day he was exposed, so he fled for his life into the wilderness. Moses went from high society to desert nomad within a day.

Moses probably felt as if his life of significance was over. But even though what he did was wrong, God did not abandon him. God took Moses' evil and turned it into a means for good by preparing him for the challenge of his life—confronting Pharaoh and demanding that he free the Hebrew slaves.

Perhaps you can relate to what Moses went through. No matter how hard your fall or how serious your character flaw—*don't give up*. Turn to the Lord for forgiveness. Then let God shape you and do something powerful in your life. Just as He did for Moses, God still has great plans for your life! There may be long-term negative consequences that you have to face. But if you will let God mold you and shape you into the person He desires you to be, you can be sure that God can use your life for good.

Those Who Have Not Heard

*That which is known about God is evident within
[men]; for God made it evident to them. For since the
creation of the world His invisible attributes, His
eternal power and divine nature, have been clearly
seen, being understood through what has been made,
so that they are without excuse.*

ROMANS 1:19–20

God makes it clear that everybody has to answer to Him
whether they've heard about Christ or not. As Jesus said in
John 14:6, "I am the way and the truth and the life. No one comes to
the Father except through me" (NIV). Have you ever thought it just
doesn't seem fair that those who have never heard the Word will be
judged the same way as those who have rejected His message?

We must keep some key things in mind. One, God is fair
and just. He is going to do the right thing. Second, this is why
the church has been given the Great Commission and called to
take the gospel to the entire world. This command should give
us a passion for the missionary endeavor to get out the good
news to everyone. Third, Romans 1:20 is clear that every person
is accountable to God for his or her knowledge of God. All are
"without excuse."

But what if we don't succeed in getting the gospel out to everyone and some people never have the opportunity to hear about
Christ? Jesus said, "I am the way to God." I believe He tells the
truth. Since every person will eventually have to answer to God,
how God deals with each person is something we must simply
leave in His hands.

Money Problems: God or Cash?

For the love of money is the root of all sorts of evil, and
some by longing for it have wandered away from the
faith and pierced themselves with many griefs.

1 TIMOTHY 6:10

There are many sayings that people think are in the Bible but are not. "Cleanliness is next to godliness." Not there. "God helps those who help themselves." Nope, not there either. But the most misquoted non-scripture has to be "Money is the root of all evil." The Bible doesn't say that at all! What the Bible does say is that the *love* of money is the root of all sorts of evil. Money is neither good nor bad. Yet God is concerned with how you acquire money, how you spend it, and where wealth ranks in your list of priorities.

God says you must decide what you're going to love most—Him or money. When we choose to love money, it can lead to all sorts of compromised decisions and makes us much more vulnerable to temptation. God's Word warns us that if we make money a priority over Him, we'll bring a lot of unnecessary grief into our lives and the lives of others.

God allows us to be the caretakers of what He provides, including our money. Let's love God first and foremost and realize that everything already belongs to Him anyway. He wants us to *love* Him and *manage* His money well.

Why, God, Why?

My God, my God, why have You forsaken me?

MATTHEW 27:46

Many Christians have a hard time understanding why on the cross Christ cried out, "My God, my God, why have You forsaken Me?" It seems contradictory to what we know of Christ, His understanding of His earthly mission, and His relationship with God. The truth is that instead of being a contradiction, these words are actually a wonderful blessing for all of us!

When Jesus said those words, it is believed to be the time He took all our sins upon Himself. And because God will have nothing to do with sin, Jesus was separated from His heavenly Father for the first time. It's a picture of God having to turn away when His Son became sin for us. Jesus cried out because He was separated from His Father for the only time in all eternity.

What is so wonderful about Christ doing this? When we face tragedy, disappointments, and rejection in our lives, our tendency is to cry out to God, "Why? Why have You allowed this?" It's so encouraging to realize that the God of the universe understands when we ask Him why. He knows the pain. He knows what it's like to say, "Why, Lord? Why?" and feel abandoned by God. Yet God had not abandoned His Son. He raised Him from the dead. Through faith in Christ, we can be "more than conquerors" as well (Romans 8:37 NIV).

What Better Day Than Sunday?

But Christ has indeed been raised from the dead, the
firstfruits of those who have fallen asleep.

1 CORINTHIANS 15:20 NIV

Christ told the truth when He predicted that He would be killed and then rise again. And He really did! So every Sunday, the day of Christ's resurrection, it is a great joy to proclaim the truth of what Jesus said and did. But where truth is concerned, humankind is divided into three groups:

+ There are those who believe that Jesus told the truth and is the truth and that He really rose from the dead. These are the followers of Christ.
+ There are also those who have never heard about all of this. The mission of the church is to tell this good news to those who have not heard.
+ And then there are those who simply refuse to believe. And God's Word is very clear—by refusing to believe, you are choosing to be eternally separated from God.

But I have good news for you. If you choose to repent and trust Christ, you will realize that He died for you too. He paid the penalty for your sins. And because He rose from the dead, He offers you the gift of eternal life.

If you have been refusing to believe, why don't you choose to believe today? When you do, every Sunday will be a special day, as we worship the One who rose on that day and who gives us the gift of eternal life.

Your First Response to Betrayal

*For it is not an enemy who reproaches me, then I could
bear it; nor is it one who hates me who has exalted
himself against me, then I could hide myself from him.
But it is you, a man my equal, my companion and my
familiar friend; we who had sweet fellowship together
walked in the house of God in the throng.*

PSALM 55:12–14

Imagine that you have a coworker, a dear friend with whom
you've been working for many years. You've spent a lot of time
together. You've had a lot of meals together, and you have worked
hard together. Then you find out that your "friend" has schemed
behind the scenes to get you eliminated from your job so he or she
could take it. Think about the sense of betrayal you would feel.
What would be your first reaction? Would it be to lash out to get
even? What *should* be your first reaction?

Follow the example of David. When David experienced that
same kind of betrayal from his personal aide, he poured out his
heart to God. He shared his pain, and God empowered him to
forgive.

Always know that Jesus can identify with your pain of
betrayal. Remember that He poured His life into twelve men. Yet
one of those men, named Judas, betrayed Him. When you are
going through a time of betrayal, be open and honest with God
about your feelings. He knows what you're experiencing. Nothing
is going to surprise Him! He wants to set us free from the bitterness and resentment and hatred that betrayal brings. Ask Him for
His help today, especially if you are struggling to forgive.

Must Christians Go to Church?

Let us consider how to stimulate one another to love and good deeds, not forsaking our own assembling together, as is the habit of some, but encouraging one another.

HEBREWS 10:24–25

I love what Billy Graham says: "Being in church no more makes you a Christian than being in a garage makes you a car." No, going to church doesn't make you a Christian, and you do not have to go to church to be a Christian, but attending church serves a threefold purpose to help us to grow in our faith.

1. We can worship with other believers, which inspires us to give our lives to God.
2. We are provided Christian fellowship to encourage our faith.
3. We can use our gifts in service and ministry to enrich our faith and the faith of others.

Failure to attend church stunts your spiritual growth. But not only that, not attending church is just plain selfish because it denies your spiritual gifts to fellow believers. Yes, you can worship God out on the lake, or on the golf course, or out hunting in the woods, but doing so only takes *from* the creation of God. We miss out on the encouragement of others, and they miss out on being encouraged by us.

Although you do not have to be in church to be a Christian, it is certainly the place where you are needed and where the committed Christian wants to be.

The Greatest Calling

Now as Jesus was walking by the Sea of Galilee, He saw two brothers, Simon who was called Peter, and Andrew his brother, casting a net into the sea; for they were fishermen. And He said to them, "Follow Me, and I will make you fishers of men."

MATTHEW 4:18–19

What do you think is life's greatest calling? You may believe it's a calling to be a missionary, or teacher, or doctor, or minister. Although these are certainly great vocations, they would rank no higher than fourth when it comes to the great callings of life! Others might say the greatest calling is to be a parent. And there's no doubt that to be a parent is one of the great callings of life, because we have the opportunity to shape a life and to raise a child God has entrusted to us. But the fact is, on any list of great callings, it would not rank higher than third. Some say, "Well, surely the greatest calling in life is to marriage and to devote your life to another person for the rest of your life." Marriage is a high calling, indeed, but on God's list, it would it be no higher than second.

The greatest calling in life is the calling to follow Jesus, the calling to be a Christian. And it's a calling that is extended to all.

If you have not accepted this amazing call, will you surrender your life to Jesus and follow Him? Life's greatest calling is to be a Christian.

It All Comes Back to Jesus

In the beginning God...

GENESIS 1:1

Look at the first four words of the Bible: "In the beginning God . . ." I can't grasp the concept of no beginning. As humans, we know that everything begins and ends—except God. He always has been, is, and always will be. I just can't comprehend that!

But let me tell you why the first four words of Genesis actually enrich my faith. John 1:1–2 says, "In the beginning . . ." Note that the gospel of John begins in the same way as Genesis. "In the beginning was the Word, and the Word was with God, and the Word was God. He was in the beginning with God." Later in the same chapter, we read, "And the Word became flesh, and dwelt among us, and we saw His glory, glory as of the only begotten from the Father, full of grace and truth" (v. 14).

Who is the Word? The Word is Jesus, and the only reason I can believe in an invisible God is Jesus. And when I struggle with those unanswerable questions—such as *Where did God come from?* or *How could He always exist?*—I come back to Jesus. If Christ rose from the dead, then any biblical claims about God are possible. If He did not, the Bible says we Christians are just a bunch of fools.

My belief in God rises and falls with Jesus—His life, His death, and His resurrection.

When Fear Is Bad

The LORD is my light and my salvation;
whom shall I fear?

PSALM 27:1

What are you afraid of? Are you afraid of spiders? Flying? How about public speaking? If so, you are in good company. I heard of a poll that asked people to list their greatest fears. Would you believe death actually came in second? What was first? Public speaking. I guess this means that at a funeral, more people would rather be in the casket than delivering the eulogy!

We face many fears in our lives. Although some fear is actually healthy, most is not. The fears that paralyze us, that make us want to quit, that make us want to give up, that cause us to not even try—these are destructive fears. We all need and want strength in facing those bad fears.

The good news is that God will give you the ability to face these fears if you'll simply trust Him. That means seeking His will in doing what is right. He will empower you by His spirit as you face the fear of rejection, or death, or even giving a speech. God gives us victory over the bad fears that cause us to miss out on the joy of walking and living in His will.

Science Versus the Bible

In the beginning [there] was the Word.

JOHN 1:1

Here is something I find interesting about the book of Isaiah. It was written about twenty-seven hundred years ago. Why is that so amazing? Because in 700 BC, the conventional wisdom was that the earth was flat. Not only did the common folk think it was flat, but the intellectuals were also convinced of this. (The prevailing scientific theory was that the earth was supported on the back of a giant turtle. What the turtle was standing on has never been fully explored.)

Yet even though humankind was convinced of the flatness of the earth, note this passage from Isaiah 40:22: "It is He who sits above the circle of the earth." Wow! The word *circle* would never have been used had a mortal written that book unassisted. But God inspired the man who wrote it, and God always knew. After all, He created it.

The Bible will always withstand scientific challenges thrown at it. In fact, science has not only never proven the Bible wrong, but over time, it has also had a way of explaining that what the Bible has been saying is actually true.

Remember, science is ever-changing as it tries to explain what God has done in creation. But God never changes, and His Word is always true.

Avoiding the Danger Zone

Can a man take fire in his bosom, and his clothes
not be burned? Or can a man walk on hot coals,
and his feet not be scorched?

PROVERBS 6:27–28

Adultery doesn't happen because a person wakes up one morning and exclaims, "I'm in the mood to commit adultery today." It begins with developing an emotional attachment to a person who is not your spouse. That attachment can easily develop in the workplace, the health club, even church, where people often share fellowship, crises, and concerns with one another. Those activities can create intimacy. We are living in a real danger zone if we begin an emotional attachment or fantasy life concerning that person.

How can you avoid having relationships cross into that danger zone? Use the "Barney Fife" rule. "Nip it in the bud!" If I would be embarrassed in any way for my wife to witness the way I'm talking or interacting with another woman, then it is time to "Nip it! Nip it in the bud!" If we can immediately nip it in the bud, we don't have to worry about falling into actual sexual sin. That will save us and our spouses a ton of heartache.

Knowing the Mind of God

*I can do all things through Christ
which strengtheneth me.*

PHILIPPIANS 4:13 KJV

Stephen Hawking, author of *A Brief History of Time*, may be the most brilliant man of the twentieth century. As a physicist, Hawking has dedicated his life to searching for a single mathematical formula that would explain all the forces of the universe. This formula is referred to as the *unified theory* because it would unite all we know about the forces that define the universe. Hawking explains his pursuit by saying that discovering this unified theory would be "the ultimate triumph of human reason" because then we would "know the mind of God."[10]

Yet none of us will ever know the whole mind of God. Expecting a human to come to know the mind of God would be similar to believing a canary could perform brain surgery. The bird has no comprehension of the subject, cannot be shown any procedure, and indeed, isn't even aware of the existence of the concept of medicine.

The gap between the mind of God and the mind of man is so much greater than between a canary and a brain surgeon. Even if any of us do make a brilliant scientific discovery, we will have only scratched the surface of God's knowledge.

But can we know the mind of God? Amazingly, we can through reading His Word, where He reveals Himself to us. Through it, we can also come to know Christ, who *is* the mind of God. Get to know Him and we won't know everything, but we'll know enough.

When Integrity Is Revealed

The man of integrity walks securely, but he who takes crooked paths will be found out.

PROVERBS 10:9 NIV

Cinderella Man is a movie about a good, honorable man who maintains his dignity even under the most intense trials. It is the story of Jim Braddock, a down-on-his-luck prizefighter trying to support his family during the Depression.

One morning, while his wife futilely attempts to scrape together a breakfast for their hungry children, a depressed Jim goes outside to get the daily milk delivery. Braddock reaches down and retrieves a note left in an empty milk bottle. His eyes tear as he reads: *No more milk until you pay the bill.*

His shoulders slump as the beaten man takes his latest slap. Perhaps the last bit of hope may have just been taken from him. Then he looks down the alley and stairways, seeing dozens upon dozens of bottles filled with rich, life-saving milk awaiting pickup by their more fortunate neighbors. Braddock, alone with the snow and cold wind, surveys the gallons of nourishing milk. The alley is quiet and empty. It is early. No one would see. Besides, who could blame him for wanting to meet his family's needs?

Yet he reenters his house. Empty-handed. In the face of excruciating temptation, he did the right thing.

Integrity is who you are and what you do when no one is watching.

The Right to Die

Do not cast me off in the time of old age;
do not forsake me when my strength fails.

PSALM 71:9

It is the concern of most elderly people that the right decisions for their welfare will be made when they come to a time in their lives when they can't care for themselves.

Why are so many of them concerned? Because the elderly, especially those who are suffering extreme disabilities, know that their very existence is threatened by today's culture of death. They see that many people declare that the quality of some lives is so low that it's really best if they no longer live, thus the logic we find in today's "right to die" movement.

With the increasing cost of medical technology, more and more children will look at these decisions not from the standpoint of respecting human life, but from the standpoint of economics. How long before a parent agrees to terminate his life because he has been made to feel guilty for spending his estate in an attempt to cling to life? In other words, at what point will the right to die become the *obligation* to die?

When they grow ill and unable to care for themselves, we honor our parents by seeing that they are provided proper care. Rather than exploring the "right to die," let's focus on honoring our parents to the end—while trusting God in His timing.

Time to Turn On the Light

"I am the Light of the world; he who follows Me will not walk in the darkness, but will have the Light of life."

JOHN 8:12

When you're staying in an unfamiliar place, do you ever awaken in the night and get up without turning on the light? Next thing you know, you're tripping over a suitcase or walking into a table. The last time that happened to me, man, did it hurt! But when you turn on the light, everything is clear.

Well, too many folks are trying to make it through life in the dark—spiritual darkness—and a lot of unnecessary falls and self-inflicted pain take place. Yet amazingly, most people in the dark feel they're doing just fine on their own. It's really kind of pitiful.

But Jesus tells us He's the Light of the world. He means He is the enlightenment about God, man, and life. Otherwise, we're in the dark spiritually. We keep stumbling, falling, and eventually, feeling frustrated by it all. Hey, isn't it time for some of you folks to turn on the light, really see God, and understand life? If you do, everything will make sense.

But God Made Me This Way!

For whoever keeps the whole law and yet stumbles in one point, he has become guilty of all.

James 2:10

How many times have you heard this nugget of logic? "Why shouldn't homosexuals be able to have a marital relationship just like heterosexuals do? After all, they didn't choose to become gay; God made them that way!"

Let's think about that. I realize that there are certain people who might have a propensity to homosexual desires. But I also agree that there are some people born with a propensity to become alcoholics. Should the church take the attitude, "You're an alcoholic? May you glory in your drunkenness! We'll have a celebration because, after all, that's how God made you!" Or there are many folks with a propensity toward heterosexual lust. Should adultery be something you glory in? Should the church say, "No problem! We'll make you an outstanding adulterer! Maybe polygamy will fulfill your needs. That's how God has created you! He's given you those desires, and those desires need to be met!"

You see, it's ludicrous for us to take one sin and say that it is simply due to the way God created a person; God doesn't create sin. And if you say one sin is no longer sin, that is unfair to those who are struggling with other types of sins. It just doesn't make sense.

In the end, Christ died for *all* sin. His forgiveness and life transformation are available for all sin. And remember, no sin is unforgivable, and no sin is stronger than the power of the cross.

No Storm Lasts Forever

"I will never desert you, nor will I ever forsake you."

HEBREWS 13:5

We will all face difficulties in our lives. It could be the death of a loved one, financial setbacks, health issues, family dysfunction, or some other painful tragedy. Events occur that can batter us, beat us down, and place us in turmoil. How can we bear such events without breaking down? Perhaps the most important thing to remember about the storms of life is this: they don't last forever. When you are facing a storm—even a hurricane—and you just don't know how you will ever work it out, realize this: every storm is temporary.

And for the believer, that's true even of death. You say, "Well, how can the storm of death be temporary?" Because when believers step over to the other side of life, we get to see Jesus face-to-face, and we get to experience a peace and a calm like we never get to experience here on earth. For Christians, death is not a storm that defeats us. It is life's ultimate storm that Jesus has conquered, and so will we. Even in death, Jesus can carry us through this storm as He does in every storm. So remember, no storm lasts forever. Hold on! Be brave! Have faith! Every storm is temporary. And we are never alone in any of them.

May

*Know that the L*ORD *Himself is God; it is He who has made us, and not we ourselves; we are His people and the sheep of His pasture.*

PSALM 100:3

The Original Sin

When the woman saw that the fruit of the tree was good
for food and pleasing to the eye, and also desirable for
gaining wisdom, she took some and ate it. She also gave
some to her husband, who was with her, and he ate it.

GENESIS 3:6 NIV

Sin began in the garden of Eden as the devil urged Eve to dis-obey God. How did he bring about this willingness to fall into sin? He told her that the words of God could not be trusted. The "original sin" occurred when Adam and Eve accepted Satan's word that God was a liar. And to this day, the devil's mode of attack is to draw us away from the will of God by attacking His Word—the trustworthiness and authority of Scripture. When Satan is successful in doing this, then man begins to make himself his own god and seeks to do what is right in his own eyes.

Sin began when Adam and Eve chose to stop trusting God and start playing god in their lives. They allowed their own desires to overrule the word of God. Sadly, this sin has become ingrained in the nature of man. It has caused man to rationalize, justify, and perform even the most heinous acts of evil.

How about you? As you face temptations and decisions, will you listen to the Word of God and obey, or will you let Satan help you justify your own desires? One way is the best. The other way makes a mess.

How Should We Pray?

*And pray in the Spirit on all occasions with
all kinds of prayers and requests.*

EPHESIANS 6:18 NIV

Most all of us feel the need to pray, but we often are uncertain how to do it right. Sometimes we're stumped and not sure where to begin. Jesus helped us with this by giving us a model, usually referred to as "the Lord's Prayer," in Matthew 6. His primary intention was not to have us recite it but to help us know how to pray and what to focus on when we pray. It was given to teach us how to talk with God, which is really what prayer is.

What does He specifically teach us?

1. We can know God as a father.
2. We need to take time to praise Him.
3. We are to pray for His will and His kingdom to come.
4. We want to pray for others while also asking God to meet our daily needs.
5. We want to ask God to forgive our sins and help us forgive others who have wronged us.
6. We want to ask for God's strength and power in resisting the temptations of the evil one.

You can enrich your prayer life by studying the prayer Jesus taught us. The God who created the universe wants to talk with you. The Lord's Prayer, which is really a disciple's prayer, is Jesus' model for us all.

Why I Believe in God

*Now the centurion, and those who were with
him keeping guard over Jesus ... said,
"Truly this was the Son of God!"*

MATTHEW 27:54

The big reason I believe in God is the overwhelming evidence of Jesus' resurrection from the dead. If He didn't, He wasn't God. But if He did, well, men like Muhammad and Buddha just don't compare. Have you examined the overwhelming evidence of Jesus' resurrection?

All the authorities had to do was produce His body and Christianity was dead on arrival. No one did.

In fear, all the disciples deserted Jesus at His crucifixion; yet they went from being cowards to courageously proclaiming His resurrection. They died martyrs' deaths for refusing to stop telling what they knew to be true.

Some said the disciples stole the body and lied about His resurrection to start a new movement. But hold on. People will die for a lie *if they don't know it's a lie*, but people don't lie for a lie they know *is* a lie. Someone would have squealed.

So much evidence and yet there is so much more. The overwhelming evidence of Jesus' resurrection is the number one reason I believe in God.

Send It Ahead

*"Do not store up for yourselves treasures on earth,
where moth and rust destroy, and where thieves
break in and steal. But store up for yourselves
treasures in heaven, where moth and rust do not
destroy, and where thieves do not break in and steal."*

MATTHEW 6:19–20 NIV

I've never seen a moving van follow a hearse. But although you can't take your wealth with you, I am happy to tell you that you can send it ahead! Now before you get too excited about signing up for this heavenly bank account, let me explain what it means to "send it ahead." You do this by investing in kingdom business, a Christ-centered ministry. You can send it ahead by giving to a ministry that is reaching people with salvation in Jesus Christ. You can send it ahead by financing the missionaries who help save the very souls you will someday meet in heaven. As an added bonus for making this investment, you get some immediate earthly rewards when you see lives saved and transformed. You get to see your reward in the changed lives of those with whom you'll be sharing eternity.

God's Word is not only talking about investing in evangelical Christian ministries, but it's also talking about sharing your wealth with other people in need—giving to the poor and sharing with friends and others who come on hard times. I hope you'll share out of your abundance. "Sending it ahead" is so much more rewarding than leaving all your wealth behind.

What Is Heaven Like?

*If I go and prepare a place for you, I will come
again and receive you to Myself, that where I am,
there you may be also.*

JOHN 14:3

What is heaven like?

The most common image is a place of clouds where people wear white robes and halos and do nothing except play harps with goofy smiles on their faces. That's a view of heaven that sounds more like hell to me! What a bore!

What is heaven really like? Jesus spoke very little of it, but He did say this: "In My Father's house are many dwelling places. . . . I go to prepare a place for you" (John 14:2). What is heaven like? It's like a home, with a loving father. It's a place of security, a permanent place to live, and a place of refuge. There's a longing within all of us to find a home. Heaven is like home with a father and loved ones as they're supposed to be.

How can you be sure you'll get to that home? Is there a map or rules to follow? No, it comes through a person, Jesus Christ Himself. As He talked about a heavenly home, He added that He is the only way for us to truly come home.

Marriage 101: The Basics

God created man in his own image, in the image of God he created him; male and female he created them. God blessed them and said to them, "Be fruitful and increase in number; fill the earth and subdue it. Rule over the fish of the sea and the birds of the air and over every living creature that moves on the ground."

GENESIS 1:27–28 NIV

When a team, an organization, or a mission gets off track, it's time to focus on the basics. With marriages and families under attack, perhaps this would be a great time to look at the basics of marriage. Specifically, why did God create marriage in the first place?

1. God created marriage for procreation (Genesis 1:28).
2. Man is to be in partnership with his wife in managing the earth, in practicing good conservation, and in caring for the environment (Genesis 1:28).
3. Marriage is for companionship (Genesis 2:18).
4. Marriage is for mutual sexual pleasure. The Bible is very clear that when a man and woman are married, their bodies are no longer just under the ownership of themselves but are for the joy of their mates (Genesis 2:24; 1 Corinthians 7:2–5).
5. Marriage is about the highest ideal of human relationships—an exclusive commitment for life that reflects Christ's commitment to His church (Ephesians 5:22–33).

This is Marriage 101: the simple basics of a championship marriage.

The Importance of Human Life

Know that the LORD Himself is God; it is He who
has made us, and not we ourselves.

PSALM 100:3

The American Constitution—normally a bastion for the dignity of humankind and protector of liberty—originally declared that some members of our society only counted as three-fifths human. This evil label in America justified slavery for another eighty years!

Think about what happened in World War II. The fascist philosophy of the Nazis said that Jewish people were less than fully human. So that was the Nazis' justification for the murder of six million innocent Jews. Throughout history, declaring any human life as less than fully human has always led to grotesque evil.

It continues today. Beginning in the 1960s, we began referring to an unborn child as merely a "fetus." This clinical word dehumanized the child, turning it from a person into a blob of tissue, thus making it easier to destroy. And since the horrific Supreme Court decision in 1973, estimates show that more than 50 million unborn children have been murdered in the United States.[11] Add to that the estimated 42 million aborted worldwide every single year, and we have a holocaust that is incomparable in all of history.[12] Abortion is one of the most grotesque evils of all time, and these are the consequences whenever man declares any human life as being less than a human.

Every life is created by God. God doesn't make mistakes. So let's respect the sanctity of human life—from conception through old age.

A Dash of Salt

Let your speech always be with grace, as though seasoned with salt, so that you will know how you should respond to each person.

COLOSSIANS 4:6

Scripture gives some wonderful advice for witnessing more effectively: *season your speech with salt*. Why is that? If somebody sprinkles salt on food and makes it taste good, you appreciate it. But if somebody hands you a spoon of salt and says, "Take this all at once," it's a little hard to swallow. In fact, you can't even digest it!

Think how the non-Christian feels when all you do is talk about God and church and Jesus. He simply thinks you don't care about him. You never talk about baseball. You never ask how work is going. You never talk about politics. You never ask about his family. You never talk about the everyday concerns of life. On the other hand, if you talk about all of these things and occasionally sprinkle in a little word about the Lord when there's the right opportunity, or an insight you learned from a sermon, or a Bible verse he might not know, then he may think, *Well, where did that wisdom come from?* His curiosity may be aroused, and longer, deeper conversations may follow. When you have the opportunity, just sprinkle the conversation with a little spiritual salt. Then God may create the perfect opportunity to share what Jesus means to you. Good witnesses season their speech with salt.

Both an Atheist and a Hypocrite

The fool has said in his heart, "There is no God."

PSALM 14:1

Books by atheists are hot today. One of the best-selling ones is *The God Delusion* by Richard Dawkins, professor of science at Oxford University. If there's any way to describe Richard Dawkins, it is this: he is an evangelist for atheism!

One thing that really fascinates me about Dawkins's book is his deep hostility toward religion. He really believes that religion is an evil influence on humankind. Although he includes many examples of Christian misdeeds, he is quite silent on the subject of the evil springing from the atheistic philosophies in the twentieth century. There's no mention of men like Mao Tse-Tung, Stalin, and Pol Pot. Nothing about the leadership of North Korea or any of the other people who have embraced atheistic philosophies and murdered millions of their own citizens. Where's the condemnation of that?

The Bible is clear that only a fool says in his heart, "There is no God." Dawkins is one of those fools. But amazingly, God loves him and wants to have an eternal relationship with him. That's why He sent His Son to die for him and for all of us. Let's pray that fools like Dawkins will quit being delusional and finally see that God is real and He is love.

Our Father

And He said to them, "When you pray, say: 'Father,
hallowed be Your name. Your kingdom come.'"

LUKE 11:2

When Jesus taught us how to pray, the first thing He did was tell us how to address God. We're to address Him as "Father" or "Dad." This is a very personal way of addressing God, and it shocked people in His day! But Jesus was telling us how we are to think about God. For some, this is difficult, for their earthly fathers don't conjure up healthy pictures. But Jesus thinks of "Father" as fathers are meant to be. He's not a cold and distant deity, but one who desires a close relationship with each of us. So based on Jesus' prayer to His heavenly Father, what does it mean to be a good father?

+ It means he is a nourisher. That's one who provides for the family and meets their material needs. A nourishing father is dependable, responsible, trustworthy, and loving.
+ He is also to be a protector. Every home wants a father who is strong, especially in the face of evil, or in threats to the home or the children's welfare.
+ He is an upholder—the upholder of values, character, and the spirit of the family.

That's really what Jesus is teaching us by using the term "Father." God is a nourisher. He is a protector. And He is an upholder. In short, God is not a good father; He's the perfect Father—a Father like fathers are meant to be.

Self-Help?

Seek from the book of the LORD, and read.

ISAIAH 34:16

Do you ever get tired of all the self-help information in society? Books, radio programs, and numerous talk shows urge you to take a look at who you are and then change yourself by your determined will. Have you tried all that information and yet you're still discouraged by repeating the same old habits?

There are some things that self-help cannot help, things like disease, overcoming certain sins, and most of all, death.

But God has a plan for us that goes beyond our own abilities. It's something supernatural. It comes through a personal relationship with Jesus Christ, who supernaturally changes us where we can't change ourselves. As a bonus to that faith, He promises us victory over death, and eternal life. So if you really want to help yourself, look beyond yourself to the only One who can save you and give you the ultimate victory—Jesus Christ.

Parenting Parents

Treat others the same way you want them to treat you.

LUKE 6:31

There are few greater challenges in the parent-child relationship than parenting our parents. It involves a role reversal that neither the parent nor the child wants. Yet it's part of honoring our parents. It is caring for them when they are unable to care for themselves.

But difficult questions arise. When does the adult child intervene? Should the parents live with the adult child or just nearby? There are no easy answers, but I offer some suggestions on how we can best honor our parents by caring for their needs.

- We honor our parents when we put their needs over what they or we want.
- Our parents need the gift of our time, love, and sacrifice—something they did for us when we were children.
- How we care for our aging parents is how our children learn to honor us when we're no longer able to care for ourselves.

Parenting our parents has long-term implications for our families, our nation, and us.

Happy Mother's Day!

Her children arise and call her blessed.

PROVERBS 31:28 NIV

Kids start to develop some pretty interesting perceptions of the world at an early age. Notice the answers some second-graders gave when asked about their mothers.

Q: Why did God make mothers?
A: To help us out of there when we were getting born.
Q: What ingredients are mothers made of?
A: God makes mothers out of clouds and angel hair and everything nice in the world and one dab of mean.
Q: Why did God give you your mother and not some other mom?
A: God knew she likes me a lot more than other people's moms like me.
Q: What does your mom do in her spare time?
A: Mothers don't do spare time.
Q: If you could change one thing about your mom, what would it be?
A: I would like for her to get rid of those invisible eyes on the back of her head.

As these kids can tell you, motherhood is the toughest, most demanding, most important job in the world. With the many choices for women today, let's not forget that there is no calling of God more important than being a mom.

The Blame Game

Then I acknowledged my sin to you and did not cover up
my iniquity. I said, "I will confess my transgressions to
the LORD"—and you forgave the guilt of my sin.

PSALM 32:5 NIV

Notice Adam's response when God asked about his sin: "The woman whom You gave to be with me, she gave me from the tree, and I ate" (Genesis 3:12). So the man blamed the woman, and he also blamed God—after all, He was the one who brought Eve into his life! Eve's defense? "The serpent deceived me, and I ate" (v. 13). (The first example of the infamous "the devil made me do it" excuse.)

The victimization blame game is rampant today. We see feminists who blame men for trouble and men who blame their problems on women. We see blacks who blame whites for the trouble in their lives and whites who blame blacks. Republicans blame Democrats, and Democrats blame Republicans. We have an entire industry, the media, in which success seems to be measured by how many people they have adequately blamed. "It's not my fault!" "It's her fault!" "It's his fault!" "It wouldn't have happened without her . . . without him . . . without the snake!" Since the dawn of humanity, the blame game is the cry of all when it comes to our sin.

Do you blame others for your mistakes and sins, or do you confess your sins and take responsibility? The first step to forgiveness from God is acknowledging responsibility for our sin. Can you take that first step in acknowledging your own sinful deeds to the One who offers unlimited forgiveness? Isn't it time to grow up and leave the blame game behind? A sure sign of maturity is accepting responsibility for our actions.

Is Scripture True or Not?

But know this first of all, that no prophecy of Scripture
is a matter of one's own interpretation, for no prophecy
was ever made by an act of human will, but men moved
by the Holy Spirit spoke from God.

2 PETER 1:20–21

Do you believe Scripture is perfect truth? Or do you believe it just contains some general principles and guidelines that can be adapted for every age, culture, or situation?

Do you believe Scripture is the written Word of God? Or do you believe that Scripture is the words of men that were shaped by prejudices concerning culture and different views all through the ages and should be adapted to the modern age?

Do you believe Scripture is our authority for faith and practice? Or do you believe each person should do what he or she feels is right?

Here is the bottom line on the truth of the Scripture: it is either complete, perfect truth, applicable for all times, or it is full of lies and inaccuracies. There is no in between. There is no such thing as partial truth or relative truth. The decision you make as to the nature of the Scripture will shape everything else you believe about God, Jesus, life, and morality. What you believe about Scripture is a huge decision of faith. So, what do you believe?

Forgive Our Sins

*If we confess our sins, he is faithful and just
and will forgive us our sins and purify us from
all unrighteousness.*

1 JOHN 1:9 NIV

A man wandered into a rural tent revival and was greatly inspired by the energetic service. One after another, people stood and poured out their hearts. After each person publicly confessed, the congregation cheered and clapped and wept tears of joy to show support for the repentant sinners. It wasn't long before the man joined in, leaping to his feet and loudly confessing one of his more recent sins. The tent suddenly became silent as jaws dropped and eyes widened as big as saucers. The preacher leaned over and said, "Brother, I don't think I would have told that one."

Was the preacher right or wrong? That depends. Jesus clearly teaches that all sin needs to be confessed to God. Yet all sin doesn't need to be confessed to men—just to those we have sinned against, to ask their forgiveness.

The man at the tent revival was right not to sugarcoat any of his sin when it came to God. For God already knew what he'd done. And God wants you to fully confess so He'll know that *you know* what you did! Don't try to explain it away, or make excuses, or have a victim mind-set. You might be able to fool a friend, but you can't fool God. Simply tell God about your sins and ask His forgiveness, and He will lift that burden from you. And when you wrong someone else, ask that person's forgiveness and seek to make things right. It may cost you, but it's worth every penny.

A Key to Contentment

If we have food and covering,
with these we shall be content.

1 TIMOTHY 6:8

In our rush to acquire wealth and possessions, we often wonder just how much is enough. Put simply, God's Word tells us that when you see God meeting the basic necessities of your life, be content. Be thankful. The apostle Paul said, "Not that I speak from want; for I have learned to be content in whatever circumstances I am. I know how to get along with humble means, and I also know how to live in prosperity; in any and every circumstance I have learned the secret of being filled and going hungry, both of having abundance and suffering need" (Philippians 4:11–12).

In other words, the apostle Paul understood. He could be content with little. He could be content with much! Let's learn to follow his example. Because Christianity is most of all a relationship, and when we are in a right relationship with God through Christ, one of the many by-products is contentment. So when the basic necessities of life are being provided, be thankful. Everything over and above is just an extra blessing!

The Writing in the Sand

But Jesus stooped down and with
His finger wrote on the ground.

JOHN 8:6

The Pharisees had just brought an adulteress before Jesus and demanded, "Now in the Law Moses commanded us to stone such women; what then do You say?" (v. 5). Silence. Jesus only stooped to write on the ground.

The Bible doesn't tell us what Jesus wrote in the sand that day. Maybe He wrote scripture. Perhaps He was writing, "Where is the man?" Doesn't adultery involve two? Or perhaps He was writing the sins of the Pharisees who were accusing this woman. Maybe Jesus was just collecting His thoughts because He was angry that they were humiliating this woman just to get at Him.

I have no idea what He wrote, but I believe that Jesus' heart was aching as He knelt in the sand. Why? Because this woman was being treated as an object, unworthy of life. He looked at the Pharisees and realized they just didn't get it. Jesus would have been totally justified to get in the Pharisees' faces and say, "You guys don't get it! I came not to judge but to save" (John 3:17, paraphrase).

But Jesus didn't blow His top and blast them. In an amazing display of self-control and compassion for this woman, He finally stood and said, "Whoever is without sin, you throw the first stone" (John 8:7, paraphrase).

They slowly drifted away, dropping their stones as they left. Jesus transferred the humiliation from the woman to the self-righteous, judgmental men. What wisdom. What a man, this Jesus. You gotta love Him. I surely do. How about you?

Self-Appointed Judges

*Therefore no one is to act as your judge in regard
to food or drink or in respect to a festival or a new
moon or a Sabbath day.*

COLOSSIANS 2:16

Jesus was attacked by legalists throughout His ministry. Perhaps the most outrageous example of this was when He healed a man with a withered hand. The Pharisees attacked Him because He had performed this miracle on the Sabbath. That's right, Jesus was accused of lawbreaking because healing was considered work and Jewish law forbade doing work on the Sabbath.

Understand this about the Pharisees: they were the self-appointed judges. They were constantly looking to accuse Jesus Christ because they felt He was oblivious to their concern for their man-made rules and traditions.

Although rarely as outrageous as that of the Pharisees, this type of legalism continues today. Some people serve as self-appointed judges—or enforcers—of man-made rules for godly living. This can happen in all religions. But it's especially sad when Christian denominations and churches impose man-made rules that are impostors to real faith. The Bible states the rules fully and unequivocally. And with so many, how great it is that Jesus' life shows us how to live them out completely. How great it is that Jesus summed them all up with the Great Commandment to love the Lord our God with all our heart, soul, mind, and strength and love our neighbor as ourselves (Luke 10:27).

So put down your gavel. God is the only judge. Besides, you don't want people judging *you* . . . do you?

Legalism Is Anti-Biblical

See to it that no one takes you captive through philosophy and empty deception, according to the tradition of men, according to the elementary principles of the world, rather than according to Christ.

COLOSSIANS 2:8

One reason fundamentalist Christians are so resented is because some, in defense of Scripture, wind up adding to Scripture. I have seen certain legalisms permeate my own denomination. Some zealous Baptists have declared all dancing to be of the devil. It's all well-intentioned. No doubt some dancing is lewd, but much dancing is wholesome and fun. Even David danced before the Lord.

Some mainline Protestants have legalistically redefined "tolerance" and "inclusion" as the ultimate values. Some reformed theologians legalistically embrace Calvinism over the Bible. Some Pentecostals insist that speaking in tongues is essential for all true believers. Some Catholics cling to their rosaries over the Word. Well-intentioned people feel there is a need to add to Scripture. They don't trust Scripture to be enough.

Man-made legalisms are an insult to God. It's like saying the Bible is incomplete and we have the knowledge to correct the Scriptures on what is right and wrong. We move into some very scary territory when we do that. God's Word plainly says, "Every word of God is pure; He is a shield to those who put their trust in Him. Do not add to His words, lest He rebuke you, and you be found a liar" (Proverbs 30:5–6 NKJV). Whew! That's strong!

So remember, the Word of God is enough. Let's obey God and trust it.

Praising God

*Praise the LORD with the harp; make music to him
on the ten-stringed lyre. Sing to him a new song;
play skillfully, and shout for joy.*

PSALM 33:2–3 NIV

Charles Haddon Spurgeon was probably the most famous Baptist preacher of all time. He preached in Great Britain to about four or five thousand people every Sunday. Spurgeon read a lot of John Calvin and was so influenced by him that he didn't allow any instruments in his worship services. Now, I know Spurgeon was a far greater preacher than I am, and Calvin was a more brilliant theologian than I could ever dream of being. But I also know for an absolute fact that they were dead wrong on this issue! Throughout the Old Testament it talks about the use of musical instruments as a way of praising and singing our praises to God.

Everyone has their own personal preference for styles of worship music. Some people like the orchestra; some like the band; some just like a guitar and drums. Many people only enjoy songs written before 1887; some feel a chorus more than five years old is a golden oldie. Some love the majesty of a pipe organ, and some are just riveted by music with a pounding bass beat. But here is the bottom line: as long as the music is centered on Christ and is grounded in the Word, then the variety of music styles all have worth. They simply serve to expand the glorification of God and allow more people to enthusiastically worship Him with all their hearts.

The Science of Astrology?

*And when you look up to the sky and see the sun, the moon
and the stars—all the heavenly array—do not be enticed into
bowing down to them and worshiping things the LORD your
God has apportioned to all the nations under heaven.*

DEUTERONOMY 4:19 NIV

I've often wondered this about astrology: *How do they know?*
Let's assume, for the sake of discussion, that when the moon is
in the seventh house and Jupiter aligns with Mars, then everyone
born under the sign of Aquarius actually *will* lose their car keys. I
mean, who figured this out? Did someone take a detailed survey
for each astrological sign concerning exact events that occurred
under every possible star alignment? And how did this person get
hold of a computer big enough to digest all this data . . . especially
thousands of years ago when astrology was first practiced? I don't
mean to mock (okay, maybe I do), but somebody please explain to
me how these "facts" were discovered and compiled.

Of course, no one has an intelligent explanation. These mystic
readings are just futile attempts by searching people looking for
answers.

But I have good news for these people. The Bible has key
answers to your life, and you can discover them by having a personal
relationship with the God who created all those stars. Wouldn't
you rather listen to the One who actually created them? He is the
only One who really knows the future. His Word reveals quite a
few insights about where the world is headed and how to be prepared for the future. So don't look to the stars. Look to the Book!

What Are Your Prayer Stats?

Pray all the time; thank God no matter what
happens. This is the way God wants you who
belong to Christ Jesus to live.

1 THESSALONIANS 5:17–18 MSG

How should we pray? "Pray all the time." This means anytime, anywhere. But prayer calls for a fourfold focus: on praise, on confession, on thanksgiving, and then on requests. Now, wouldn't it be fascinating if God gave us the statistics showing how much prayer time we spend on requests versus how much time is spent thanking God, praising God, or confessing our sins? That would be an interesting stat! I know that if He did it for my own prayer life, I would see those requests way up there on that list!

God's Word tells us that when we pray, we need to focus on the greatness and goodness of God. With praise comes an attitude of thanksgiving. We want to be thankful to the Lord for the many blessings in our life. The greatest blessing of all is the salvation we have in Jesus Christ, and the bonus is His indwelling Spirit and even more—abundant eternal life. We are called to confess our sins to God. This, too, gives us an attitude of thanksgiving for being free of guilt and filled with joy. Then it's time to share with God our requests—for others and ourselves.

Strive for this fourfold balance in your prayer life, and see how it draws you closer to the Creator of the universe.

Rest for the Weary

*"Take my yoke upon you and learn from me,
for I am gentle and humble in heart, and you
will find rest for your souls."*

MATTHEW 11:29 NIV

The idea that the pace of life seems to continually increase stress and worry is a universal concept. There seems to be no end to the demands on our time and energy. Are you tired of the rat race?

There is a solution. It isn't one that offers escape from the demands of life, but one that guarantees rest in the midst of the rat race. Jesus said, "Come to me if you are tired and burdened. I'll make your load lighter and help you carry your burden" (Matthew 11:28, paraphrase). Jesus offers us rest amid the fast pace of life.

Christ doesn't always take us out of life's demanding situations. Instead, He invites us to allow Him to help us handle the demands. He wants to face each day and each challenge with us. Walking with Jesus Christ daily and trusting Him for guidance and wisdom to handle whatever comes is the way to experience rest *in* the rat race.

How to Be a Good Boss

*Masters, grant to your slaves justice and fairness,
knowing that you too have a Master in heaven.*

COLOSSIANS 4:1

Here are some biblical principles for being a good boss:

+ *Be a person of integrity.* People need to be able to trust the boss.
+ *Make expectations clear.* Take the time to teach, train, and respond to questions.
+ *Hold people accountable.* Expecting excellence is good for all.
+ *Be fair to all concerned.* Playing favorites is demoralizing to the troops.
+ *Lead by building up* the team and individual rather than leading through intimidation.
+ *Genuinely care* about the employee's success just as much as your own. This makes your chance for success far greater.
+ Most of all, remember you have to answer to God.

God has entrusted authority to you to serve Him and others through leadership. Jesus was the perfect example of servant leadership when He humbled Himself to become one of His own creations and, even more so, when He gave His life for those He came to lead.

Jesus is the ultimate CEO, the ultimate boss, the ultimate servant leader.

When Christianity Is Worthless

But if there is no resurrection of the dead,
not even Christ has been raised.

1 CORINTHIANS 15:13

Do you know what would make Christianity worthless?

If Christ did not rise from the dead, Christianity would be built around a big lie. It would mean Jesus was a liar because He said He would be killed and rise again. It would mean that the Bible is filled with lies because over and over it writes of Jesus' resurrection. It would mean that of all people on earth, Christians are to be pitied the most, for we have bought into a colossal hoax.

But if Christ rose from the dead, it means that when Jesus says He is the Son of God, He is believable. It means there is hope beyond the grave. It means every miracle in the Bible is believable. After all, if a man rises from the dead, what's the big deal about parting the Red Sea or making the lame walk? Christianity rises and falls on the resurrection. No resurrection, and Christianity is worthless. But if He did rise, it means everything. I believe He did. How about you?

Grace Be with You

The grace of the Lord Jesus be with you.

1 CORINTHIANS 16:23

Paul normally closed his letters by saying, "Grace be with you." Now, it's interesting that Paul used that particular phrase because he had been a most unlikely candidate for receiving the grace of God. Paul spent his first career terrorizing first-century Christians. He literally persecuted the church and oversaw the killing of Christians. That was his mission.

Then Christ appeared to him, forgave him, and saved him. And Paul, perhaps more than anyone who has ever lived, was focused on the grace of Christ because he knew he didn't deserve to be forgiven. Here's where it hits home. None of us does either. Not one of us deserves to have the God of the universe go to a cross and pay that awful penalty for us so that we might be forgiven and have eternal life.

Paul's salutation reminds us that a Christ-centered church will focus on the grace of God that's found in what Jesus did for us on the cross. It will emphasize the grace of God, remembering the price Jesus paid in giving us something none of us deserves—forgiveness, salvation, and eternal life.

May the grace of the Lord Jesus be with you.

How Can We Repay
Their Sacrifice?

*"Greater love has no one than this; that he lay
down his life for his friends."*

JOHN 15:13 NIV

The opening scene of the movie *Saving Private Ryan* shows the incredible carnage and sacrifice that occurred during the invasion of Normandy. From this scene emerges a humble schoolteacher, Captain John Miller (Tom Hanks), who is assigned an unusual mission—to lead a small platoon across Germany and retrieve Private James Ryan. Ryan's three older brothers had all been killed on a single day, and General Marshall wanted to bring the sole surviving son back to his mother.

Captain Miller eventually located Private Ryan. Because of Ryan's loyalty to his fellow soldiers, Miller had to use every bit of persuasion he had to finally convince Ryan to leave his comrades in battle. Before he could leave, a counterassault by the Nazis mortally wounded Captain Miller. Miller addressed his last words to Private Ryan, "James—earn this. Earn it."

What a powerful charge. How could a single soldier possibly pay back all that sacrifice? He couldn't—but he could choose to be a good citizen.

Christ sacrificed His life for us. How can we ever pay back Christ? We can't! We can never earn His favor. We simply have to accept His gift on faith and then love God and our neighbors as ourselves. It is called being a good citizen of the kingdom of God.

More Than Life Itself

*"Anyone who loves his father or mother more than me
is not worthy of me; anyone who loves his son or
daughter more than me is not worthy of me."*

MATTHEW 10:37 NIV

If Jesus ever made a scary statement, one that causes me to examine my heart to its very core, it has to be Matthew 10:37. Read the above scripture again. Now, that is a stunning statement, one that challenges me greatly. Because I love my wife. I love my children. I love my grandchildren and parents and siblings. I even love my in-laws. Because of my deep love for my family, Jesus' statement makes me very uncomfortable. In fact, it terrifies me.

Similar to God's statement to Abraham when He told him to sacrifice his son Isaac, Jesus was saying that when it comes to our family members, He must be in *first place*, or else He will be in *no* place at all when it comes to our lives. As hard as that is to take in, Christ wants to make it clear that if we want to follow Him, He must be first. If we love anyone (or anything) more than Jesus, we are not worthy of Him. And if that's not tough enough, He went on to say that we must love Him more than we love *our own lives*. Jesus sets high expectations for His followers. Am I willing to meet His expectations? I am willing, as tough as it is.

How about you?

Better Read That One Again

And we know that God causes everything to work together for the good of those who love God and are called according to his purpose for them.

Sometimes we should take a closer look at the Scriptures. For instance, the Bible doesn't say that money is the root of all evil; it says the *love of money* is the root of all sorts of evil. And Adam and Eve ate the forbidden fruit; it never says it was an apple. Likewise, God does not guarantee that all things work together for good. Do you think for people in hell things have worked out for their good? He declares that all things work together for good "for those who love God and are called according to his purpose." In other words, things most certainly work out for good for you if—and this is a big if—you are a follower of Christ and are willing to seek, trust in, and fulfill His will. Under those conditions, all things do work together for good!

No matter what kind of setback you face, no matter what kind of rejection by man, no matter what kind of suffering, hurt, and evil you have to endure in this life, God can bring good out of any situation. If you choose to trust God, He can bring good out of the darkest, most dismal of circumstances. Why don't you start looking for the good that God wants to bring? This is what God's Word means when He talks about all things working together for good.

Intercessory Prayer

Pray hard and long. Pray for your brothers and sisters.
Keep your eyes open. Keep each other's spirits up so
that no one falls behind or drops out.

EPHESIANS 6:18 MSG

What is intercessory prayer? Paul bragged to the church in Colosse about Epaphras, a member of the church: "Epaphras [is] … always laboring earnestly for you in his prayers, that you may stand perfect and fully assured in all the will of God" (Colossians 4:12). Epaphras prayed for the people in the church to be spiritually mature, for them to be complete and whole, and also for them to fulfill the will of God. That is an example of intercessory prayer; it focuses on fulfilling the ministry and the mission of the church.

One of the concerns we often have about our prayer ministry is that the requests we receive are *overwhelmingly* for those who are sick. There is no doubt that the church is called to pray for the sick. But so often it seems the church is obsessed with praying sick sinners out of heaven and totally oblivious to praying lost sinners out of hell. We need to have the right priority when it comes to our intercession. It's about praying for Christ's kingdom to come and His will to be done on earth as it is in heaven. That means focusing on the spiritual welfare of the church and its mission as we remember the physical needs of those who are sick.

June

*"Peace I leave with you; My peace I give to you;
not as the world gives do I give to you. Do not let
your heart be troubled, nor let it be fearful."*

JOHN 14:27

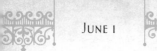

AWOL Fathers

Fathers, do not provoke your children to anger, but bring them up in the discipline and instruction of the Lord.

EPHESIANS 6:4

No statistic is more troubling than this: about 40 percent of births in America are illegitimate. That means that for about 40 percent of all children, their lives begin without the presence of a father in the home. But it's even more tragic in the African-American community, where almost 70 percent are illegitimate. Yet no matter what a child's ethnic background, for those fortunate few who have a dad in residence, often the light's not on. Either he is passive in his leadership role with the children or so involved in his career that he is essentially nonexistent in the home. Certainly, what we are seeing in our contemporary society is the crisis of the absentee dad. This doesn't bode well for our nation's future.

God's Word is clear that the father is to be the spiritual leader in the home. This is not a dictatorial or authoritarian leadership; it's Christ-centered servant leadership. It means that loving his wife is the best way to be a good father (not to mention a good husband). It requires understanding the fragile psyche of a child that needs to be built up and not torn down. It means acknowledging the importance of discipline in the child's life. And it involves loving instruction, explaining what is right and wrong.

The first step in being a good father is simply showing up. Then, when we show up, let's move it up a notch to be the kind of dad God expects each of us to be.

One of the Greatest Mission Fields in the World

But when the time had fully come, God sent his Son, born of a woman, born under law, to redeem those under law, that we might receive the full rights of sons.

GALATIANS 4:4–5 NIV

There are thousands of unreached people groups, people who have never been told of the love of God in Jesus Christ. Yet one of the most overlooked people groups in the world are the millions of orphans without homes. Adoption and foster care are great ways to reach out to these children in need. And what better way to share the love of Christ with a lost child than to bring him or her into a loving Christian home?

God's Word gives us a theology of adoption. Without Christ, we are all spiritual orphans. Through faith in Christ, we are adopted children of God—no longer fatherless but able to know God as Father.

When we think of missions, of reaching the lost, don't overlook children in need of a family. It's one of the greatest mission fields in the world.

Contentment Through a Godly Life

Godliness is actually a means of great gain when accompanied by contentment.

1 TIMOTHY 6:6

Would you like to be rich? I guess we all would, but let's look at God's definition of *rich*. God's Word explains it something like this: *If you really want to be rich from a lasting perspective, then you want to live a godly life.* Now, don't make the mistake of feeling that you can live a godly life by trying to be religious, by trying to be good, by trying to do all the things you're supposed to do in church. Realize that godliness is a by-product of a personal relationship with Jesus Christ.

Godliness comes out of growing closer to Christ so that His Spirit begins to guide and convict us through the Word of God to live lives that are more pleasing to Him—to walk with Him.

Godliness is to be our primary goal when it comes to thinking about money and riches. There's no lasting significance in money, but there is lasting significance in godliness. God says, *When you live a life of godliness, this is a life of great gain* (1 Timothy 6:6, paraphrase). There's no ultimate meaning in money, but there is ultimate meaning in having a godly walk with the Lord. You can never lose this. Oh yes, you can stray from God, but you will never lose that relationship with God. It's eternal! Unlike financial riches, your relationship with God is forever. It goes beyond the grave, beyond death. Let godliness be your primary concern, and out of that will come contentment.

Made in God's Image

Then God said, "Let Us make man in Our image,
according to Our likeness; and let them rule over the
fish of the sea and over the birds of the sky and over
the cattle, and over all the earth."

GENESIS 1:26

What does it mean that man was made in God's image? Does it mean that God has two arms, two legs, and a long flowing beard as depicted on the ceiling of the Sistine Chapel? (Michelangelo also painted a belly button on God, something that really makes no sense on so many levels.) Being made in the image of God means that, like God, humans can think and reason. We appreciate beauty. And unlike animals, we have an inner sense of morality and the ability to grasp deep concepts. This gives us the ability to communicate with God. And that is the real reason God made us in His image—He desires a relationship with us all.

In the same passage, God addresses our relationship with the earth. One reason God made us in His image is to make us responsible for caring for all of God's creation. We're God's appointed managers over all of His creation. How can we manage it unless we stay close to God, think like Him, and want to fulfill His will? Part of having a relationship with God is managing His creation well.

Being created in His image is an awesome gift, as well as a sacred responsibility.

Today Is the Day

*Peter got up the nerve to ask, "Master, how many times
do I forgive a brother or sister who hurts me? Seven?"
Jesus replied, "Seven! Hardly. Try seventy times seven."*

MATTHEW 18:21–22 MSG

Having healthy relationships is central to what God wants for the body of Christ. They are to be healthy, loving, and forgiving. And this is true not only within our immediate circle of fellow Christians but also with our neighbors, business acquaintances, and even our enemies! What this means is that we must seek forgiveness when we have wronged others and we must forgive others when they have wronged us.

Do you have relationships where things aren't right? It could be in your marriage, with your children, with your parents, or with somebody at your church. Someone close that you trusted may have burned you. Or it may be that you've let somebody else down and you're estranged because of what you have done. Let this be the day when you say, "Lord, forgive me. Help me to forgive and have the courage to go and seek forgiveness from the person I have wronged."

The ultimate meaning of life is found in healthy relationships with God and with our fellow man. Don't wait. Decide to get those relationships right. Today is the day.

No Sin Is Too Great

In him we have redemption through his blood,
the forgiveness of sins, in accordance with
the riches of God's grace.

EPHESIANS 1:7 NIV

Abortion makes me sick—most of all for the most innocent of all human creation, the unborn child. But it also makes me sick at the thought of doctors, who are called to save lives, taking part in the murder of human life. In addition, look what it does to the feminine psyche, in a perverted hardness of heart to the basic calling of motherhood, not to mention the unnecessary guilt that can be haunting for life.

Yet understand this: if you have had an abortion or taken part in an abortion, it's vital for you to remember the good news of Jesus Christ. There is no sin so great that Christ can't forgive it through the cross. *Not one!* Christ has paid the penalty for every sin you and I have committed. The only unforgivable sin is to reject Him. So when you and I acknowledge our sin, confess it to God, and come to Him with a repentant faith, God cleanses us. He forgives us.

As fellow repentant sinners, we welcome you into God's house and into Christian fellowship. We invite you to receive the love and forgiveness of Christ. Brothers and sisters in Christ are eager to embrace you and pledge to you acceptance, respect, and assistance. True love and acceptance from the body of Christ are available to you if you are willing to receive them.

Remember, no sin is too great for Christ to forgive.

A Horse Story

"In everything, therefore, treat people the same way you want them to treat you, for this is the Law and the Prophets."

MATTHEW 7:12

Perhaps you have read the book or seen the movie about the famous American racehorse Seabiscuit. This story is certainly inspiring. It's also a fascinating glimpse at American social history during the 1930s. The horses were treated better than the jockeys! These jockeys were paid very little and didn't even have medical insurance, even though theirs is one of the most dangerous professions in the world.

The words of Jesus could not be clearer. We are to treat others as we want to be treated. We are to be fair. But it doesn't just mean adequate pay and benefits. An employer must treat employees fairly, and that fairness extends much further than compensation.

It also means not showing partiality. What does that mean? If you've ever seen a situation where a parent shows favoritism to one child over another, you know how incredibly demoralizing it can be to the entire home. It works the same way in the workplace. Think of the demoralizing effect partiality has on employees. It's the perfect place for Jesus' golden rule to be applied: do unto others as you would have them do unto you.

If supervisors treated employees this way and employees treated supervisors and fellow employees this way, morale would soar, productivity would increase, and profits would rise. As a matter of fact, because the good owner of Seabiscuit actually treated his jockey this way, Jesus' golden rule became golden for them both.

Last Words

"Do not lay up for yourselves treasures on earth, where moth and rust destroy and where thieves break in and steal; but lay up for yourselves treasures in heaven, where neither moth nor rust destroys and where thieves do not break in and steal. For where your treasure is, there your heart will be also."

MATTHEW 6:19–21 NKJV

I've had the privilege of being with many people as they neared death, yet I never had any of those folks tell me, "You know, Bryant, I wish I had made more money." I've never had anybody say, "I wish I had accomplished more." But what people do say usually has something to do with a lament about relationships. "I wish I had spent more time with someone," or "I wish I had focused more on the relationships that count."

I'm sure you nodded your head while reading that paragraph. Bet you were thinking, *I know that. Nothing new there.* Hold on a second. Although everyone does seem to understand this lesson in their heads, true realization rarely seems to make it to their hearts. The fact is, when people ask me, "What is the ultimate meaning of life?" I always respond one way: "Ultimate meaning is found in relationships." Your most important relationship is, of course, with God, but your last moments on this earth will be so very empty if they are spent agonizing over failed relationships with people: family, friends, or those you may have wronged. Act now to ensure that your last words are not about regretting your relationships on earth but instead are spent praising the glory of heaven that awaits you.

Time

[The Lord] has saved us and called us with a holy calling, not according to our works, but according to His own purpose and grace which was granted us in Christ Jesus from all eternity.

2 TIMOTHY 1:9

Do you hear the clock ticking? Time keeps moving on. It never stops for anyone—no matter how important you are. We just can't find enough of that stuff. But one thing's for sure—God wants us to be good stewards of our time, but we'll never be able to until we're clear about our purpose for living. The starting point is knowing why we're here.

First, ask God to help you develop a life-purpose statement. It will take some time, but it's the best time you'll ever invest. Know why you're here. Second, decide each day what's most important for you to do that day, and do it. By having a clear purpose and doing the most important thing each day, God can revolutionize your life and help you make the most of your time.

Your Secret Time

"But you, when you pray, go into your inner room, close your door and pray to your Father who is in secret, and your Father who sees what is done in secret will reward you."

MATTHEW 6:6

In the Sermon on the Mount, Jesus advised us to spend quiet time with God each day. In fact, He not only suggested that this time be private, He actually used the word *secret*.

Some people take this verse so literally that they say you should never pray in public, but that's not what Jesus was talking about. He was talking about the spirit of prayer. He was talking about having time alone to pray to God and not be showy about it.

Why did Jesus place such emphasis on this? Why is it so important? Because Christianity is a *relationship*. And in any meaningful relationship, we need time with the other person, to talk and to listen, to communicate, to share our lives together.

Make it your daily priority to have a quiet time with God. These meaningful moments alone with your heavenly Father are your opportunity to grow your relationship with your Lord. What happens with the Lord in secret will be a blessing to others in public.

Literal Translation

When he was alone, the Twelve and the others around him asked him about the parables. He told them, "The secret of the kingdom of God has been given to you. But to those on the outside everything is said in parables so that, 'they may be ever seeing but never perceiving.'"

MARK 4:10–12 NIV

When a well-meaning Christian declares, "I believe everything in the Bible, literally," that person is lying to you. Why is that? Well, look at the teachings of Jesus. In the Sermon on the Mount, Jesus said, "If your right eye makes you stumble, tear it out and throw it from you; for it is better for you to lose one of the parts of your body, than for your whole body to be thrown into hell" (Matthew 5:29). If the person claims to believe that everything in the Bible should be taken literally, but he has eyes, then he is lying to you, because we all stumble with our eyes through lust, greed, or envy.

Jesus was not actually urging us to pluck our eyes out. He was talking about the seriousness of sin, and how we must repent of sin, lest we wind up in hell. But if every word Jesus uttered is taken literally, every one of us must immediately gouge out both eyes.

Remember that Jesus taught in parables, metaphors, and allegories. He used these devices to make the broader spiritual point. Does that water down Scripture? Absolutely not! Jesus was simply using memorable illustrations to communicate perfect truth. And that's where the guidance of the Holy Spirit comes into play: to help us to distinguish between literal truth and a parable, thereby allowing us to understand the rich truths of our faith.

The Role of the Holy Spirit: The Helper

"The Helper, the Holy Spirit, whom the Father will send in My name, He will teach you all things, and bring to your remembrance all that I said to you."

JOHN 14:26

The verse above is from the New American Standard Bible; it translates the Greek word *paraclete* (which means "the Holy Spirit") as "the Helper." Compare this with other translations.

- The King James Version translates *Helper* as *Comforter*.
- The New International Version translates *Helper* as *Counselor*.
- The New Living Translation translates *Helper* as *Advocate*.

All four translations give us a more complete picture of the Holy Spirit. He is Helper, Advocate, Counselor, and Comforter.

Helper = He empowers us with a "want to," or a desire to follow Christ in faith.

Advocate = He reminds us that God is for us and loves us.

Counselor = He is our teacher and guide in how to understand and apply God's Word to our everyday lives with wisdom.

Comforter = He is our greatest, most compassionate encourager in a time of need.

To know God is to know Jesus in faith. To know Jesus is to receive a great gift—the gift of the Holy Spirit.

The Role of the Holy Spirit: to Help Us Resist Temptation

I pray that from his glorious, unlimited resources he will empower you with inner strength through his Spirit.

EPHESIANS 3:16 NLT

During times of temptation, it can be difficult to show our love for God. In temptation we realize that love for God is contrary to all of our emotions. When we give in to temptation, the result is guilt. But if we keep repeating a sin over and over, we develop hearts of stone. And that is not a pretty sight. But there is good news for the Christian in the face of temptation. The Holy Spirit convicts us to push back, to say no, and to do what is pleasing to God. Sometimes He brings to mind a verse on the example of Jesus. He is the source of what is truly supernatural in resisting temptation.

So often Christians try to live the good life on their own, by their own strength. This is doomed to failure. When we face temptation, we are up against spiritual powers of darkness and evil that are stronger and smarter than any of us. If you are a Christian, don't be an arrogant fool and try to make it on your own. Claim the power of the Holy Spirit, and find victory over temptation.

The Role of the Holy Spirit: to Convict Us of Sin

"When [the Holy Spirit] comes, [He] will convict the world concerning sin and righteousness and judgment."

JOHN 16:8

Let's face it: no matter how hard we try, all of us will rationalize all sorts of evil plans. As my dad has said many times, "For many people today, there is no such thing as sin; everything is explainable." The Holy Spirit cuts right through this nonsense.

The Holy Spirit is God's gift to convict us of sin. When we are not in close relationship with God, the Holy Spirit uses the preaching of the Word of God to convict us of our need for the forgiveness and salvation of God in Christ. If we are followers of Christ, then the Holy Spirit dwells within us to convict us of the need to get things right with God when we do wrong.

Realize that the most miserable person in the world is not the non-Christian. The most miserable person in the world is the Christian who is rebelling against God, because that individual is going through a war inside. When the Holy Spirit convicts us of sin, He gives us an inner desire to confess our sin to God and then to seek forgiveness from those we have wronged. In the process, we get right with God once again.

The Holy Spirit is there to convict us—because God loves us and wants the best for our lives. His conviction is all about God's love.

No Backing Down

"Blessed are those who have been persecuted for the sake of righteousness, for theirs is the kingdom of heaven. Blessed are you when people insult you and persecute you, and falsely say all kinds of evil against you because of Me. Rejoice and be glad, for your reward in heaven is great."

MATTHEW 5:10–12

Let me tell you of the day I face with dread. There will be a call telling me that one of the missionaries our church has sent out into the mission field has been arrested, or kidnapped, or even killed.

Whether it is a fellow minister, a doctor on a special mission trip, or even one of our teenagers building houses for the poor during their spring break, I pray that if such an event occurs, in our grief, we will not stand around wringing our hands, saying, "You know, this is getting too dangerous! We gotta back off some of this!" No! May it never be! Christ didn't say that when we face persecution, we should retreat like a bunch of cowards. He said "when" we are persecuted. Expect it. Then continue the mission of the church, for those who are persecuted face extraordinary blessings!

Jesus Christ gave us a clear mission: to take the gospel to every people group on the earth. The mission of the church is what He has called us to fulfill, no matter what the cost! God is calling on us to be filled with the Holy Spirit so that we will be faithful witnesses for Christ to the very end, no matter what sacrifice we have to pay.

When George Got a Whippin'

The fear of the LORD is pure, enduring forever.

PSALM 19:9 NIV

What does it mean to "fear" the Lord? When you think about God, do you picture an angry God who's looking to zap you when you do something wrong? Wrong image, and it inspires the wrong kind of fear. To "fear" God has to do with reverence and respect. It's done by trusting that God knows what is best in our lives. If we ignore what God says is best, we know we're going to face some negative consequences, so we obey Him. That demonstrates a healthy fear of a loving God.

One day, when my oldest son, George, was about two years old, I saw him walking around with a screwdriver. I told him to give it to me, but he ignored me. Before I could take it from him, George stuck it in an electrical socket. And—*BOOM*! He flew back on the floor and sat there, stunned. Then he started to cry, and then he got a whippin' on top of that!

You may think, *What a mean ole daddy!* No, that's a loving daddy. I wanted it seared in George's brain that certain actions bring about negative consequences. I assure you he got a lot of love and comfort after that, and as far as I know, he didn't repeat the deed. We as parents are not loving unless we create a healthy fear in our children! It's so similar in having a healthy fear of the Lord. Our heavenly Father loves and cares enough about us to teach us what is best. If we ignore Him, there *will* be negative consequences.

Wisdom from Dad

*As water reflects a face, so a man's
heart reflects the man.*

PROVERBS 27:19 NIV

A young girl asked her mother "the question": "Where do babies come from?" Mom calmly explained that when Mom and Dad love each other, Daddy will . . . Okay, you know how this story goes. The little girl then asked, "Where do kittens come from?" Mom replied, "Pretty much the same place." The girl had a proud look on her face as she declared, "Wow! My daddy can do anything!"

Kids are quite proud of their parents and listen carefully to what we say. So for Father's Day, let's look at some of the things we dads say—or don't say—to our kids.

The most frequent things dads say: "Because I said so." "Who said life was fair?" "You'll understand when you're older." "If your friends jumped off a bridge, would you jump too?"

And the top things most dads never say: "I must be lost. I'll pull over and ask for directions." "Sweetheart, now that you're thirteen, I think you are old enough to start dating." "Rather than going to a ball game, what do you say we just go to the mall?"

And the greatest thing a Dad ever said: "That's My boy—I'm proud of Him" (Matthew 3:17, paraphrased). God the Father said this about Jesus at His baptism.

May all of us fathers seek to be like the greatest Father of all—Jesus' Dad.

The Shadow You Cast—Part 1

As a result, people brought the sick into the streets and laid them on beds and mats so that at least Peter's shadow might fall on some of them as he passed by.

ACTS 5:15 NIV

Jesus' shadow fell over Peter. Peter's shadow fell over people of his day with such an awe that they brought the sick and lame on pallets and carts by the road in hopes that Peter would walk their way, his shadow would fall over them, and they would be healed. Peter casts a long shadow for Christ to this very day.

In the 1930s, my grandfather, a Baptist minister, stepped to the pulpit to preach from Acts 5:14–15. His title was "The Shadow You Cast." My grandfather's shadow for Christ fell over my father. My father's shadow for Christ fell over me. Now, my shadow falls over my sons, my church, and people I'll never know. I hope when I've finished with this world, my boys and others will say, "He surely loved Jesus."

What kind of shadow do you cast? What kind of shadow will you cast? I hope it is a long shadow for good, for Jesus.

The Shadow You Cast—Part 2

Brethren, join in following my example, and observe
those who walk according to the pattern you have in us.

PHILIPPIANS 3:17

A Bible school teacher told me she noticed a boy sitting in the hall with a stern look on his face, barking orders to the other children. "What are you doing?" she asked. "I'm pretending I'm the pastor," he said. "How are you playing the pastor?" she asked. He explained, "I ain't doing nothing. I'm just telling everybody else what to do!"

We sometimes never know where our shadows fall and how they influence others. Martin Luther cast a long shadow over Germany, Europe, and the rest of the world—a long shadow for good. About four hundred years later, Adolf Hitler also cast a long shadow over Germany, Europe, and the rest of the world—a devastatingly evil shadow. Two lives, two Germans—one filled with the Spirit of the Lord, the other filled with the spirit of the devil.

You will probably never influence the entire world as Luther or Hitler did, but I guarantee you will have tremendous influence on some part of it. It may be as a parent, coworker, neighbor, or friend. It may be as a coach or a teacher. You won't always be conscious of where your shadow falls. It goes with you wherever you go, always falling on others. As I asked yesterday, what kind of shadow do you cast? Is it for good or for bad? Is it to encourage or to discourage? Is it for Christ—or something else? Only your shadow knows.

The Accuracy of the Manuscripts

Every word of God is tested.

PROVERBS 30:5

Bible scholar Norman Geisler explains why he trusts the accuracy of the Bible: "Compared to any other book from that period, the New Testament has more manuscripts, earlier manuscripts, and more accurately copied manuscripts." He further explains:

- *More manuscripts:* Although most ancient books survive with about a dozen copies, over fifty-seven hundred Greek manuscripts of the New Testament still exist.
- *Earlier manuscripts:* Most ancient manuscripts were copied about a thousand years after the original composition. The earliest New Testament manuscripts are from 25 to 150 years after the original.
- *More accurately copied manuscripts:* Surviving copies of the New Testament can be restored with about 99.5 percent accuracy. This is so accurate that not a single doctrine of the Bible is affected.[13]

A further note: many seminary students compare copies of the ancient manuscripts, looking for differences. They are amazed by the fact that they just can't find many. There's a *the* where there's an *a* in another copy. There's an adjective that's a little bit different from that found in a different text. But never is the theme different. The message is the same. Now that's accuracy. The trustworthiness of God's Word through all of history really is a miracle.

A Regular Meeting

*Very early in the morning, while it was still dark,
Jesus got up, left the house and went off to a
solitary place, where He prayed.*

MARK 1:35 NIV

One of the reasons I love to be in the Sea of Galilee region in Israel is because it's one of those places where you can still see what it was like in Jesus' day. It's a place where you can very easily visualize Jesus wandering up in the hills—whether in the early morning, or even in the middle of the night—and finding a quiet place, just to spend time with His Father. So I ask you, if Jesus, the Son of God, needed to spend time with His Father, don't you think you do as well?

Let me share a personal insight. On my own, I am too selfish, too lazy, and too busy to arrange regular time alone with God. I just don't have the discipline to make that happen. And I'll bet you have the same issues standing between you and a close relationship with your heavenly Father. If so, here is my secret to overcoming my self-made obstacles and creating a lifestyle of regular time alone with God—ask for His help. Simply ask God to give you the hunger to know Him and the determination to make it happen. He'll be glad to give you that desire and to teach you how to create the discipline to have a regular meeting with Him! Why don't you do what Jesus did and spend regular time alone with the Father?

It Doesn't Always Have to Be Tough

But how can they call on him to save them unless they believe in him? And how can they believe in him if they have never heard about him? And how can they hear about him unless someone tells them?

ROMANS 10:14 NLT

A local pastor tells of a teenager at his church who is responsible for leading dozens of his friends to Christ. How does he accomplish this? It's actually pretty simple. He invites schoolmates to come to church with him. Most accept the invitation, begin attending regularly, and become involved in the activities the church provides for the youth. He is a great missionary by simply bringing his friends to church and then letting the teachers and pastors take it from there. His pastor says, "No one ever told him that witnessing was supposed to be hard!"

Indeed, it need not be. There are a lot of simple, nonintimidating things you can do to help someone begin his or her journey toward Christ. For instance, you can send a copy of this book to a coworker or friend and note in the book a devotional or two that may be particularly helpful to him or her. Follow up with an e-mail asking what the person thought. Was it helpful? You can call a friend and let him know you were thinking of him and ask if there is any way you could pray for him. These are just a few simple ways to reach out, and sometimes the Lord may bless you with an opportunity to share with others what Jesus means to you.

Pretty easy, isn't it? Witnessing doesn't always have to be tough.

Forgive *Who???*

*"In prayer there is a connection between what God
does and what you do. You can't get forgiveness from
God, for instance, without also forgiving others."*

MATTHEW 6:14 MSG

In the spring of 1981, both Ronald Reagan and Pope John Paul II were shot and seriously wounded in assassination attempts. Each survived, and both the president and the pope made it a priority to forgive the very people who had tried to kill them.

Ronald Reagan said, "I realized I couldn't ask for God's help while at the same time I felt hatred for the mixed up young man who had shot me. Isn't that the meaning of the lost sheep? We're all God's children and therefore, equally beloved by Him. I began to pray for his soul and that he would find his way back into the fold."[14]

Pope John Paul II's forgiveness was even more dramatic. I can still see those amazing pictures, on the cover of *Time*, of Pope John Paul II visiting the man who tried to kill him and in his prison cell—sitting face-to-face, forgiving him.

These are not normal responses when someone tries to kill you. Where did these great men learn such actions? From Jesus! This ability and motivation to forgive under those circumstances could only come from one source—the One who said, "Father, forgive them, for they don't know what they are doing" (Luke 23:34 NLT).

If Jesus can provide these leaders with the ability to forgive their assassins, don't you think He can give you the power to forgive those who have mistreated you?

Facing Rock Bottom

And He has said to me, "My grace is sufficient for you,
for power is perfected in weakness." Most gladly,
therefore, I will rather boast about my weaknesses, so
that the power of Christ may dwell in me.

2 CORINTHIANS 12:9

When reminded that God does not give us any burdens we cannot handle, Mother Teresa replied, "I know, but sometimes I just wish He didn't think so highly of me."

Although it's true that tough times can challenge us and shape our character, most of us would prefer that God would find another teaching method!

Hitting rock bottom is not fun, but crises do offer opportunities for growth and service. For instance, sometimes God allows us to go through hard times so that we can learn to truly trust Him. You see, when we do choose to trust God—even when there is no concrete evidence of His presence—we demonstrate real faith. And that faith is not only demonstrated to God; it is a powerful witness to everyone who sees what we have gone through.

Look at the example shown by Joseph in Genesis. After thirteen years of miserable setbacks, the first thing he did was stand before Pharaoh and share his testimony of his faith in God. What a magnificent witness to the glory of God!

So when facing tough times, recognize the opportunity you have to build trust in God, deepen your faith, and become a powerful witness for your heavenly Father.

It All Comes with the Package

"Do not think that I came to bring peace on the earth."

MATTHEW 10:34

There are a lot of well-intentioned Christians who get confused and are pridefully divisive in their self-righteous judgment of others. In their blindness to their own sin, they are quick to point out the sins of others. In that process, they become divisive, and then they often take on a martyr complex. "Oh, I'm being persecuted for my faith." Really? I doubt it. They're probably just being persecuted because they're jerks!

But Christ does want us to understand that when we trust in the person of Jesus Christ and then claim what He claims about Himself—that our ultimate goal is not to be peacemakers—it will not be an easy road.

There is a lot of focus these days on unity. This concept of unity is a big deal to a lot of church folks. ("Hey, can't we all just get along?") But understand this: when church folks take on the mind-set that unity is more important than truth, they have completely misunderstood the person of Jesus Christ! He was very clear that when He comes into a person's life, there will be a lack of peace in certain relationships because some are for Him and some are not. There will be division. When we follow Christ, we're going to face ridicule, division, and sometimes even persecution. It all comes with the package.

Remarriage

*"But if you do not forgive men their sins, your
Father will not forgive your sins."*

MATTHEW 6:15 NIV

Here is a horrific statistic: 70 percent of second marriages fail. Why is this? Often it is because the new marriage began while unresolved issues still lingered from the divorce. Take the time to resolve these issues and not carry unnecessary baggage into a new relationship.

How can you resolve these issues? First, ask forgiveness from the Lord, as well as from your ex—even if you were the one who was sinned against. Ask the Lord to help you deal with unhealthy behavior on your part so that the same sinful patterns don't repeat themselves. Seek forgiveness from your children as well, recognizing the devastating effect the divorce has had on their lives and the potentially destructive effect it can have on their future. And then the toughest and most important step—*give* forgiveness to your ex, cleansing your heart of the resentments, pain, and ill feelings that may still remain.

Before entering into a new marriage, be sure that you have healed from the loss of your previous marriage. If this has not occurred, then you are certainly not ready for remarriage. If you are feeling doubts, God may be telling you to slow down or even leading you to break off the new relationship. Seek God's will, and be willing to follow His leading.

Identifying Counterfeit Religion

"For false Christs and false prophets will appear
and perform great signs and miracles to deceive
even the elect—if that were possible."

MATTHEW 24:24 NIV

It should have been easy for members of his cult to know that David Koresh was lying when he claimed to be Jesus. He died with many of his followers in Waco years ago when his compound caught fire while surrounded by federal agents. Why should they have known better? He wore glasses! Jesus was perfect and sure wouldn't need thick glasses sitting on the end of His nose! Unfortunately, false prophets and false teachings aren't always that easy to spot.

We can learn how to identify false teachings by examining how U.S. Treasury agents are taught to spot counterfeit money. Agents spend many days doing nothing but looking at piles of real money. They carefully study authentic bills, saturating themselves in true currency and its features. And then, when a counterfeit is introduced, it is so obvious to the agent that the bad bill practically jumps out of the stack!

It works the same way with identifying false teachings. If you study the Word of God, learn it, and know it from cover to cover, you will be able to discern false teaching when it comes along. The best way to identify a false prophet is to know the real Christ through knowing His Word.

A Great Prayer for Your Children

We have not ceased to pray for you.

COLOSSIANS 1:9

We need to pray for our children. For many years, my wife has prayed a prayer from Scripture for our three sons. Her prayers are based on Colossians 1:9–12. Here are some ideas for you to try:

- *Pray that they will increase in the knowledge of God.* Most parents' greatest hope for their children is that they will be happy, but a fulfilled life comes from knowing God. Without God, there is a nagging emptiness. Lots of people know about God, but knowing Him personally is different. We all know a lot about our nation's president, but only a few know him personally.
- *Pray that they live worthy lives.* Pray that their lives have an impact for good and that they will be people of trustworthy character.
- *Pray that they're strengthened in God's power.* The world and evil influences will seek to pull our children down. They need God's power to be strong, to resist temptation, and to do the right thing.
- *Thank God for each child.* They are unique creations of God.

We all need to pray for our children. Why don't you do it right now?

Achieving Greatness

"Whoever wishes to become great among you shall be your servant; and whoever wishes to be first among you shall be slave of all."

MARK 10:43–44

Deep down inside, don't you want to be great? What does it mean to be great? Probably the most common way that the world defines *greatness* is accomplishment, achieving great things. You might look back and think about Alexander the Great; he conquered the known world by the time he was thirty-three years old and then wept that there were no more worlds to conquer. Or you may think about Thomas Edison, with more than a thousand patents to his name. Or consider Einstein and his amazing discoveries in quantum physics.

Others would say real greatness is all about power. In Jesus' time, Caesar Augustus would be considered truly great because of all the power he held. In the modern world, look at U.S. presidents—that is the big enchilada because there is no position more powerful.

Actually, anyone can become great, and Jesus tells us how in our Bible passage for today: "Whoever wishes to become great among you shall be your servant; and whoever wishes to be first among you shall be slave of all." Jesus, the greatest man to ever live, said He didn't come to be served; He came to serve, even to the point of giving His life for our salvation. The greatest man was also the greatest servant. And that is what He calls us to be. He calls us to serve God and those around us. It's the only lasting road to greatness.

Stockholm Syndrome

It is for freedom that Christ has set us free.
Stand firm, then, and do not let yourselves be
burdened again by a yoke of slavery.

GALATIANS 5:1 NIV

Stockholm syndrome is a term used to describe the behavior of kidnap victims who become sympathetic to their captors. The name derives from a 1973 hostage incident in Sweden. After six days of captivity in a bank, the hostages actually resisted rescue attempts. Months later, the victims still refused to testify against their captors at trial.

What causes this seemingly odd behavior? Out of a fear of violence, hostages identify with their captors, initially as a defense mechanism. Small acts of kindness by the captor become magnified. Rescue attempts are often seen as a threat since it's likely the captive would be harmed during such attempts. The behavior is considered a common survival strategy for victims of abuse and has been observed in battered spouses, abused children, prisoners of war—even occupants of concentration camps.

When it comes to dealing with Jesus, many people react with their own version of Stockholm syndrome. Jesus, the Liberator, wants to free you from the bondage of slavery to sin; He wants to free you from being a prisoner to worldly values and to spare you from judgment. Many people would actually rather stay in bondage, clinging to their own personal captors, feeling it's the only way they can survive. But the good news of the gospel is that Jesus Christ came to pay that ransom so you could be set free!

July

Delight yourself in the LORD;
and He will give you the desires of your heart.

PSALM 37:4

Don't Just Pray—Do Something!

Then the LORD said to Moses, "Why are you crying out to me? Tell the Israelites to move on. Raise your staff and stretch out your hand over the sea to divide the water so that the Israelites can go through the sea on dry ground."

EXODUS 14:15–16 NIV

Imagine a family about to leave for vacation and the father says, "Let's pray for God's guidance on this vacation." They begin to pray, and days later they're still in the garage, praying.

There's a time to pray, and there's a time to move in faith.

Israel had their back against the wall when Moses led them from Egyptian slavery. There was the Red Sea on one side, the Egyptian army charging toward them on the other. Then Moses prayed, and God miraculously parted that great sea. The children of Israel could have just stood there after God parted the water, continuing to pray fervently although the seabed was dry. But they didn't. They stepped out in faith, believing that God had provided a way out for His people.

If they had just prayed and never stepped out in faith, they would have been like a lot of Christians today. Many cultural Christians believe the Bible with "head knowledge." Yet when it comes to trusting God, they are standing just on the edge of the sea.

Just like the Israelites, we must trust God to save us. Then step out in faith to show it. Remember the lesson from the Israelites: there is a time to pray and a time to move. There is no real faith until we step out and trust God with our own lives, no matter how much we pray.

Murder—Is There Forgiveness?

*"I, even I, am the one who wipes out your transgressions
for My own sake, and I will not remember your sins."*

ISAIAH 43:25

The definition of *murder* is the premeditated taking of human life. So because life begins at conception, abortion is murder. If you have had an abortion—or performed an abortion—you are guilty of the sin of murder.

But here is a message for those of us who have never been involved in an abortion—we, too, are guilty of murder. In fact every person who has ever lived is guilty of the sin of the murder of the Son of God! This is not wordplay. The sins each of us have ever committed directly caused the murder of Jesus Christ. We often speak of aborted children as "innocent life," but understand that there has never been a more innocent life than Jesus Christ! And our sins are responsible for His death.

But here is incredibly good news. When we seek forgiveness by believing that Jesus paid the penalty for all our sins on the cross, we are cleansed by the loving sacrifice of the Son of God.

Accept that forgiveness. Let God discard your guilt, and know the internal peace that your loving Father gives to all of us sinners. We all deserve death for our sin, but in Christ, we have forgiveness and eternal life.

Equally Yoked

Do not be bound together with unbelievers; for what partnership have righteousness and lawlessness, or what fellowship has light with darkness? Or what harmony has Christ with Belial, or what has a believer in common with an unbeliever?

2 Corinthians 6:14–15

Did you know that Christians are called to marry Christians? Why? First, it's just common sense. If Christ is your priority and you marry someone whose priority is politics, music, work, sports, or anything other than Christ, in time you'll find yourselves drifting apart. God's practical instruction that Christians are to be bound with Christians allows us to be joined together in a deep relationship of love, respect, compassion, and understanding of mutual interest.

But that's not all. If it's important that Christians marry Christians, then it is just as important that Christians should seriously *date* only Christians! Why? Well, we tend to marry people that we date! Christians must be cautious about getting into serious relationships with those who are not committed to following Jesus. Determine their commitment up front. Don't ask them if they are Christians—80 percent will say yes. Ask them what is most important in their lives and how they would describe their relationship with God. Their answers will reveal if it's real.

Remember, when a Christian marries a non-Christian, he or she is choosing to put that unsaved person above Jesus by choosing to ignore God's Word. But if you are a Christian who did this, God wants you to make the most of your marriage for life and seek to be a good witness to your spouse.

The Day America Told the Truth

Every man did what was right in his own eyes.

JUDGES 17:6

In the book *The Day America Told the Truth*, authors James Patterson and Peter Kim found that in every region of the country, 90 percent of the people believe in God. But when they asked people how they made up their mind on issues of right and wrong, they found that people do not turn to God or religion to help them decide about moral issues of the day. They concluded, "There is absolutely no moral consensus at all."[15] In other words, people believe there is a God, but He has no relevance to their everyday lives. They do what is right in their *own* eyes.

True belief in God is about trust and obedience. We trust Him to know and want the best for us, so we obey His command in His Word. It's radically countercultural, but it's the best way to live.

Having Jesus as Lord means loving God enough to trust and obey Him and loving your neighbor as yourself. It connects morality with God in a way that is good for all.

The Gnostic Gospels

*You shall not add to the word that I command you, nor
take from it, that you may keep the commandments of
the LORD your God that I command you.*

DEUTERONOMY 4:2 ESV

The Gnostic gospels received widespread attention after they were referred to in the novel and movie *The Da Vinci Code*. It thrust the Gnostic writings into pop culture. This has caused a lot of conflict and confusion as people wonder why these "lost gospels" were not included within our Bible.

The answer to that is easy. The Gospels in the Bible were all written within twenty to sixty years after the life of Jesus, soon enough that the actual witnesses to Jesus' words and deeds were available as primary sources. The Gnostics, however, were written in the second century, long after Jesus' contemporaries had died. To give credibility to their stories, the Gnostics falsely attached the names of people who had long been dead, such as Thomas, Mary, and Philip. So not only was the gospel of Thomas not written by Thomas; it wasn't even written by someone who had ever met Thomas!

The Gnostic gospels are not gospels at all, and here's something I find interesting. The Gnostics are sometimes referred to as the "secret gospels." (Now, *there* is an oxymoron!) If God is going to inspire a gospel, He most certainly isn't going to allow it to be kept secret! Why would God inspire something for every generation only to allow it to be lost? Believe the true Gospels and you will never be lost.

When Your Back Is Against the Wall

Do not fear, for I am with you; do not be dismayed, for I am your God. I will strengthen you and help you; I will uphold you with my righteous right hand.

ISAIAH 41:10 NIV

I'm sure you have seen movies where the bad guys chase the hero into an alley. He runs across empty barrels, through hanging laundry, over a stack of rubbish, and comes to . . . a brick wall! Panicked, our hero turns to face the bad guys, and his back is literally against the wall. And while you watch this scene, you subconsciously recognize it as a metaphor for many fearful moments in your life.

Often God leads us to what seems like a dead end, and we can be overcome with a sense of doom. Our human tendency is to take our eyes off of God, look at the problem before us, and feel overwhelmed with fear and anxiety. And when fear floods in, faith floods out! How can you handle these times that seem so hopeless? When your back is against the wall, choose faith over fear. Stand firm in the faith, and put your trust in God.

These frightening moments are only a temporary dead end. God will lead us to the point when we can no longer help ourselves and must trust in God alone. Then God goes to work, and He is glorified in a way greater than ever before. We are called to choose faith over fear and to trust that in God's plan there are no permanent dead ends!

Actually, Money *Can* Buy Happiness

If there is a poor man among your brothers in any of the towns of the land that the LORD your God is giving you, do not be hardhearted or tightfisted toward your poor brother.

DEUTERONOMY 15:7 NIV

Here's an interesting news article I recently read. A research team at Harvard Business School has found that spending as little as five dollars a day on others will significantly boost your own personal happiness. A psychologist heading the study said, "We wanted to test the theory that how people spend their money is at least as important as how much money they earned."[16] So they had their subjects make a list of income as well as detailed expenditures, especially donations to charity and gifts to others. Then they rated their happiness levels and discovered that the more you spend on others, the happier you'll be.

I'm not sure how much this study cost, but I think I could have saved them a whole bunch of money. In God's Word, Jesus already said, "It is more blessed to give than to receive" (Acts 20:35 NIV). Giving to God—by giving to others—is a tried-and-true way to a happier, more fulfilling life.

Can't We Just Sort It All Out in Purgatory?

*It is appointed for men to die once and
after this comes judgment.*

HEBREWS 9:27

It would be nice if we could, but there's a big problem. The idea of purgatory is not found in the holy Scriptures. It's a concept found in the Apocrypha—Jewish books of sacred writings—that were never believed to be on the level of holy Scripture. Some may be thinking, *What's purgatory?* One definition is to be in limbo.

So what does Scripture say happens when we die? As the above-referenced scripture, Hebrews 9:27, says, "After this comes judgment." God makes a judgment on whether we'll spend eternity with Him in heaven or spend eternity separated from Him in hell. There's no in-between holding zone. When we die, it's one or the other.

What would it take for God to make the judgment that we deserve eternal life in heaven with Him? Either of two things:

1. Our being perfect. Bad news: only one Man has been perfect and it ain't you—or me.
2. Our believing in the perfect Man, who gave His life for every single sin in your life and mine. Jesus is that Man. He paid the penalty for our sins so that if we trust in Him, we will be blameless before God and receive eternal life.

If you died today, what judgment would it be? Heaven or hell? One thing is for sure: it won't be purgatory.

The Sword of the Lord

*Above all, taking the shield of faith, wherewith ye
shall be able to quench all the fiery darts of the
wicked. And take the helmet of salvation, and the
sword of the Spirit, which is the word of God.*

EPHESIANS 6:16–17 KJV

Do you ever find it a challenge to fight temptation? Of course
you do; we all do. The best way to fight temptation is to reject
it the way Jesus did. When Satan tempted Jesus with bread, power,
and freedom from harm, Jesus responded by quoting Scripture.
Again and again Satan would throw out a great prize, and each
time Jesus shot him down with God's Word. Follow Jesus' example,
and you'll have a much easier time overcoming the devil's attempts
to tempt you into sin.

Perhaps you are thinking right now, *Bryant, that makes a lot
of sense, but I'm just not able to memorize things.* Let me offer you
some advice. If you are not good at memorizing the exact words,
then capture the spirit of the passages. There are two reasons for
this. First, worrying over the exact words might pose a barrier to
your learning and may even be so frustrating that you give up. All
Bibles today are translations of Old Testament Hebrew and New
Testament Greek. Second, it's the point of the verse that God uses
to give us victory over temptation. But whatever you do, don't
change the meaning in any way, or the devil will have a field day
with you.

God's Divorce Recovery Program

"When you stand praying, if you hold anything against anyone, forgive him, so that your Father in heaven may forgive you your sins."

MARK 11:25 NIV

Perhaps today you are suffering from the consequences of divorce. Maybe your spouse deserted you or ran off with another person and you are feeling rejected, hurt, even humiliated. Or you may be still struggling twenty or thirty years later with the breakup of your parents and have a festering resentment against them. Or maybe you've been separated from your grandchildren because of divorce—something completely out of your control—and your heart is full of bitterness.

If you are suffering from the consequences of divorce, know this: your pain will not go away until you release your resentment and forgive those who have wronged you. If you are a follower of Jesus Christ, know that this forgiveness is not "just another option." It is not something God simply encourages. Jesus Christ *commands* forgiveness. I know this is hard; in fact, some pain is just too deep for us to forgive on our own. Only by the power of Christ can we forgive in certain cases. So claim that power. Ask God to help you do what you can't do. Let God bring cleansing and healing to your life. It's the best divorce recovery program of them all.

Insight into the Scriptures

*"For just as Jonah was three days and three nights in
the belly of the sea monster, so will the Son of Man be
three days and three nights in the heart of the earth."*

MATTHEW 12:40

Sometimes you might be troubled while studying the Bible.
Sometimes you'll come across passages that just don't seem
to add up. They may even appear contradictory, and that's dis-
concerting because the Word of God just shouldn't contradict
itself. For instance, in my early days of Christian growth, I was
troubled by the above passage in Matthew. This really bothered
me because, when I counted, I couldn't count that Jesus was in the
tomb for three nights! But several years later, a teacher explained
that first-century writers would count a day and a night if it were
any part of that day or night. So Jesus died on Friday and was
dead for Friday night, Saturday night, and *part* of Sunday—thus
the people of that time considered it to be three nights. That
insight pulled it all together for me; it finally made perfect sense.

If you're struggling with a problematic passage, be thankful
that we have the Holy Spirit and wise teachers to help us understand things we don't see at first reading of the Word. That's why
Bible studies are so vital and why we need Spirit-filled teachers to
guide us. Most of all, that is why we need the Holy Spirit to give
us insight into areas we can't understand on our own.

Earth Pains

*We know that the whole creation has been groaning as
in the pains of childbirth right up to the present time.*

ROMANS 8:22 NIV

Things just ain't what they're supposed to be. Consider man's
violence against man, the animal kingdom's survival of the
fittest, or pollution poisoning our air and streams. And it's incredible how the earth, with all its beauty and wonder, can become
a destructive force against itself through earthquakes, volcanoes,
hurricanes, and floods.

The Bible says, "The whole creation groans and suffers the
pains of childbirth" (NASB). There is a reason. In the beginning,
before man sinned, everything was in sync. There was such peace
on earth that people were vegetarians (Genesis 1:29–30). There
was no killing of any kind. But now the earth has entered into a
period that God likens to a mother giving birth, and like childbirth, things will get worse before they get better.

All creation longs for things to be made right, and one day
they will be—the day when Jesus returns. It will be a time of
salvation and judgment. Judgment will be for those who are not
right with God; salvation, for those who are. His arrival will usher
in a new age of harmony and peace on earth. Won't it be great?
If you're ready, yes. If you're not, no. The key question for you is,
will you be ready? The only way to be ready is through faith in
Jesus Christ.

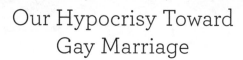

Our Hypocrisy Toward Gay Marriage

"How can you say to your brother, 'Let me take the speck out of your eye,' and behold, the log is in your own eye?"

MATTHEW 7:4

Here are some humbling statistics: The level of premarital sex among teenage Christians is no different from those who are not Christian. And divorce rates in the church are no different from those outside the church. When you look at these statistics, is it any wonder that gay activists look at us and cry, "Hypocrites!" And most troubling of all—their charge is valid.

Jesus made it clear that God never desires divorce and that premarital sex, adultery, lust, and homosexuality are *all* sins. But too often the church focuses on homosexuality and ignores several sins God's Word lists alongside it. We often park on one sin and neglect the multiplicity of sins that are continual within the body of Christ. Gay activists see the obvious hypocrisy and use it to self-righteously justify their own actions.

When we deal with subjects like same-sex marriage, let's be sure we first look in the mirror. Let's recognize that all sin displeases God. May we repent of our sins and seek to reach out with the love and hope of Jesus Christ to all humanity. Remember that no sin is too difficult to be forgiven and overcome by the power of the cross.

Taking Up the Cross

"If anyone would come after me, he must deny himself and take up his cross daily and follow me."

LUKE 9:23 NIV

I find it interesting that Christ had not yet been crucified when He said, "He who does not take [up] his cross and follow after Me is not worthy of Me" (Matthew 10:38). How do we make sense of that? For a first-century Jewish man living in a land occupied by Rome, it would not be unusual to see condemned men carrying their crosses to their execution sites. He used this image to explain the high expectations He had for His disciples' devotion. He told them what He is telling us now: "If you're going to follow Me, you've got to be willing to die for Me."

So I ask myself this question, "Bryant, are you willing?" When Jesus gives this challenge, I think about how weak I am. I think about how cowardly, selfish, and sinful I am. And I think about Christian martyrs today, knowing that there is more persecution of Christians going on right now than there has been in all of history. I think about people living in that situation, and I wonder, *Would I be willing to go through torture for Christ? Would I be willing to give my life for Christ?* I surely hope so.

If you call yourself a Christian, what about you?

The Prince of Peace?

"Do not suppose that I have come to bring peace to the earth. I did not come to bring peace, but a sword."

MATTHEW 10:34 NIV

Many Christians are a bit unsettled when they learn that Christ—the Prince of Peace—proclaimed, "I did not come to bring peace, but a sword." What He meant is that He would bring division in this world. How does this reconcile with His mission on earth? Understand this: the reason Christ brings division is because when He left His throne in heaven and came to the earth to be the Savior for humankind, He invaded enemy territory. The evil one has so many in the world in captivity. And all through history, slave owners have not willingly given up their slaves. Think of the response of the Egyptians when Moses said, "Let my people go!" They resisted mightily; they didn't want to lose all that free labor. Think about the Old South, when abolitionists called for freeing the slaves: the response was the same.

Well, it's the same with the devil. When he has a person enslaved to sin, he fights like the dickens when someone tries to free that individual from his captivity. That's exactly why Christ came—to save those in captivity and to confront the evil one who enslaves people to sin. That battle creates division in our world— a division that is a natural by-product in the war for your soul.

Parenting Preschoolers

*Train up a child in the way he should go, even
when he is old he will not depart from it.*

PROVERBS 22:6

This directive from Proverbs gives us great instruction on rearing
our children:

Train up means to lead and to teach; you must teach your
preschooler to obey and to understand who is boss. In the early
days of childhood, there is a battle of the wills between the parent
and the child. This is a battle the parent can't afford to lose. Mom
and Dad need to be in charge.

In the way he should go means being a student of your children.
God has created each of them uniquely, and we want them to discover who God wants them to be. This means understanding our
children's interests and weaknesses. It means teaching them right
and wrong and that there will be consequences for doing wrong.

When he is old he will not depart from it. "Old" doesn't mean
teenager or young adult, but aged man. Some kids "get it" sooner
than others when it comes to God, right and wrong, and what
their purpose is. Others take a long time.

Along the way, some kids break their parents' hearts, but
God's Word offers hope that they will eventually come around.
Take time to be both a leader and a student of your children when
they're small, and there's a far better chance they'll listen to you
and do what's right when they're old.

Solomon on Leadership I:
The Faith of a Child

*Now, O Lord my God, you have made your servant king
in place of my father David. But I am only a little child
and do not know how to carry out my duties.*

1 Kings 3:7 niv

Think back to when you finally got out of the military or college and took that first job. Or maybe when you had your first child, and all of a sudden you realized you had to act like an adult. I'll never forget those feelings when I finished college and took a job in corporate America. It was several years before I went into the ministry. I'd wake up in the morning and think, *I'm supposed to be an adult, but I feel like a kid*. I was scared to death.

That's what Solomon felt when he suddenly became king of Israel. He felt overwhelmed with all the responsibility. He was called to lead a great nation that began with the patriarchs—a nation with extraordinary, godly leaders like Moses and Joshua, even his own father, David. As Solomon reflected on all of this, he thought, *I feel like a little child*.

Children are utterly dependent on their parents. So Solomon spoke to his heavenly Father (since his earthly father had died). He expressed an utter dependence on his heavenly Father. That is not a bad place for a king to begin—or for us to begin either. Approach your life as a little child, completely dependent on your Father. He will provide; He will never disappoint. With the faith of a child, we can live like mature adults.

Solomon on Leadership II: The Right Wish

The Lord was pleased that Solomon had asked for this. So God said to him, "Since you have asked for this and not for long life or wealth for yourself, . . . I will do what you have asked. I will give you a wise and discerning heart."

1 KINGS 3:10–12 NIV

I remember as a child playing the game "Three Wishes." We would all tell what we would wish for if a magic genie appeared and granted us anything we wanted. Of course, there would be wishes for lots of money or to be a hall-of-fame baseball player or have superpowers. I always thought I was so clever in asking for unlimited wishes.

Years ago, a young king of Israel asked for and received the greatest wish from God. He could have asked for long life or great wealth. Instead he asked for wisdom. Solomon asked for the understanding in his heart to know the right decisions for the best interests of the people. He wanted the wisdom of how to rule. Few things are more important to great leadership than wisdom.

Know this: wisdom is not knowledge. A lot of brilliant people have no wisdom at all. Wisdom is the ability to assimilate your knowledge to make decisions that are right, wise, and best for all concerned. God gives us the key to wisdom: willingness to listen to the Word of God and obey it. Solomon "wished" for the right thing. We should follow his example whenever we find ourselves placed in a position of trust, responsibility, and authority.

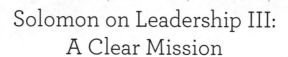
Solomon on Leadership III:
A Clear Mission

I intend, therefore, to build a temple for the Name of
the LORD my God, as the LORD told my father David,
when he said, "Your son whom I will put on the throne in
your place will build the temple for my Name."

1 KINGS 5:5 NIV

The first thing to understand about Solomon is that God's mission for him was clear from the very beginning. He was to build a great temple for the Lord. Interestingly, Solomon's father, David, also had the same vision, but it was not his mission to carry it out. God knew David was a warrior, not a builder, so He saved this particular goal for David's son Solomon.

Solomon gave the goal and the mission to the people of Israel, helped them to understand his mission, and challenged them to carry it out. The timing was right for this. The enemies had been defeated. It was a time to follow God's will.

Are you clear on your life mission? Are you clear on your life's purpose? Can you express it in a brief sentence, as Solomon could? Are you clear on your organization's mission and the role you are to play in it? Are you very clear about the goals God has given you to help fulfill it? Are you communicating that mission clearly? Follow Solomon's example: begin with a clear mission, and communicate that mission to those who are helping you meet that goal. It's an absolute key to successful living.

Solomon on Leadership IV: Networking

Without consultation, plans are frustrated,
but with many counselors they succeed.

PROVERBS 15:22

President Bill Clinton and British prime minister Tony Blair were often considered "soul mates." As the first baby boomer leaders of their nations, they also had similar political philosophies. People marveled at how well these two charismatic leaders got along. But it's also interesting to note that when George Bush succeeded President Clinton, Tony Blair reached out to him. The two also seemed to get along splendidly and worked together quite well. Blair proved that he was not just a friend of the president, but really a friend of the United States.

There was a similar relationship between Solomon and Hiram, the king of the Phoenicians. Solomon recognized that he needed others to help him fulfill his mission. He needed people with insight and resources he did not have. The Phoenicians were great ship builders and a great seafaring people. Hiram had been a friend of King David, and when he heard that Solomon was the new king, he reached out to him and offered his assistance. Solomon had enough humility as a leader to recognize that he needed not only people within his own nation but people of other nations, outside his place of responsibility. Good leaders reach out to others, collecting wisdom and support from every source available. Remember, God's Word tells us to seek wise counsel. It worked for Solomon; it will work for you.

Solomon on Leadership V: Organize and Delegate

King Solomon conscripted laborers from all Israel— thirty thousand men.

1 KINGS 5:13 NIV

Solomon was a builder. Why? Because he had extraordinary organizational ability. He had exceptional administrative ability to help gather good people around him and clearly explain their individual responsibilities for carrying out the mission. He knew how to organize. He knew how to delegate.

Look at the massive workforce Solomon organized. First Kings explains, "Now King Solomon levied forced laborers from all Israel; and the forced laborers numbered 30,000 men. He sent them to Lebanon, 10,000 a month in relays; they were in Lebanon a month and two months at home" (5:13–14). In other words, he had these forced laborers, probably slaves, working four months of the year. And then for eight months they could stay and work as laborers on private farms. But that's not all. The Bible also describes other sectors of this massive workforce. "Now Solomon had 70,000 transporters and 80,000 hewers of stone in the mountains, besides Solomon's 3,300 chief deputies, who were over the project and who ruled over the people who were doing the work" (vv. 15–16). Hundreds of thousands of people were involved in this extraordinary project.

Solomon organized all these various subcontractors, yet everybody was clear on their own responsibilities. Solomon set the example of the need for a leader to organize and delegate.

Solomon on Leadership VI: Provide Resources

Then the king commanded, and they quarried great stones, costly stones, to lay the foundation of the house with cut stones. So Solomon's builders and Hiram's builders and the Gebalites cut them, and prepared the timbers and the stones to build the house.

1 KINGS 5:17–18

I know a surefire way to kill a project I don't want to do," the businessman bragged. "All I have to do is ask for funding." Many of you can relate to that. Isn't it aggravating to be given an assignment but not be provided the tools, manpower, or money to get it done?

Solomon clearly understood that it was his role to see to it that the project of the building of the temple had the funding and supplies it needed to be successful. He was an organizational genius in this time of peace in ancient Israel. He also knew exactly what he wanted to build and what it would take to accomplish the goal. If you are a leader, always remember that when you give someone the responsibility to do something, also give the worker the resources to get it done. There is an old management formula that states, "Responsibility = Authority." Authority can be interpreted as having the resources and clout to accomplish the assignment. And when we've been given a mission from God, through Him, the ultimate Authority, we also are given everything we need to carry it out.

Creation or Evolution?

By faith we understand that the worlds were prepared
by the word of God, so that what is seen was not made
out of things which are visible.

Hebrews 11:3

There's a lot of discussion today about creation and evolution. It's really very important, for understanding our origin is central to understanding who we are, why we're here, and what we're supposed to do on this planet.

Creation is based on the idea that we're here by intelligent design, and evolution is based on the idea that we're here by chance. Which makes the most sense? If I were to tell you that your personal computer actually evolved by chance from an explosion in a factory that makes radios, you'd laugh in my face. Yet is the computer more complex than a human mind? Absolutely not! It's amazing to me that intelligent people know computers are made by intelligent design, yet when it comes to life and earth's design, they choose to believe, "Well, it just evolved by chance." I just don't have enough faith to believe that. Science helps us fill in some of the details of creation, but God is the intelligent Designer behind it all.

Meeting Death

What man can live and not see death?

PSALM 89:48

The great Scottish preacher Peter Marshall used to tell the legend of the merchant of Baghdad. The merchant sent his servant to the market in the ancient Middle Eastern city. The servant returned, pale and trembling, and the merchant asked him what was wrong. The servant told him he had bumped into someone, looked up, and saw Death in a dark hooded robe, pointing at him. He begged the merchant, "Please let me borrow your horse so I can flee to Samara where Death can't find me."

The merchant agreed. Later that day, the merchant went to the crowded market and saw Death standing to the side, and the merchant asked him, "Why did you frighten my servant?"

Death responded, "I did not intend to frighten him. I was only shocked to see him in Baghdad, for tonight I have an appointment with him in Samara."

We each have an appointment with death. For every life, there is death. The statistics on death are 100 percent. But the fear of death is removed by receiving the promise of eternal life through faith in Jesus Christ. With faith, we can concentrate on living this life to the fullest.

We all have a rendezvous with death. Are you ready?

Finding Your Calling

With this in mind, we constantly pray for you, that our God may count you worthy of his calling, and that by his power he may fulfill every good purpose of yours and every act prompted by your faith.

2 THESSALONIANS 1:11 NIV

Whether you are a big sports fan or not, it's easy to get caught up in the action whenever a celebrated sports figure is on TV. Why? Athletes play at such a high level that it is an inspiration to watch them when they're in "the zone." What does it mean to be in the zone? Well, that's when someone's actions seem effortless, almost as if he could score at will.

We can all think of a bad day at work, but can you think of a time when you were in the zone—a moment when you were enjoying your task, and you were so caught up in your work that you lost track of time? What were you doing at that moment? What skills were you using? What was it that caused you to be passionate about the work? Understanding the answers to these questions will often help you better understand how to best use your time and talents—a calling.

A calling is when we are passionately using our God-given gifts in a way that pleases Him to build up and encourage the body of Christ—the church. We are not talking about your personality profile, but about those God-given gifts listed in the Bible, like teaching, wisdom, generosity, administration, and prayer, among many others. And that's how we discover our true calling from God.

Have you discovered your calling? If not, pray and search for God's will. Over time, He'll reveal it to you.

Reaping What You Sow

*Do not be deceived, God is not mocked; for whatever
a man sows, this he will also reap.*

GALATIANS 6:7

A young teenager wanted to aggravate the hardworking farmer who lived next door. He led some of his pals to sneak into the farmer's field one night and planted kudzu all over the farm. It soon took hold. Kudzu is a vine that will devour trees, fields, and anything else that gets in its way. He laughed every time he saw the farmer vainly trying to get rid of it.

A few years later, long after the teenager had forgotten his prank, he fell in love with the farmer's daughter, and they were married. When her father died, he inherited the farm, and for the rest of his life he battled that sorry kudzu he had planted.

The Bible says, "For whatever a man sows, this he will also reap." In short, when we're hard on others, they tend to be hard on us. It's the law of the harvest. When you plant tomatoes, you don't get squash, for the harvest never lies.

What kind of seeds are you sowing? What kind of harvest are you reaping? Let's remember . . . in life, we reap what we sow.

Are You Sure That's What
It Says in the Bible?

*"You will not surely die," the serpent said to the woman. "For
God knows that when you eat of it your eyes will be opened,
and you will be like God, knowing good and evil."*

GENESIS 3:4–5 NIV

There are a lot of religious fanatics out there spouting strange doctrine. At first, they may actually sound reasonable because they quote from the Bible. But the problem is, these false prophets will take a verse out of context and base their whole theology around it. Although this is often done unintentionally, there are some who will twist a few words on purpose, resulting in an interpretation bearing no resemblance whatsoever to God's actual message.

This is an effective technique the devil has mastered well. Think about the consequences for humankind when the devil twisted God's words in the garden of Eden! And remember how Satan tried to tempt Jesus in the beginning of His ministry? He twisted the Word of God just a little bit, making it seem right, when he was saying the exact opposite of the actual meaning.

How can you battle this prostitution of God's Word? Always study Scripture in light of Scripture. Study the Old Testament in light of the New. Study the Gospels in light of the Epistles so that you can have the theological and doctrinal understanding of the life of Christ, why He came, what He's all about. You want to study a verse in the context of the chapter and in the context of the book. The more you study the Bible, the easier it will be to defend yourself from false—or ignorant—prophets.

Forgiveness When Rejected for Your Faith

"Blessed are you when men hate you, when they exclude you and insult you and reject your name as evil, because of the Son of Man."

LUKE 6:22 NIV

Have you ever felt rejected because of your faith? Has anyone ever avoided you, left you out of the clique, or even rejected you outright just because you are a Christian? No, that's not paranoia; this happens to every dedicated Christian at one time or another. Jesus wants you to know that when you are rejected by others or shown hostility for your beliefs, you are not the one being rejected. People are hostile at Jesus, not you. They are rejecting Him, not you. Never forget that.

And that is where we need to follow the example of Jesus most of all. When you are rejected due to your devotion to Christ, you need to respond just as Jesus did when He was rejected on the cross. He said, "Father, forgive them. They don't know what they're doing" (Luke 23:34 GW).

In your devotion to Christ, if you are rejected, face hostility, or are even persecuted, you need to forgive as Christ forgave on the cross. Because if you want to see something that is unique about Christianity over every other religion, look at Jesus and His spirit on that cross, forgiving those who had rejected Him. Are you willing to follow Jesus if it means facing rejection?

The Road to Financial Security

*How blessed is the man who finds wisdom
and the man who gains understanding.*

PROVERBS 3:13

A re you on the road to financial security? Let me suggest a few goals to strive for in seeking personal financial security.

- You need to know what you make, and if you're on commission, estimate conservatively what it'll be.
- Spend less than you earn. I know it seems obvious, but it is so overlooked that it has to be mentioned.
- Have a personal or family budget. Budgets help us prioritize and meet our goals.
- In developing that budget, focus on five major categories:

  1. a goal for giving
  2. a savings and investments goal
  3. an estimated amount for taxes
  4. your fixed expenses, such as car, house, groceries, etc.
  5. a goal for discretionary expenses, like entertainment, vacation, furniture, clothing, etc.—all good things but things you don't have to do and can postpone

From where does all this practical insight come? It's based on principles right out of the Bible. You'll be amazed that when you look to Scripture, you'll find the keys to financial security.

Saving Our Marriages from the Start

And be subject to one another in the fear of Christ.

EPHESIANS 5:21

Here are some devastating statistics from *SBC Life*, in an article titled "Kingdom Families."

Each day of the year in America, more than 3,571 marriages end in divorce. More than 50 percent of the children in America's public schools live in single-parent homes. Of the nation's children who live apart from their biological fathers, 50 percent have never set foot in their father's home.[17]

Sometimes I'll be performing a wedding ceremony, and as we go through the reciting of the vows, we'll get to "till death do us part," when I realize that, in reality, the marriage outlook is so often, "It's all about me-do-us-part!"

The answer to this selfish focus is found in our verse today from Ephesians. In the New American Standard Version, it reads, "Be subject to one another in the fear of Christ." What does it mean to *be subject to?* "Be subject to" is an old military term in the Greek. It means "to rank under"; someone has authority over another. God's solution to the "me-focus" is found in this rather militaristic phrase. Both husband and wife must be subject to each other, concentrating on the needs of the family rather than on the urges of the individual. After all, that's what you signed up for when you promised before God "till death do us part."

Knowing the Truth

And the Word became flesh, and dwelt among us, and
we saw His glory . . . full of grace and truth.

JOHN 1:14

To know Jesus we need to know Scripture, for Jesus taught that God's Word is truth (John 17:17). Do you believe this?

Today, very few believe in absolute truth, yet Scripture records that Jesus said He is the truth. Jesus claimed to be "absolute truth." Truth is found in a person, not a religion, not a philosophy, and not a code of morality. The absolute truth about God is found in Jesus. And the truth of Jesus is discovered in Scripture. Thus, Jesus and Scripture are not mutually exclusive. They are like two sides of a coin. We can't know the real Jesus without the written Word of God. We can't know His teachings without God's Word.

We cannot know truth unless we know Jesus. We cannot know Jesus unless we know Scripture. Therefore, we have to decide if what Jesus said about Scripture is true. So are Jesus and the Word absolute truth? Absolutely! God reveals Himself in a person, and God reveals that person in His Word, for Jesus said, "Thy word is truth" (John 17:17 KJV).

August

And not only this, but we also exult in our tribulations, knowing that tribulation brings about perseverance; and perseverance, proven character; and proven character, hope.

Romans 5:3–4

Midlife Blues

*Whatever you do, whether in word or deed, do it all
in the name of the Lord Jesus, giving thanks to
God the Father through him.*

COLOSSIANS 3:17 NIV

Midlife has come (and for some, gone) to the baby boomer! The thought of millions of boomers in a midlife crisis can unsettle even the most stable mind. Midlife is the time when hard-driving adults begin to grow weary of all their responsibilities. They can feel trapped. Boredom may kick in as they realize their goals. Depression may set in from goals that have not been realized and never will be.

Bob Buford calls this stage of life "halftime." In sports, halftime is when the teams regroup, catch their breath, go back out, and do better in the second half. Buford says that the key to getting through a midlife crisis is shifting our focus from success to significance.[18]

I propose that the key to lasting significance lies in meaningful relationships—relationships with God, family, and friends. It's found in doing your best with the gifts and talents God has given you. It's found in living life God's way, with godly character.

Midlife is a key time to get those things right, before the second half begins. If you're at midlife, seek to shift your focus from success to significance. If you do, your second half can be even better than your first.

Evidence of Life After Life

*Mary Magdalene came, announcing to the disciples,
"I have seen the Lord."*

JOHN 20:18

All through the ages, man has speculated about life after life. Dante's *Divine Comedy* seeks to describe it. Modern medical science has added to the speculation with its study of near-death experiences. All kinds of religions offer their theories.

But the greatest evidence of life after life is based on the historical evidence that Jesus rose from the dead. Christianity is the only faith founded by a man who died and came back to life. No other religion makes that claim.

Historical accounts of His appearances to His disciples and more than five hundred people at once were written within twenty years of the event. His disciples faced martyrs' deaths for refusing to quit preaching of His death and resurrection. People don't willingly die for something they know is a hoax.

The one thing that could have stopped Christianity in its tracks would have been for Rome or religious authorities to reveal the dead body of Jesus. They never did. The best evidence of life after life is the historical evidence of Jesus' resurrection. Believe it, and one day you'll live it.

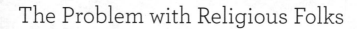

The Problem with Religious Folks

*"Woe to you, scribes and Pharisees, hypocrites, because
you shut off the kingdom of heaven from people."*

MATTHEW 23:13

Isn't it interesting that the group Jesus had the hardest time with
were the religious folks? And the people He was most drawn to
and who were most drawn to Him were the obvious sinners?

Why was that?

1. He had no patience with self-righteousness, and the religious
   had an abundance of it.
2. He condemned hypocrisy, and the religious leaders were
   eaten up with it.
3. He knew that legalism put people in guilt-inducing bondage,
   and He came to free people of this demanding "yoke."

Yet obvious sinners were drawn to Him because of His love
and acceptance. Oh, He wasn't flippant about their sin. It would
cost Him an agonizing death. But amazingly, while they were yet
sinners, He loved them anyway (Romans 5:8). "Them" is "us."

Hey, Christians—let's be more like Jesus than "religious folks."

Lying

Deliver my soul, O LORD, from lying lips, [and]
from a deceitful tongue.

PSALM 120:2

An excited husband called to tell his wife that he had been asked to accompany the boss on a fishing trip to Canada. The husband had to leave that evening and asked his wife if she would mind packing a few things for him. He added, "Be sure to include my new silk pajamas."

She thought that sounded fishy but said nothing. When the man returned from his trip, his wife asked how it went.

"Great," he said.

"Did you catch anything?" she asked.

"Yes, pike, walleye—what fun!" Then he asked, "But why didn't you pack my blue silk pajamas?"

"I did," she said. "They were in your tackle box."

Lying is, most of all, about stupidity. We will be found out. You may be getting away with it for now, but in the end, the truth comes out. It may not be until you die, but God has on file everything we've ever said. So you'd be wise to seek His forgiveness and start telling the truth. Always! Otherwise, you'll eventually look like a fool.

Bodily Abuse

*Or do you not know that your body is a temple of the
Holy Spirit who is in you, whom you have from God,
and that you are not your own?*

1 Corinthians 6:19

Christianity teaches that the body is the temple of God's Spirit and that we are to take care of our bodies. Although gluttony and obesity in America are at epidemic levels, many people, primarily teenage girls and young women, struggle with another form of bodily abuse—an eating disorder.

Often the original intent of those who suffer from eating disorders was to take care of their bodies by eating less. But over time they become obsessed about controlling their food intake.

There are three main types of eating disorders:

- *Anorexia*—eating too little or being rigidly obsessed with avoiding perceived unhealthy foods.
- *Bulimia*—binge eating and then throwing up or taking laxatives to avoid weight gain.
- *Exercise bulimia*—an obsession with exercise without enough caloric intake to replace the caloric output.

Each of these disorders is addictive and can bring great harm to the body. And like all addictions, whether food, booze, drugs, or sex, an eating disorder substitutes for the place of God in the addicted person's life. If you or someone you know suffers from an addiction, seek God's forgiveness and His help. Then find others who can assist you in achieving victory over the unhealthy addiction.

The Real Beauty of a Rainbow

As the appearance of the bow that is in the cloud in the day of rain, so was the appearance of the brightness round about. This was the appearance of the likeness of the glory of the LORD. And when I saw it, I fell upon my face, and I heard a voice of one that spake.

EZEKIEL 1:28 KJV

Most of the rainfall in Israel comes in the form of brief but heavy showers followed by a brilliant sun—a perfect formula for rainbows. In fact, these conditions often treat us to double rainbows; occasionally the sun is so bright that it will generate one. The sight of the rainbow is so beautiful and powerful that it is often used in the Bible as a reminder of God's covenant with us.

We can indeed find prominent use of the rainbow in the beginning, middle, and end of Scripture. Near the beginning in Genesis, God sent a rainbow as a sign of His covenant that He would never again flood all the earth as punishment for human sin. In the middle, in Ezekiel, the rainbow symbolizes the coming of Christ, as well as declaring the glory of God. And in Revelation, at the end of God's Word, John described Christ as "clothed with a cloud: and a rainbow . . . upon His head" (10:1 KJV), a symbol of peace and reconciliation with God.

God never intended the rainbow to be a symbol of diversity or a symbol to represent as good what God calls evil. God gave us the rainbow as a symbol of the trustworthiness of His promises— as a symbol of hope in Him.

Victory over Temptation

No temptation has seized you except what is common to man.
And God is faithful; he will not let you be tempted beyond
what you can bear. But when you are tempted, he will also
provide a way out so that you can stand up under it.

1 CORINTHIANS 10:13 NIV

Let's talk about temptation. How do you keep a decision to do wrong from getting the best of you?

Realize that temptation is a part of life. The Bible tells us that Jesus was tempted in every way we are—every way. The big difference between Him and all of us is that He never gave in to it.

So how can we keep temptation from getting the best of us?

- *Just say no.* Don't take time to flirt with it or even argue. Just say no.
- *Then scram.* Get out of there! This is one time in life when running is not cowardly, but the bravest thing you can do.
- *Ask God's help resisting it.* For things too tough to resist, things you battle constantly, simply admit they're too tough, and ask God's help in resisting them. The power of the only Man never to give in to temptation is available to all of us. We just need to confess our weakness and admit our need for Him and His strength.

Remember, God promises us that we'll never face temptation that is too tough for us to resist through His power.

What Is the Sword?

"I've come to cut—make a sharp knife-cut between son and father, daughter and mother, bride and mother-in-law—cut through these cozy domestic arrangements and free you for God."

MATTHEW 10:34–35 MSG

Gentle Jesus—meek and mild. "Jesus loves me," we sing to children. If that is your image of Jesus, you probably have a tough time reconciling it with His statement that He came to "make a sharp knife-cut." The verse before it is even more pointed: Jesus said He didn't "come to bring peace, but a sword" (v. 34 NASB).

Relax. Throughout the New Testament, the word *sword* is used to describe the Word of God, not a military weapon. Ephesians tells us of "the sword of the Spirit, which is the word of God" (6:17). And again in Hebrews, God's Word teaches us about itself: "For the word of God is living and active and sharper than any two-edged sword, and piercing as far as the division of soul and spirit, of both joints and marrow, and able to judge the thoughts and intentions of the heart" (4:12).

The sword, the Word, is a powerful way to explain how the Word of God pierces our hearts, exposing us for who we are. It is so powerful that it exposes our real desires, our real thoughts, our sinfulness. Now *that* is the power of the Word of God. It is even sharper than a two-edged sword, for it doesn't just expose our sins, but like a scalpel in the hands of the Great Physician, it shows us the way of ultimate healing and salvation from sin. That may not always bring us peace with our fellow man, but it sure brings peace with God and peace within.

Why They Blow Themselves Up

"You worship what you do not know; we worship what we know, for salvation is from the Jews."

There was an article in a 2002 edition of *Time* magazine written by a Palestinian medical doctor explaining why Islamic terrorists blow themselves up. He said they commit these acts (a practice the physician actually defends!) because of a desire for revenge against the Jews, whom they believe have oppressed them for hundreds of years (which doesn't explain why they often blow up fellow Muslims and innocent bystanders). Also, the suicide bombers believe that the teachings of Muhammad imply that they will have an automatic ticket to paradise if they sacrifice their lives in jihad to destroy Jews, those who support Israel, and infidels at war with Islam.

Here is one of the dramatic differences between their messenger and our Savior. Muhammad personally oversaw and took part in the beheading of more than six hundred Jews who refused to convert to Islam. Jesus never killed anyone; in fact, He died to save everyone who, in faith, receives Him! He gave His life to reconcile us with God so that we can have the opportunity to spend eternity in paradise with Him. Jesus paid the full price for our entry into heaven. It's a free gift, available for all who choose to accept it, even the Islamic terrorists. They die to kill. But He died to save.

Giddy Giving

Each man should give what he has decided in his heart to give, not reluctantly or under compulsion, for God loves a cheerful giver.

2 CORINTHIANS 9:7 NIV

Here is something preachers sometimes say: "Give until it hurts." You'll be happy to know that's *not* my message today, because it's nonsense. The Bible says to give until you feel giddy. Am I kidding? Nope.

Lesson 1: It all belongs to God. Everything we have. It's His.

Lesson 2: The starting point (not the destination) in faithful giving is the tithe (10 percent of what we earn). The first 10 percent, not the last. If we don't do this, God's Word says we are robbers. What? Yes, we're robbing God, and robbers are simply low-class thieves. Malachi 3:8 says, "Will a man rob God? Yet you rob me. But you ask, 'How do we rob you?' In tithes and offerings" (NIV). We don't even need to pray about whether or not to tithe. That would be like praying about whether we ought to rob a bank. On certain actions, the Bible is clear about what to do.

Lesson 3: Giddy giving is biblical. In 2 Corinthians 9:7 the Greek word for *cheerful* actually means "hilarious" or "giddy." Once we realize that all we have is God's and show we believe that through tithing, then the real adventure in giving begins. Seeking God's will about where to give and how much to give is a spiritual decision that begins with the tithe and goes up from there as God blesses. So don't give till it hurts . . . give till you're giddy!

The Holy Spirit Speaks to *All*

"When [the Holy Spirit] comes, he'll expose the error of the godless world's view of sin, righteousness, and judgment."

JOHN 16:8 MSG

In earlier devotions we focused on how the Holy Spirit convicts Christians about their sins and the need to get right with God. But what is most amazing to me is that the Holy Spirit convicts everyone, even those who are not believers. You may be a skeptic or even completely disinterested. Regardless, the Holy Spirit has led you to this devotional today.

Sometimes the Holy Spirit convicts nonbelievers when they hear of God's love for them through Jesus Christ. Sometimes He convicts nonbelievers of the need to surrender and give their hearts and lives to God. And when that occurs, it becomes the most crucial moment of decision making in your life. It is a decision to either keep doing things your way or to begin doing them God's way. The Holy Spirit convicts, but you must decide whether to give your life to God through the person of Jesus Christ. If you do that, then the Holy Spirit will come and dwell within you and give you an inner desire to obey the commands of God.

It all begins with the fact that God has first loved us through Jesus Christ. Christ is the reason we want to love Him back and obey His commands. This is what the Holy Spirit convicts us all to do.

Why Prayer Is Disappointing

"Yet not as I will, but as You will."

MATTHEW 26:39

Do you ever feel your prayers are not answered? God's Word gives us the key in James 4:3: "When you ask, you do not receive, because you ask with wrong motives, that you may spend what you get on your pleasures" (NIV).

The major reason prayer doesn't seem to work is because we tend to pray with selfish motives. God promises to meet our needs, but needs and wants can be two very different things. So much prayer is focused on how we can use God to get what we want.

But the greatest example of prayer is found in the words of Jesus. The night before His crucifixion, He asked His Father to spare Him the agony of the cross, but then added, "Yet not My will, but Yours" (Luke 22:42). Prayer is about getting to know the will of God, and Him providing the power to do it.

Earthly Consequences Remain

*Wash me thoroughly from my iniquity, and
cleanse me from my sin. For I know my
transgressions, and my sin is ever before me.*

PSALM 51:2–3

In February of 1998, Karla Faye Tucker became the first woman executed since the Civil War. Tucker was convicted of killing two people with a pickax. What made the execution even more unusual was that thousands of people asked that her sentence be reduced to life in prison. This compassion was because while she was in prison she became a devout born-again Christian. This case begs an interesting question. Why do we suffer the punishment for our sins even after God has forgiven us? Did He forgive her or not?

Yes, of course God forgave Karla Faye, just as He forgives anyone who genuinely repents. Jesus died for our sins, but understand that the sacrifice was to get us right with God, not to protect us from earthly consequences.

Look at the story of David. After being guilty of adultery, abuse of power, murder, and cover-up, the guilt of his sin clung to him. Then he confessed his sin to God before a priest and was instantly forgiven by God. But although God instantly forgave David, He did not remove the negative consequences of his sins. For the rest of his life, David dealt with those consequences through a disillusioned family.

With repentance and confession, God forgives instantly. But He doesn't remove the consequences of our sin. We have to live with them.

Is There Other Life in the Universe?

*Lift up your eyes on high, and see who has created these stars,
the One who leads forth their host by number.... The
Everlasting God, the LORD, the Creator of the ends of the earth.*

ISAIAH 40:26, 28

America's spaceship on Mars produced magnificent views of space. Scientists are seeing unlimited potential for space exploration, and their excitement is contagious. There's so much more to know and explore!

Could there be life on other planets? How do these new discoveries affect our view of God? Do we need to revise our understanding of Him?

Well, the answer depends on how big your concept of God is. You see, we need to recognize that God is almighty, far greater than anything the human mind can conceive. The discoveries of science excite us, but it's even more exciting when we recognize the greatness of the Creator of it all. God is limitless. His creative genius surpasses man's ability to comprehend.

We don't need to fear science or what's out there in space, for in the end, science simply explains to us the creative genius of God. God is over all!

No Greater Gift

*When you were dead in your transgressions and the
uncircumcision of your flesh, He made you alive together
with Him, having forgiven us all our transgressions,
having canceled out the certificate of debt consisting of
decrees against us, which was hostile to us; and He has
taken it out of the way, having nailed it to the cross.*

COLOSSIANS 2:13–14

Do we really comprehend the incredible gift we were given when Jesus died for our sins? Not that we take this act for granted, but we have spoken about it so routinely that we might not absorb the full scope of this gift.

It's as though all of our sins were listed on a chalkboard, and then Christ came along with a cloth and erased them forever. It's as though they had never been there. And then on that board, some-body put a receipt that said, "Paid in Full." That's what the nails on the cross did—paid the penalty for our sin in full. Christ has done it all. Our sins have been nailed to the cross; they've been taken care of. Nothing more is needed for forgiveness other than our accepting this amazing gift. Have you done that? Have you claimed the liberating forgiveness, knowing that Christ has paid the full debt for your sins? If not, why not let Christ give you a clean slate? After all, He's already "paid in full." Our choice is simply to accept His gift in faith.

Alone, But Not Lonely

"I am with you always, even to the end of the age."

MATTHEW 28:20

Some feel it in a crowd; others feel it when alone. Sociologists say that never before in history have so many people lived so close together and felt so far apart. Loneliness is a major problem for many today. There's no doubt that singles bars are filled with people battling loneliness. A divorced person, tired of one-night stands, recently said, "Sex is readily available in the American singles scene, but friendship is not."

I propose to you that one can be alone but not lonely. As a matter of fact, a person will never find victory over loneliness until he or she learns to enjoy being alone. You see, at the root of all loneliness is alienation from God.

Years ago, a man named Augustine espoused that God has made us for Himself. Our soul is restless until we find rest in Him. We may seek to fill the void of a restless soul with activities, crowds, and noise, but a nagging loneliness will always be there until we have a personal relationship with God. When we find that, we have found the key to being alone but not lonely.

Being More Like Jesus

Jesus went through all the towns and villages, teaching in their synagogues, preaching the good news of the kingdom and healing every disease and sickness.

One of the things that troubles me about evangelical Bible-believing churches is the total neglect of one important aspect of Jesus' ministry—healing. Why does this neglect happen? Well, many Christians see exaggerated claims of supernatural healing in some charismatic or Pentecostal churches. Others see charlatan faith healers on TV and say, "We don't want to be involved with anything like that!" And sadly, in reaction against that, some Christians put their major trust for healing in medical science. They forget that doctors have never healed anyone! They may enhance the healing process with the treatment they provide to patients, but only God can heal. Jesus went about teaching, preaching and healing; and if the church is to be like Jesus in spirit and character and mission, we need to do the same. How?

1. Pray for the sick through prayer meetings, prayer chains, and prayer ministries.
2. Have spiritual leaders, like elders and ministers, pray for the sick by laying hands on them in private or in worship (James 5:13–16).
3. Offer the ministry of presence: the body of Christ (not just paid ministerial staff) is to reach out to the sick with love, compassion, and encouragement.

The Audit

"Where your treasure is, there your heart will be also."

MATTHEW 6:21

Let's suppose Jesus walked up to you and said, "I want to see your books. Let Me see your investments, your paychecks, and your checkbook. I want to see how you're spending your money." If Jesus looked at all of that, would He then say, "Salvation has truly come to this house. I can tell where your heart is by how you manage your money"? Or would He look you in the eye and say, "I know you profess to be a Christian, but there's nothing in the books indicating that you are. You know, you may profess to be a follower of Mine, but in reality, you're in bondage to your money, to your possessions"?

I can also see Jesus adding, "But I have good news. If you will trust Me for salvation, I will give you the Holy Spirit to empower you with an inner 'want to' to become a good manager of what I entrust to you. If you will trust Me fully, I will put you on the road to financial freedom, where you will no longer be living in the financial slavery that is so evident by your books! Won't you trust Me?"

That's the question Jesus is asking you today. Do you trust Him, especially when it comes to all the money and possessions He's allowed you to manage? Or are you afraid to let it go? What would His audit say?

The Myth of Quality Time

*He must manage his own household well, with all
dignity keeping his children submissive.*

1 TIMOTHY 3:4 ESV

There can be nothing more important than the different experiences that we share together as families, where we have the opportunity to talk, to listen, and to really understand one another. In contemporary culture, one of the biggest lies of the devil when it comes to parenting is this: "It doesn't matter about the quantity of time; it's the quality of time that's important." What a lie! There is no such thing as quality time unless there is a quantity of time with our children! Because only in a quantity of time do we have the opportunity to respond to our children as they are dealing with everyday issues of life. It is through spontaneous conversations when we experience everyday life together that we can teach our children our values and faith. It is through unplanned dialogue that our children can ask random questions or share a thought that just pops into their heads. We just can't plan for these times; we have to be there when they happen.

So whether you use a BlackBerry, an iPhone, or just a plain calendar, make it a point to schedule a large quantity of time with your family. In time, you'll be amazed at the quality.

Old Age Ain't for Sissies

And even to your graying years I will bear you!
I have done it, and I will carry you; and I will
bear you and I will deliver you.

Old age sure ain't for sissies. Based on the book of Ecclesiastes, it seems as though King Solomon would agree. He wrote of how the things we take for granted when we're young cause us to lose delight in living when we're old.

Our eyesight grows dim—we start with reading glasses and then move to bifocals. Our hearing grows weak. We're constantly saying "Huh?" to our spouses. We have time to sleep late, but we wake up early. Our hands start to tremble. Our desire for sex diminishes.

Old age isn't for sissies. Our bodies just don't work like they used to. Aches and pains are a daily reality, and morning stiffness is our companion every day as we get out of bed. It can all be very depressing, and without God it can be meaningless. But with God, there is wisdom, strength, joy, and the hope that when the body finally gives out, there is life—real life—in heaven with God. It's something to remember when you're young and when you're old.

David's Deathbed Advice to His Son, Part I

"I am about to go the way of all the earth," he said.
"So be strong, show yourself a man."

1 Kings 2:2 NIV

King David had passed the throne to his son Solomon. On his deathbed, David called his son before him to give him his charge.

First, understand the pressure Solomon was going through. From the time he was a little boy, he had heard the stories about his father—how he was a legend even before becoming the king of Israel, and how as a teenager he had killed the giant Goliath and led the Israelites to a great victory over the Philistines. Solomon had heard how his father courageously endured the suffering under King Saul and survived Saul's continuing threats. He knew of his father's military triumphs and his capture of Jerusalem. Solomon knew his father was a larger-than-life personality. And now King David was calling to him as he was about to die. You can imagine the sense of anxiety and fear young Solomon had. How would he ever meet his father's expectations? Was it even possible to fulfill this responsibility?

But David understood his son. He knew that courage is not the absence of fear but the willingness to do right in the face of fear. And the first thing he told Solomon was, "Be strong, therefore, and show yourself a man" (1 Kings 2:2 NASB). What tremendous words to share on this occasion—words any father can share with his son when he is embarking on his life's calling.

David's Deathbed Advice to His Son, Part II

"Keep the charge of the LORD your God, to walk in His ways, to keep His statutes, His commandments, His ordinances, and His testimonies, according to what is written in the Law of Moses."

1 KINGS 2:3

King David, upon passing the throne to his son, offered two pieces of advice. David's first advice to his son Solomon, as we read yesterday, was to "be strong." But that wasn't all. He also encouraged his son to walk with the Lord. David's concern for his son was not only that he be strong but also that he walk with God, obey the Word of God, and be encouraged by Scripture. Most of all, David wanted his son to be a man of God, so he gave Solomon God's formula for success (Joshua 1:7). What is that? It is to obey the Word of God; by doing so he would fulfill God's destiny for his life.

As we look at this counsel of a father charging his son, we realize this could be a father's counsel to any child: "Be a person of God, and then you will fulfill your destiny and understand ultimate success. This means being in the will of God, doing the will of God, and doing what God has called you to be and do." Good advice for David to give Solomon. And good advice for you to give your child.

The Paradox of Modern Science

*They exchanged the truth of God for a lie,
and worshiped and served created things rather
than the Creator—who is forever praised.*

ROMANS 1:25 NIV

Several years ago, the local school board required high school science textbooks to have a sticker attached. This sticker said simply, "This textbook contains material on evolution. Evolution is a theory, not a fact, regarding the origin of living things. This material should be approached with an open mind, studied carefully, and critically considered."

Notice that there was nothing on the sticker that advocated a belief in God. Neither did it even mention creationism. It simply advised the students to ask questions and form their beliefs based on what they conclude from the evidence. This was really all about good education, about considering different theories with an open mind. Part of learning is to be able to consider different outlooks about life. Despite this, the federal courts demanded that these simple stickers be removed from all textbooks.

Education is supposed to be about the free flow of ideas. When you have a theory as controversial as evolution that is taught through indoctrination more than examination, it is not education. Good science requires that theories stand up to probing questions. Why do evolutionists fear similar questioning? What do they have to fear?

Open-minded people don't fear the truth—they seek it, for truth has no fear. It's the paradox of modern science.

What If?

I have set before you life and death, the blessing and the curse. So choose life in order that you may live.

DEUTERONOMY 30:19

History buffs enjoy playing a little game called "Alternative History." Entire books have been written exploring questions such as, "What if the British had won the Revolutionary War?" or "What if the Japanese had been repelled at Pearl Harbor?" One of my favorites: "What if the French had not defeated the Muslims in AD 732?" We would have grown up going to mosques rather than churches because Europe and, eventually, North and South America would have been Muslim. When playing this game, we soon see how one seemingly small event dominoes into hundreds of subsequent events, changing the course of human history dramatically.

Think of the consequences of some of the biblical events. What would have been the consequences if Abraham had trusted God and not fathered Ishmael through his maid, and Isaac had been his true firstborn? There would have been no Jewish/Arab animosity. Would the Islamic faith have ever existed? What would be the current political situation in the Middle East? Would 9/11 have occurred?

Perhaps we can look to Harry Truman for the answer to some of these questions. When he was asked, "What if the South had won the Civil War?" he curtly replied, "They didn't!" Still, it is interesting to ponder the long-term consequences of man's poor use of his free will. Hopefully it makes you pause and reflect on the long-term effects of your own day-to-day decisions.

Two Very Different Sons

When the boys grew up, Esau became a skillful
hunter, a man of the field, but Jacob was a
peaceful man, living in tents.

GENESIS 25:27

Esau and Jacob. Same mother, same father, twins. Raised the same way with the same belief system. But you would never meet two more diverse persons on the face of the earth.

Parents will often lament to me about problems they're having with one child while another child is doing splendidly. A parent will say, "You know, Pastor, I've raised 'em the same way." And I think to myself, *That's the problem.* You cannot raise all children the same way and expect it to be a fruitful venture. Children are not robots. They each have their own unique talents, interests, and temperaments.

The role of the parent is to seek to shape our children and to understand how to parent them uniquely. We should raise them with love, fairness, discipline, and teaching in hopes that our children will one day be able to grasp the grace of God. We pray that one day they'll claim the grace of God and allow Him to transform their lives through Jesus Christ. And in the process, some of our children are going to choose to claim that grace and repent, and some are not. Do your best, pray for God's guidance, and leave the results in the hands of God.

Fighting Internet Porn

"The lamp of the body is the eye. If therefore your eye is good, your whole body will be full of light. But if your eye is bad, your whole body will be full of darkness. If therefore the light that is in you is darkness, how great is that darkness!"

MATTHEW 6:22–23 NKJV

Do you talk to your children about what they're seeing? Do you warn them about the dangers not only of pornography but also of other sites on the Internet and ask them to report to you when certain dangers arise? Let them know you want to help them stay away from danger. If you're not doing this now, you should start immediately.

And what about you? Ask yourself this: "Would I be the least bit embarrassed if my mom or dad, my husband [or wife], or especially my children were seeing what I'm viewing on the Internet? How about God?" (He sees everything we do!) These are great questions to ask, because they are a great check in our spirits about what can be so devastating to our minds and spirits.

Be sure that you're an involved citizen. Do you realize our public libraries can become the modern-day adult bookstores? The modern-day adult theaters? And unbeknownst to most of us, pornography even works its way into school libraries and computer labs. We have to be active as parents to see that protection is in place so this enemy doesn't reach out and kidnap innocent minds. This is a constant battle worth fighting.

Patience

*A patient man has great understanding, but a
quick-tempered man displays folly.*

It has been said that life is a test in patience. Where do you struggle with being patient?

I struggle with lines—whether it's traffic or waiting at a restaurant. I'd rather drive five miles out of the way than sit still in traffic. I get impatient with people when I'm facing a deadline and get interrupted, or when someone says he'll do something and it doesn't get done.

Where do you struggle with patience? Do you ever pray, *Lord, give me some patience—now!* Let me suggest a few practical ways to learn patience:

1. Take a breath and pray for self-control.
2. When people anger you, if possible, retreat for a moment. Take time to back off and get control of your emotions.
3. Confront fairly and seek to listen, understand, and, where needed, forgive.
4. Remember, the greatest motive for patience is remembering God's patience with us.

Patience is a precious commodity, for it's a powerful way to win the respect of others and turn a potential enemy into a friend.

To Be More Like Jesus

For all who are being led by the Spirit of God,
these are the sons of God.

ROMANS 8:14

There's a lot of talk these days about core values, those distinctives that identify priorities for your company, your church, your family, or your life. Let me share with you the number one core value in our church: *to be more and more like Jesus.*

Think about it. Jesus poured His life into the lives of twelve ordinary men, investing most of His time with them. At one point, He even washed their feet—the act of a slave or a servant. He healed the sick. He loved the poor. He was concerned about the widow, the orphan, and the person who was left out. He loved kids. He got angry when the religious leaders put the legalism of the law before the love of God and the love for people. Even when humanity was murdering Him on the cross, He chose to forgive.

Jesus was totally dedicated to doing the will of God, yet He was loving and compassionate and forgiving with people. Do you have that kind of balance in your life? We all fall short, but what a model to follow His ideal in everyday living.

The number one core value at our church is to be like Jesus in spirit, character, and mission. What's yours?

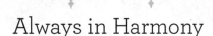

Always in Harmony

For there are three that bear record in heaven,
the Father, the Word [Jesus], and the Holy
Ghost: and these three are one.

1 JOHN 5:7 KJV

The biblical concept of the Trinity of God has confused men for two thousand years. It is important to recognize that we don't believe in three gods. We believe in one God in three persons: God the Father, God the Son, and God the Holy Spirit, *always in harmony with one another*. The Holy Spirit will never guide us to do something that is contrary to the commands of God.

In 2004, there was a *USA Today* headline declaring, "Gay Episcopal Bishop Says, 'Holy Spirit Led Us.'" The article went on to quote the new priest as saying that, although he genuinely regrets the pain that his ordination caused some believers, he saw no reason to repent because the leaders who made the decision were led by the Holy Spirit.[19] Now, my friends, when pseudo-spiritual leaders give credit to the Holy Spirit for guiding man to do something that God says is evil, this is nothing but blasphemy of the Holy Spirit.

God loves all sinners. He sent His son to die to pay the penalty for all sinners. The Holy Spirit convicts us of sin and the need to repent and receive God's gift of salvation through Christ. God the Father, God the Son, and God the Holy Spirit are always in perfect harmony. Everything the Holy Spirit counsels us to do will be in obedience to the commands of God. He never counsels us to disobey the Word of God. The Trinity is about the perfect harmony of one God in three persons.

Hypocritical Preachers and Religious Leaders

*If someone says, "I love God" and hates
his brother, he is a liar.*

1 JOHN 4:20

Don't you just hate hypocrisy in the church? For many of you, it's a major reason why you don't come to church. In the old movie *The Apostle*, starring Robert Duvall, we see a preacher who gets in trouble. He even kills a man but runs to a new town and continues to preach. It's really a pretty good movie that deals with the haunting power of guilt from sin that we just can't run from.

Yet certainly over the last thirty years, Hollywood has done a number on preachers and priests. And time after time they are painted in a very unflattering way, usually as hypocrites or a bunch of out-of-touch airheads or mean, cruel sickos. If you combine all of that with the charlatan TV evangelists, well, it's not a pretty picture.

But the truth is, all of us preachers struggle with hypocrisy and not always practicing what we preach. I sure do. But I have good news. I've only known one preacher in my life who had no trace of hypocrisy. And He's alive today—His name is Jesus. All the rest of us fall short, but Jesus never does. So put your focus and your faith in Him.

How to Use the Holy Spirit as Your Matchmaker

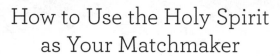

"But when he, the Spirit of truth, comes,
he will guide you into all truth."

JOHN 16:13 NIV

When you're in a serious dating relationship, don't overlook the importance of praying for God's will, letting the Holy Spirit guide and direct you. Here are a few practical questions to consider before marriage.

+ "Is this person my best friend?"
+ "Do we have similar beliefs and values? Does this person help me grow closer to God?"
+ "How do my family and friends feel about the relationship?"
+ "Am I willing to commit my life to this person?"
+ "Do I want this person to be a parent to my children?"
+ "Does he or she have some unacceptable habits that I think I'll be able to change someday?" (Believe me, you won't!)
+ "At the same time, do I recognize and accept his or her flaws and idiosyncrasies?" (If not, it's not real love; it's infatuation.)

If you haven't been able to say "yes" to these questions, maybe you need to slow down and give the relationship more time. Maybe you're headed toward choosing second best, rather than God's best for your life, and you need to back off. Spend more time in prayer, asking God to reveal His plan for you. His plan is always best.

September

"Come to Me, all who are weary and heavy-laden, and I will give you rest. Take My yoke upon you and learn from Me, for I am gentle and humble in heart, and you will find rest for your souls."

MATTHEW 11:28–29

Practicing for the Big Game

Study to shew thyself approved unto God, a workman that needeth not to be ashamed, rightly dividing the word of truth.

2 TIMOTHY 2:15 KJV

Football coaches have a saying about preparing for the big game: "As you practice, so you play." It works the same way in our spiritual lives. Regular time alone with God is how we practice staying close to God each day. And certainly if we're going to have meaningful weekly worship with other believers, it's always more meaningful when we've spent time alone with God.

Have you ever been to a worship service that just seemed to fall flat? Maybe you thought your pastor let you down and gave a sermon that was just plain boring! Or maybe the music didn't connect with you or wasn't the style you were in the mood for that day. Some days things just don't connect, and you think, *Well, that was a wasted hour.*

No doubt we preachers sometimes fall short, and no doubt some music gets on our nerves. Yet when a weekly service disappoints, it may be because you haven't been in practice all week. As you practice, so you play the game. You'll be amazed how much anticipation there is for weekly worship when you have regular time alone with God.

Enemies in the Home

. . . so that there will not be among you a man or a woman, or family or tribe, whose heart turns away today from the LORD our God.

DEUTERONOMY 29:18

There are many enemies within the home seeking to destroy the family. Let me share a few:

Busyness: Everyone is overcommitted, mostly through workaholism and "activity-itus." With our over-scheduled children's activities, this is true for our young ones as well.

Lack of spiritual and moral leadership by the father: Approximately 40 percent of all births in the United States are to single moms. Even in some families that have a dad, he's often absent or practically nonexistent.

Negative influence of media and technology: Kids spend more time with the TV, computer, and video games than they do with their parents, and their influence can be overwhelmingly negative. Electronics are a poor substitute for family communication. And now Internet pornography is devastating marriages and perverting how some men and boys view women.

Parents, a vibrant relationship with God through Jesus Christ is the best way to battle the many enemies within the home.

Laziness and Work

*What does a man get for all the toil and anxious
striving with which he labors under the sun? All his
days his work is pain and grief; even at night his mind
does not rest. This too is meaningless. A man can do
nothing better than to eat and drink and find
satisfaction in his work. This too, I see, is from the hand
of God, for without him, who can eat or find enjoyment?*

ECCLESIASTES 2:22–25 NIV

A re you giving work your best shot? Or are you tending to do
what you can to get by? One thing for sure, we live in a culture that doesn't glorify laziness. And although we can let work
get out of hand, laziness is not a quality that God admires either.
He wants us to do what we do with all our might, because laziness will allow our lives to pass by without us ever experiencing
significant accomplishment.

You may not be that happy in your job, but remember, fulfillment and purpose in your work will not come apart from God.
When we work to please ourselves or the people around us more
than God, we will always be controlled by the successes and fail-
ures our work produces. When we work to please God, we find
that He gives us direction and a sense of meaning even when it's
hard—even when our talent is underutilized.

You may not be happy where you are. But to please God,
give it your best shot, because you sure aren't of any use where
you are not.

Who's Responsible?

*He who has the Son has the life; he who does not have
the Son of God does not have the life.*

1 JOHN 5:12

Here is a tough objection to Christianity we must deal with
when discussing our faith with skeptical friends: what happens to those who die without ever really hearing about the
salvation found in Christ? It is a difficult question to answer, but
Jesus said this, "I am the way and the truth and the life. No one
comes to the Father except through me" (John 14:6 NIV). Couldn't
be clearer. Because of that, the church is given a mandate; we're to
take the gospel to every tribe and nation.

But what about those who never have a chance to hear because
the church simply has not completed its job? The Bible says the
person who has never been able to hear of Jesus is still going to be
responsible for responding to God with the natural revelation of
God that he or she *has* received (Romans 1:20). Now, how God
does this, I don't know. And yet we know that God, who has sacrificed His Son for our salvation, wants us to receive that salvation.
And He is going to be fair, just, and loving. We must trust Him
to make the right decision regarding those who have never heard.
He will do the right thing.

But here is what is most important to the person reading this
devotion. You have heard. And those who have heard are without excuse when it comes to trusting Christ. Be sure you choose
Jesus—the only way to God.

What Is Your Ultimate Authority for Making Decisions?

All Scripture is inspired by God and profitable for teaching, for reproof, for correction, for training in righteousness.

2 TIMOTHY 3:16

What is your ultimate authority for making important decisions? Is it your knowledge? Intuition? Your experience? Is it people you want to please? Is it contemporary culture? Is it a synagogue, church, or certain spiritual leader?

I want to suggest God's Word. God has created you for a purpose. He knows how you work best. The way He speaks is through His written Word. It is perfectly true. It applies to every age, race, and nation.

On some things, the Bible is clear, things like murder, stealing, adultery, and forgiveness. When it doesn't speak to a specific issue (like which mutual funds to invest in, whom to marry, or whether to accept a new job), it gives perfect principles we need to know to make the best decisions—those that are pleasing to God.

So try reading it. Start with the New Testament. Ask God to speak to you through His Word. When it comes to living well, God's Word knows best.

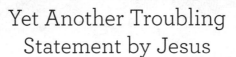

Yet Another Troubling Statement by Jesus

"For I came to set a man against his father, and a daughter against her mother, and a daughter-in-law against her mother-in-law; and a man's enemies will be the members of his household."

MATTHEW 10:35–36

Today's verse is probably very troubling to read. Christ said, "Look, when I come, you're going to see a son set against his father, a daughter become an enemy of her mother, even a daughter-in-law set against her mother-in-law." (Well, the last one is not too hard to believe.)

Was Jesus advocating that someone who becomes a Christian become a troublemaker in the home? No, of course not. What Jesus was telling us is that when a person comes to Christ within a family of unbelievers, the unbelievers are probably going to be unhappy about that decision and possibly even reject the believer. Why? Because they feel the new Christian is claiming to have the truth and declaring that everyone else in the family is wrong. There will be natural divisions in the family, often including anger toward and rejection of the Christian member. If you are in this situation, Jesus wants you to realize that it is not you being rejected; it is Christ Himself. Jesus will help carry the hurt you feel from this misdirected rejection. And never lose hope. When rejected, hope, pray, and love. Someday they may believe too.

Childlike Faith

"Let the little children come to me, and do not hinder them, for the kingdom of heaven belongs to such as these."

MATTHEW 19:14 NIV

Parents pushed and shoved their children, hoping the famous Man would touch them. His assistants, thinking they were protecting Him from unwanted demands, tried to shoo the kids away, but this important Man was indignant with His assistants. He said, "Let the little children come to me." He took them in His arms and hugged them, and the kids loved Him. The Man's name was Jesus. He showed His well-intentioned disciples how important children are to God.

Question: Dad, Mom, do you make time for your kids, as Jesus did—the Man who lived an incredibly busy life but was not too busy for children?

Very often, a child's importance is shown by giving him a listening ear or a hug when a little time is what he wants and needs. When it comes to your kids, ask the Lord to help you be like Jesus. No job is more important than that, even if you're the Son of God.

Sex in Marriage

*Marriage is to be held in honor among all, and the
marriage bed is to be undefiled; for fornicators
and adulterers God will judge.*

HEBREWS 13:4

How's your sex life?

Have you bought into the idea that the best, most enjoyable, most intense sex is always found outside of marriage? We are constantly bombarded with this message by the media: TV, movies, books, and songs.

This message is a lie. It is the exact opposite of what God had in mind when He invented sex. Any sex that is outside the context of committed love in marriage is always less than the best. It brings emotional harm, broken relationships, turmoil, and guilt. Now, that may sell movies and books, but in the end, it will destroy a person's life. God intended sexual intimacy to be His great gift for marriage and marriage alone. He knows how it is best enjoyed.

So seek to trust the Inventor of sex in order to experience the sacred enjoyment God has in mind for you. Quit settling for second best. Seek God's best for the best sex.

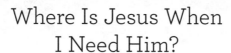

Where Is Jesus When I Need Him?

"And lo, I am with you always, even to the end of the age."

MATTHEW 28:20 NKJV

Have you ever faced a storm in your life and the frustration was multiplied because it did not seem that Jesus was there for you? The disciples faced this very situation. Jesus told them to take their boat to sea while He stayed behind to pray. Suddenly, a powerful storm came up. The terrified disciples faced it for several hours before Jesus, making a pretty dramatic entrance, showed up to comfort them. So why didn't Jesus come to them right away?

Well, think about it this way. When we are going through storms, it's human nature for us to have the mind-set that *I've just got to work this out by myself*! The disciples knew that Jesus was on land and probably assumed there really wasn't anything He could do anyway. But Christ was praying on the shore, and He knew the exact location and needs of His disciples. You should realize that Jesus is watching over you in the midst of your storm as well.

Know this: the storms of life will unsettle us—even terrify us, but *there is no storm in life stronger than Jesus*. He is watching over you always. And sometimes in storms, He'll show up in amazing ways, so trust Him even when it seems He's far away.

Going Home

"So he got up and came to his father. But while he was still a long way off, his father saw him and felt compassion for him, and ran and embraced him and kissed him."

LUKE 15:20

Robert Frost wrote, "Home is the place where when you have to go there, they have to take you in." There's no place like home. No matter how bad we mess up or how disappointing life gets, it's the one place they have to take us in.

Jesus told of a wayward son who messed up big time, wasting all his dad had blessed him with. He became homeless and so hungry that he wanted to eat leftover slop fit only for animals. But when he came to his senses, he thought about home. He knew he didn't deserve to go there, but he went anyway. And his dad was so overwhelmed with joy that he welcomed him home.

The dad represents God, and the wayward son represents you and me. It's Jesus' way of telling us that we all mess up—but nobody messes up so badly that when he decides to come home to the Lord, the Lord won't welcome him back to a right relationship with Him. Is it time for you to come home to the Lord?

Who Is Jesus to You?

*"But what about you?" he asked. "Who do you say I
am?" Simon Peter answered, "You are the Christ,
the Son of the living God."*

MATTHEW 16:15–16 NIV

I was riding in a cab to Washington's Dulles Airport. As we passed the Pentagon, I asked the cab driver, "Which side of the building was hit on September 11?" When he answered, I could tell he had an accent, and I asked where he was from. He said he was from Iran. I said, "Tell me about your faith; do you have any?" "Oh yes! I'm a Muslim," he answered and then went on to state that he was currently on a spiritual search.

I asked what he thought about Jesus. "I believe in Jesus," he enthusiastically replied. "He is in the Koran. He is a great prophet." "But do you believe in Him as the Son of God?" He quickly answered, "Oh no! There is only one God, and that is Allah." We continued this conversation during the long ride to the airport. As I left him, I encouraged him to read the Gospels with an open mind and ask God to reveal to him who Jesus really is.

Who do you say He is? This is what Jesus wants to know. This is the most important question you'll ever answer. How you answer that question will determine your spiritual destiny forever. The only correct response is the one Peter gave when asked that question by Jesus Himself. He replied, "You are the Christ, the Son of the living God!"

Revenge—The Wrong Way to Pray

"Do not judge, or you too will be judged. For in the same way you judge others, you will be judged, and with the measure you use, it will be measured to you."

MATTHEW 7:1–2 NIV

Do you ever wish that certain people got what you felt they deserved—especially people who have wronged you? Do some people seem to get away with murder and not face any kind of punishment or repercussion?

You may have seen the cartoon with three panels:

+ Panel #1: A zealous character is praying to the Almighty. He says, "God, smite my worst enemy!"
+ Panel #2: The man praying this prayer is struck by lightning.
+ Panel #3: The man groggily says, "God, let me rephrase that!"

Be careful what you pray for, because sometimes you may find that your own worst enemy is yourself. Jesus Christ said, "Do not judge lest you be judged. For in the way you judge others you will be judged as well" (paraphrase).

I hope that today you won't be so hard on others, because one day the gavel may fall down on you.

Appointments

Commit your works to the Lord and your
plans will be established.

Proverbs 16:3

Most of us have a pretty full plate, and that BlackBerry or iPhone or calendar can fill up quickly. How do you keep your priorities in place?

Let me suggest three appointments you don't want to miss:

1. *A regular daily appointment with God.* Pick a time of the day to meet with God to communicate with Him through prayer and Bible study. When it comes to appointments, this one is the most important.
2. *A weekly appointment in church.* This is key if you claim to be a Christian or have an openness to investigate Christianity. Remember, being in a church doesn't make you a Christian any more than swimming in the ocean makes you a fish. Yet it does help you stay close to God and get right with those around you.
3. *A weekly date with your spouse,* if you're married. You don't have to be a Christian to do this. The weekly date helps you stay close with your spouse all week long, and it can rekindle those romantic fires.

These are three of life's most important appointments to keep on your calendar. Give 'em a try.

Financial Wisdom

*He who tills his land will have plenty of bread, but he
who pursues worthless things lacks sense.*

PROVERBS 12:11

Money can, indeed, solve a lot of problems. There are many good things that can be done with dollars. But there are also terrible human tragedies that await those who believe money will solve most of their problems.

One of the reasons I don't support the states legalizing and encouraging gambling—be it the lottery or casinos—is because it appeals to the idea that we can get rich by doing nothing. I realize that for many, gambling is a form of entertainment. Yet very often the people who have the least are the ones who buy into this mind-set. It just tugs at my heart when I see a poor individual standing there in the convenience store, buying all those lottery tickets—sometimes with young children resting on both arms. I cringe when I think about how much of their already meager wages are going into this pipe dream that they will find instant wealth. This type of thinking just doesn't make sense. It's a sign of a person's lack of understanding. And unfortunately, the state encourages it. And even worse, in my state, the lottery is a sick way of taking money from the poor to pay for affluent kids' college educations. How unjust can that be?

We must not only learn how to spend money wisely; we need to make sure we understand how to pursue money in a way that makes sense. Playing the lottery just isn't one of them.

What's Your Identity?

*A righteous man is cautious in friendship, but the
way of the wicked leads them astray.*

PROVERBS 12:26 NIV

People will often wrap themselves in the identity of other groups or people. Some will choose to be identified as Republicans or Democrats, conservationists or environmentalists, or maybe just part of the elite. Many people, especially here in the South, will embrace the identity of the college they attended, be it UGA, Auburn, Tennessee, or for the wisest among us, the University of South Carolina. They will wrap themselves in the colors and excitement of that college, even to the point that their mood for the entire week depends on whether their football team won or lost the previous Saturday. (I wish I didn't battle this disease.)

How about you? Is there someone with whom you have chosen to identify? Be careful with that decision, because the person you become will reflect whomever you choose to follow and befriend. And the image others have of you will reflect those with whom you identify. Knowing that, it only makes sense to choose to be identified with Jesus Christ. Even those who don't follow Him never question His character.

Have you chosen to follow Christ? To let His Spirit give you the desire for Him to be your role model? Do your actions indicate that you identify with Him? Do others see Jesus in you? What's your identity?

First Basic in Victorious Living

Ho! Every one who thirsts, come to the waters.

ISAIAH 55:1

Great football teams focus on the basics of blocking and tackling, over and over and over. Victorious living focuses on the basics as well. And the number one basic discipline for victorious living is regular time alone with God.

The prophet Isaiah said, "Ho! Every one who thirsts, come to the waters." Ho, whoa, slow down! We tend to be like a bunch of racehorses, charging out of the starting gates, rushing into the day without a thought for God. Ho! Slow down and thirst for God. Charging out to make money doesn't satisfy; it leaves your soul empty. God is the source of satisfaction and fulfillment.

So thirst for God. Ask God to give you a thirst to know Him. Ask God to give you a desire and discipline to spend time with Him, talking and listening to Him through prayer and Bible study for both renewal and strength. Regular time alone with God is the first basic in victorious living.

Set Free from a Tangled Web

"I tell you the truth, everyone who sins is a slave to sin."

JOHN 8:34 NIV

Have you ever noticed that sin has a way of multiplying in a person's life? The Bible paints a very graphic picture of a person who becomes entrapped by his own sin. It says, "And he will be held with the cords of his sin" (Proverbs 5:22). Now, what does that mean?

Have you ever seen a little bug caught in a spider's web? The more that bug struggles to become free, the more entangled in the web it becomes. That's what this verse is talking about. When a person is trapped by his sin—even when he comes to his senses and recognizes the need to change—he cannot escape by his own strength. He just gets more tangled.

But there's hope for the person caught in his sin. We can all be set free from bondage by admitting our sin to God and giving Him control of our lives through Jesus Christ. Only He can untangle us from the tangled web of sin! Only Jesus truly sets us free.

Bothering Friends

A friend loves at all times.

PROVERBS 17:17

They've been there. You are having a problem or even a crisis. They are people who could help you. You sure would like to talk with them. You reach for the phone, and then your hand stops in midair. *No*, you tell yourself, *I really shouldn't bother them.* So instead of getting the advice and comfort of a friend, you continue to deal with the issue all alone.

We have lots of reasons for ignoring the potential comfort of friends. Maybe you are afraid they will think your issues are silly. Perhaps you haven't spoken to that old friend in years. Maybe you've had a spat. Or perhaps you fear your friend just wouldn't understand.

Let me ask you a question. If that person were to call you up and ask for your advice, would you help him or her? I bet you would. In fact, you would probably go to extraordinary lengths to help. Most everyone likes being asked for advice or assistance. It makes us feel important and valued. So why not show your friends that same respect and give them the opportunity to serve?

Most of all, remember: whether you have a friend to call or not, there is always Someone you can reach out to for help. You don't even have to pick up the phone. His name is Jesus, and you can connect to His line anytime through prayer. He's waiting— why don't you give Him a call?

Torture or Separation?

"The rich man also died and was buried. In hell, where he was in torment, he looked up and saw Abraham far away, with Lazarus by his side."

LUKE 16:22–23 NIV

No one in the Bible spoke more about hell than Jesus. He painted a pretty complete picture of what hell is like. In some cases He spoke literally, and in others He spoke more figuratively. Christ spoke about the suffering of hell. It means being permanently separated from God. It is going to be a place of totally unrestrained evil, where the devil and his demons reside along with all those who have rejected Christ. That's not a pretty picture and not a place you want to be.

Although nothing in Scripture says that hell is an eternal torture chamber, it does say it will be unbearably hot. It will be eternal suffering and a clear awareness of what you have missed out on. If you go there, you will realize that your whole life was a waste because you never responded to Christ. There will be the realization that you are permanently separated from God. That will create great agony.

Whatever it may be, you sure don't want to wind up there. And you don't have to. The good news that follows this bad news is that Christ came to save us from hell. He came to forgive us of our sins and make us right with God. Have you claimed this good news in faith? Do so today. Hell is a place you want to be saved from.

The Real Target of Their Wrath

"And forgive us our debts, as we forgive our debtors."

MATTHEW 6:12 KJV

Before the apostle Paul came to Christ, his Jewish name was Saul. He was a religious terrorist—persecuting, arresting, and at times approving the killing of Christians.

Know this: his real hostility was not so much at the church as it was with Jesus. Christians, realize this important point. When you are mocked by others, when you feel excluded by them, when you feel the pain of their persecution, recognize that they are not as hostile with you as they are with Jesus. It's still true of religious terrorists today. Persecution of Christians is not so much a hatred of the individual Christian. Persecutors may not realize it, but who they really hate is Jesus!

Whoever it is that gives you a hard time for being a Christian, don't take it personally. Remember who they really hate—even though many would never admit it. Instead, seek to love them, forgive them, and pray for them. Who knows? Your positive witness to them may convict their hearts of their need for Jesus. They may want what you have. It happened with Paul as he watched the first Christian martyr die—a man named Stephen. It prepared his heart for the time Jesus would confront him on the road to Damascus with the question, "Saul, Saul, why do you persecute me?" (Acts 9:4 NIV).

God's Family

That is, it is not the children of the flesh who are children of God, but the children of the promise are regarded as descendants.

ROMANS 9:8

There are good families and bad families—good ones we're drawn to and bad ones we want to get away from. But no matter what type of family you have, no earthly family lasts forever. They all end in separation through death or man's choice.

But I have good news. There is a family that lasts forever. It begins here on earth and is only realized in perfection after we die. When a person decides to become a follower of Christ, he or she enters a giant family of faith—the church.

Now, there's no perfect church. If you find one, please don't join it; you'll mess it up in a skinny second because we're all sinners who fall short of God's best. But in the family of faith, we're forgiven sinners who begin a process of being transformed into the people God wants us to be. Looking for a family that lasts? Know Jesus and enter into the only family that lasts forever.

The Most Difficult Job

Behold, children are a gift of the LORD.

PSALM 127:3

Have you ever considered what is the most difficult job in life? It's the job of parenting, the challenge of guiding a child through the demands of growing up in this world and helping that child become all he or she was created to be.

The Bible provides timeless insight. "Train a child in the way he should go, and when he is old he will not turn from it" (Proverbs 22:6 NIV). "The way he should go" means "according to his bent." This means we have to be students of our children—learning to recognize their God-given abilities and interests. We're also to help our children develop their strengths as well as curb and check their weaknesses.

Once we become students of our children and teach them right and wrong—with a lot of prayer—the promise of God can be realized. The challenge is a great one, but the rewards of seeing our children become mature, productive adults make all the hard work worthwhile.

What on Earth Am I Here For?

Many plans are in a man's heart,
but the counsel of the LORD will stand.

PROVERBS 19:21

What on earth am I here for?

Have you ever asked yourself that question? Rick Warren asks that question in *The Purpose Driven Life.*

Are you clear on your life purpose? Can you write it down?

It seems the average American thinks life is all about working hard, raising a family, doing your best, making enough money to retire (the earlier the better), and then finally doing what you want to do when you want to do it. But by midlife, this philosophy makes a person cry, "What on earth am I here for?" It's like slowly drowning in an ocean of emptiness.

But I have good news. We can know what on earth we're here for. It begins when we get to know our Creator through the person of Christ. Our Creator, God, loves us and has a purpose for our lives. Our role is to trust Him and obey Him through His written Word.

So don't waste your life. Get to know your Creator personally. I promise you'll become clear about what on earth you're here for.

Touchdown

In that day His feet will stand on the Mount of Olives,
which is in front of Jerusalem on the east.

ZECHARIAH 14:4

I love football season—the fans cheering, the big games, the great rivalries. With every new season there's always anticipation and hope. Will the players rise to the challenge, or will some bad play cost the team a game? Or even a season? And certainly no play in football is more important than the touchdown . . . the goal of every drive.

Did you know the Bible speaks about a touchdown, the greatest touchdown ever? It's something biblical Jews and Christians alike will agree on. The Bible says it's going to happen just as time is running out, at the end of the game. The Messiah is going to touch down on the Mount of Olives in Israel. The Scriptures teach us the great touchdown will be made by a Man named Jesus.

He's coming for those who are on His team and to judge those who are not. His touchdown will mean victory for His team and lasting defeat for the opponents. The question is, are you going to be one who celebrates His touchdown, or one who loses the ultimate game of life?

Just as I Am

*"All that the Father gives me will come to me, and
whoever comes to me I will never drive away."*

JOHN 6:37 NIV

There is no way to verify this, but I believe that no song is more associated with people's public profession of faith than the hymn "Just as I Am." Though written in 1835, the hymn's popularity reached its apex in the second half of the twentieth century, when it was so often played at the end of Billy Graham's crusades and church services as people were invited to "walk down the aisle" and give their lives to Jesus.

And no wonder. Does any hymn summarize the declaration of a spiritual journey more succinctly than "Just as I Am"? Focus on these powerful, beautiful words of a sinner deciding to place his soul, just as he is, in the hands of Jesus.

> *Just as I am, without one plea,*
> *But that Thy blood was shed for me,*
> *And that Thou bidd'st me come to Thee,*
> *O Lamb of God, I come, I come.*
>
> *Just as I am, tho' tossed about*
> *With many a conflict, many a doubt,*
> *Fightings and fears within, without,*
> *O Lamb of God, I come, I come.*

Have you come? Will you come today—just as you are?

God Is the Giver of Life

*Then the LORD took note of Sarah as He had said, and
the LORD for Sarah as He had promised. So Sarah
conceived and bore a son to Abraham in his old age, at
the appointed time of which God had spoken to him.*

GENESIS 21:1–2

If you are struggling with infertility, you should take special interest in the stories of the first ladies of the faith—Sarah, Rebekah, and Rachel. Sarah was ninety years old when God fulfilled His promise and she conceived Isaac. Rebekah did not give birth to her twins until she had been married for twenty years. And Rachel struggled for years to have a child, whereas her older sister, Leah, had many. So many of you who are struggling with infertility can find a great point of identification in these ladies. Their struggle is your struggle. And note that when each was finally able to have a child, it gave her a greater sense of appreciation for God's blessing in her life.

It's also so important to notice how, for each of these women, prayer was central. It was specific answered prayer when God brought about life in the barren wombs of these women. And men, pay attention to the active role that their husbands played in praying to God to open their wives' wombs. No matter what course you may take, don't forget to pray, to seek God's will. If He blesses you with a child, remember that God is the Giver of life. If He doesn't, may God give you the grace to accept it and clarity as to whether giving a godly home to a child through adoption is the route God is leading you to take. Either way, God is the Giver of all life.

The Real Nature of Tithing

Bring the whole tithe into the storehouse, so that there
may be food in My house, and test Me now in this, . . .
[see] if I will not open for you the windows of heaven
and pour out for you a blessing until it overflows.

MALACHI 3:10

It is said that God's instruction on stewardship is that we give a tenth of our income. But is that what He actually says? Take another look at the verse. It begins with an interesting choice of words. It says, "Bring the whole tithe into the storehouse." The first word in that verse is not *give*; it is *bring*. This wording is intentional and indicates the true nature of what a tithe is.

Think about it. If you're going to give a present to someone, you must first be the rightful owner of what you are giving away. You can't just walk into a store and grab something to give to someone without paying for it. A gift must first be owned before it can be given away. So Scripture is very clear here: we are not the owners of the tithes we bring before God; we are simply stewards of the blessings God has entrusted us with. When we tithe, we are just *bringing to Him* what is rightfully His. Are you willing to bring a tithe to God? You'll never regret it. When we *bring* a tithe to God, He promises us we'll be blessed. Why would you choose to miss His blessings?

Why Do Good Things Happen to Bad People?

For I envied the arrogant when I saw the prosperity of the wicked. They have no struggles; their bodies are healthy and strong. They are free from the burdens common to man; they are not plagued by human ills.

Psalm 73:3–5 niv

I had lunch with a man who mentioned that something was really bugging him. "I really don't have a problem with the fact that sometimes bad things happen to good people. I understand that God gives man free will and that sometimes those choices—even good ones—have bad results. I'm actually okay with that."

"Then what is bugging you?" I asked.

"Well, I don't understand why *good* things happen to *bad* people. Why do corrupt politicians have their sins exposed and yet see their popularity soar? And why is it that an atheist famous for calling Christians "a bunch of losers" is allowed to accumulate fame and wealth beyond imagination? Why has he been so blessed?"

"Well, let's see," I began. "If I'm not mistaken, the fellow you are talking about has had several marriages fail, right?" My friend nodded. "So here is a man with a miserable family life, and unless he changes his views on Jesus Christ, he will never see heaven. And you call him *blessed?*" I continued. "Let me ask you something. Despite his fame and riches, would you trade places with this man?"

"No way. Not even for a second," he replied.

"Well," I said, "maybe what you call 'blessed' ain't so good."

Popularity and money are temporal. True blessings last.

Heaven Is Like Home

*"But the father said to his servants, 'Quick! Bring the
best robe and put it on him. Put a ring on his finger and
sandals on his feet. Bring the fattened calf and kill it.
Let's have a feast and celebrate. For this son of mine
was dead and is alive again; he was lost and is found.'
So they began to celebrate."*

LUKE 15:22–24 NIV

My favorite parable is the story of the prodigal son. There's that
wonderful scene when the wayward son finally comes to his
senses and begins to walk home. And what does that father do?
He runs and embraces him. And there's joy and celebration.

I know that's a picture of redemption. I know Jesus is talking to us about what it's like when we confess our sins and finally
come home to the Lord. But I also think it's a beautiful picture of
finally coming home to heaven after the weariness and demands
of this very difficult life and world. When we finally come *home*,
our heavenly Father is there. He runs to embrace us! And He's
full of joy. He's got those tears in His eyes, as only a Father can
have when His son comes home. And the celebration begins, and
it never, ever ends! Because heaven will be like coming home. It's
like home is supposed to be. So I ask you, my friends, when your
days in this life are done, will you be headed home?

A Model for Forgiveness

*Be . . . quick to forgive an offense. Forgive as quickly
and completely as the Master forgave you.*

COLOSSIANS 3:13 MSG

Is there someone you've been unwilling to forgive? Who immediately comes to mind? Unfortunately, unwillingness to forgive is refusal to give control to God. You have to leave the getting even up to Him.

Now, I assure you that in some situations you're not going to be able to forgive people in your own strength. The hurt is too deep. In these cases you need to ask God to help you do what you cannot do. Ask for His supernatural power to begin to forgive that person!

How do you know when forgiveness is complete? For me, it's when I'm able to see the person who hurt me without having a knot in the pit of my stomach. There's no sense of bitterness or resentment—just acceptance. But does forgiveness mean you have to trust your offender? Oh no—that's for fools. But you choose to love that individual. It's a great miracle that God brings about when we ask His help in forgiving others. And what freedom—to finally let go.

If you're really struggling in this area, remember, Jesus is our ultimate example. Nobody got the shaft like Jesus. He had no sin. We murdered Him on the cross with our sins. And while we were murdering Him, He said, "Father, forgive them" (Luke 23:34). If Jesus can forgive us for that, then through His power we can forgive others who have wronged us. Ask God to help you do this *today*!

October

The Lord will indeed give what is good,
and our land will yield its harvest.

Psalm 85:12 niv

But It Takes Two to Tango, Right?

*One evening David got up from his bed and walked
around on the roof of the palace. From the roof he saw a
woman bathing. The woman was very beautiful....
Then David sent messengers to get her. She came to
him, and he slept with her.*

2 SAMUEL 11:2, 4 NIV

The whole fiasco began with David and Bathsheba committing an act of adultery. Then came a clamoring of dominoes involving deceit, murder, lying, and cover-up. Yet despite the horrendous consequences of the consensual act, the Bible's perspective seems to only condemn David. What about Bathsheba?

She was a beautiful woman, and that is great power. Don't kid yourself: Bathsheba was aware of her power when she bathed outside by the moonlight; she knew the king was in town and her husband was away.

But here's what is so relevant today. The Bible puts the responsibility of this sin on David, which is consistent with our contemporary laws on sexual harassment. The person in authority is the one held responsible for the deed. David was the man in power. He was the king, and he had the major responsibility for this sin, no matter how cooperative Bathsheba may have been.

It takes two to tango, but the one in power is *always* the most responsible. If you are the one who holds the power, be sure you don't abuse it by giving in to temptation.

The Local Church and Neighborhood Bar

. . . not forsaking our own assembling together, as is the habit of some, but encouraging one another; and all the more as you see the day drawing near.

HEBREWS 10:25

Have you ever thought of the similarities between the local church and the neighborhood bar?

In both places:

+ people come looking for fellowship
+ people cling to anonymity while hoping for friendship
+ people want to go where they are accepted
+ people want to go where their spirits will be lifted
+ people are united around one theme
+ people go where they like the music
+ people tell others, whether bartenders or ministers, about their troubles

But the differences are profound: The bar is centered on booze, and the church is centered on Jesus Christ. The bar offers a way to escape problems. The church offers a way to face them, get through them, and overcome them. The spirit inside the bar lowers one's guard when it comes to temptation and sin. The spirit of the true church encourages people to turn from sin and turn to God.

In short, the neighborhood bar may be a substitute for the church, but it never comes close to providing the meaning and purpose found in a Christ-centered church.

In the Spirit

The high priest questioned them, saying, "We gave
you strict orders not to continue teaching in this
name, and yet, you have filled Jerusalem with your
teaching and intend to bring this man's blood upon
us." But Peter and the apostles answered,
"We must obey God rather than men."

ACTS 5:27–29

I realize today that the call to obey God's law rather than man's when they conflict is a dangerous message. Why?

1. *The Christian Fool Syndrome.* In every body of believers, there are some Christian fools. They hear a sermon to obey God over man-made morality, so they go out with the best of intentions to tell those in authority where they are wrong. They confuse defiance and rebellion with godliness, when in most cases, they are simply obnoxious fools. Can't you picture God, from heaven, looking at them, shaking His head, and saying, "Bless their hearts!"?

2. *This one can be really dangerous*—being led by the Holy Spirit and God's Word. When God gives us an open door to speak about our faith in Christ, we need to do it in the Spirit. And yes, there may be repercussions, and yes, there may be objections, and yes, there may be legitimate persecution for doing so. But it's not because we are acting the fool. It's because we are obeying God rather than man, under the leadership of the Holy Spirit.

So, Christian, seek to be filled with God's Spirit. Follow His prompting, and then leave the results up to God.

Strength for the Day

But those who hope in the LORD will renew their strength. They will soar on wings like eagles; they will run and not grow weary, they will walk and not be faint.

Every Christian has to consider whether he or she would be willing to suffer for, even die for, Jesus. For me, though, being willing is not the tough question. My fearful question is: would I actually be able to? I always find hope in the fact that God promised that He would always be with us. When we come to Christ, He fills us with His Spirit, and that Spirit of the Lord will be sufficient in the day of the crisis. He does not give us strength for tomorrow's crisis today. He gives us strength for today's crisis today.

It's understandable that each of us would gulp and say, "I hope I am willing," and then wonder deep inside if we really would be. Well, I want you to know, as cowardly, weak, and selfish as I am, I know I could not do that in my own strength. But I'm going to trust that the power of the Holy Spirit would give me strength in that moment of crisis—strength that I just can't imagine having today.

The Secret Weapon

Do not fear, for I am with you; do not anxiously look about you, for I am your God. I will strengthen you, surely I will help you, surely I will uphold you with My righteous right hand.

ISAIAH 41:10

Years ago, Baylor University had a great football team. They stormed through the old Southwest Conference that year. But late in the season, they were discouraged by a shocking loss to an unranked team. And their hopes were further threatened because a good Arkansas team was next.

Then Baylor's head coach pulled out a secret weapon. He invited a former team member, one who had been paralyzed in a freak football accident earlier in the season, to speak to the discouraged players. He sat in a wheelchair before them as they gathered in the locker room before the game. He thanked his teammates for their prayers and support. Then, referring to their loss the week before, he said, "Guys, you've got to turn a setback into a comeback." With that bold declaration, he slowly rose from the wheelchair and took a step forward, to the shock and amazement of his teammates. They began to cheer and cry, and then they ran out on the field and whipped the tar out of Arkansas.

What setbacks have you faced? What are you facing today? God's power and strength are available to help us all turn a setback into a comeback. After all, the ultimate "setback" of the cross was followed by the ultimate "comeback" of the resurrection.

Should You Tithe?

"Bring the whole tithe into the storehouse..." says the
LORD Almighty, "and see if I will not throw open the
floodgates of heaven and pour out so much blessing
that you will not have room enough for it."

MALACHI 3:10 NIV

Should you tithe? Here are five good reasons why you should give the first 10 percent of what you earn to God:

+ *God has always chosen the tithe as a way for people to show their faith in Him.* Hundreds of years before the Law of Moses, Abraham and Jacob both tithed.
+ *The tithe acknowledges God's ownership of all we have.* When we tithe, we're saying, "He's entrusted all this to me, but this is the owner's fee." This is a basic expectation. It's not an offering.
+ *It shows we trust God.* The only time in Scripture God says for us to test Him is regarding the tithe!
+ *It shows God we put Him first.* Bring the tithe to the Lord first, and see how God will bless you.
+ *Tithing naturally forces better stewardship.* If you know you must live on 90 percent of your income, it forces you to be a better steward of God's money.

If you are tithing to the church where you worship and serve, keep it up. If you are not tithing, why don't you put God to the test and see if His promises are true?

What a Wife Most Needs from Her Husband

*Husbands, go all out in your love for your wives,
exactly as Christ did for the church—a love
marked by giving, not getting.*

EPHESIANS 5:25 MSG

Dr. James Dobson was asked, "Why are men so insensitive to women's needs today?"

He answered, "I question whether men have really changed all that much. I doubt if men *ever* responded as women preferred. Did the farmer of a century ago come in from the fields to say, 'Tell me how it went with the kids today'? No. He was as oblivious to his wife's nature then as husbands are today."[20]

So men, if you're struggling to meet your wife's needs, here are a few tips:

+ *security*—physically, financially, and emotionally
+ *romantic love*—who do you think buys all those romance novels and likes to watch chick flicks?
+ *understanding*—this means listening more than telling her what to do
+ *reassurance*—knowing that you think she's beautiful, in a society of constant comparison
+ *spiritual leadership*—not dictatorship, but servant leadership, as Christ provides for His church

A wife most needs love from her husband, and these are ways to show it.

What a Man Most Needs from His Wife

Each individual among you ... is to love his own wife even as himself, and the wife must see to it that she respects her husband.

EPHESIANS 5:33

So many wives are clueless about what their husbands need the most. They often make the mistake of thinking that his greatest need is like hers—the need for love. But the husband's greatest need is for respect. This is how God has wired him. So, wives, how can you respect your husbands?

Praise him. Build him up in a world where he often gets beaten down. Just think how much you like to hear the words "I love you," and praise him just that much and more.

Seek to be his best friend. From his wife, he needs support, not competition. Men as a whole are not as relational and verbal as women.

Be willing to follow his lead. You're kidding! In the twenty-first century you want me to follow his lead?

Well, if this makes you mad, argue with God. It's His teaching in His Book. This is how you really respect your husband. When he senses this, it's amazing how much he will love you in return.

Running from the Light

*"For everyone who does evil hates the Light,
and does not come to the Light for fear that
his deeds will be exposed."*

JOHN 3:20

There are four things that don't like the light. One is cockroaches. Two, rats. Three, teenagers making out in a dark room when a parent comes in and turns on the light. And four, cat burglars. None of those four like the light. Why? Because the light says, "You're up to no good!" And so there's a tendency for roaches, rats, smooching teenagers, and cat burglars to run for cover when the light comes on. They don't want their deeds exposed.

Really, this is true for all of us. The closer we get to the light, the more our sins are exposed. The closer we are to Christ, the more aware we are of our sinfulness. The further we are from Christ, the more unaware we are of our sinfulness, so we tend to think that we are basically pretty good people. So when the Light exposes who we really are, we prefer to flee toward the darkness.

But there is good news in all of this. John 1:9 says, "There was the true Light which, coming into the world, enlightens every man." And 1 John 1:9, "If we confess our sins, He is faithful and righteous to forgive us our sins, and to cleanse us from all unrighteousness." In other words, in Jesus we are made clean—we don't have to fear exposure. He enlightens us about God. He enlightens us on living.

A Magnificent Failure

We are assured and know that [God being a partner in their labor] all things work together and are [fitting into a plan] for good to and for those who love God and are called according to [His] design and purpose.

ROMANS 8:28 AMP

With only twelve official legal holidays in the USA, it requires a remarkable occasion to have a holiday. We have holidays to celebrate our independence, memorialize our veterans, and contemplate all the things we are thankful for. We also honor great people and their accomplishments. Holidays are so scarce that all forty-three of the men who have been our president have to share a single day! When you think about it, there are only two people who have achieved such distinction that they have their own holidays—Martin Luther King Jr. and Christopher Columbus. And you know what is strange about that? Columbus was a failure!

That's right. Christopher Columbus was on a mission to find a shorter trade route to India, but instead he missed it by more than nine thousand miles. Nine thousand miles! But that failure put a spotlight on new lands that motivated future explorers, attracted settlers, and eventually resulted in the creation of great nations. It was one of history's biggest blunders, yet we celebrate the failure every year with one of our national holidays.

The next time you think you've made a big mistake, think about the legacy of Christopher Columbus. You'll see that God can turn your blunder into an unexpected good.

The Original Religious Terrorist

"But I say to you, love your enemies and pray for those who persecute you."

MATTHEW 5:44

Do you know who is the most famous religious terrorist of all time? He is introduced in the book of Acts. A crowd was stoning a Christian named Stephen. A zealous Jew named Saul stood by, enthusiastically endorsing the execution. He was an up-and-coming aristocratic Jew who saw Christianity as a dangerous heresy that had to be stopped. As a religious terrorist, Saul continued "ravaging the church, entering house after house, and dragging off men and women . . . [to] prison" (Acts 8:3).

But I wonder if Saul was haunted by the picture of Stephen as he died, so pure, so at peace. Maybe Saul could not release from his mind how Stephen had prayed for those who were killing him, asking God to forgive them (Acts 7:59–60). Perhaps God was using a martyr's prayer to prepare Saul's heart for a personal encounter with Jesus Christ.

As Saul traveled to Damascus to persecute Christians there, he had that encounter. And he moved from being a religious terrorist to becoming Christianity's greatest missionary and theologian.

It should give us hope to know that God can transform even the life of a religious terrorist. Perhaps that is one reason God demands that we pray for everyone, even our enemies, even those who persecute us, even religious terrorists. Christ died for all and desires all to be transformed into a new creation through His power.

Becoming Like the Crowd We Run With

Do not be misled: "Bad company corrupts good character."

1 Corinthians 15:33 niv

The last line of George Orwell's *Animal Farm* is a stunner: "The creatures outside looked from pig to man, and from man to pig, and from pig to man again; but already it was impossible to say which was which."[21]

One of the greatest influences we have for determining the way we live our lives is the group of people we run with. The fact is, we tend to become like those we choose to be with. As we spend time with people, we adopt their styles, values, and interests. If you associate with unethical people, you may find yourself progressively compromising on ethical decisions. If you surround yourself with men and women of godly character, you will find the ethical path much easier to navigate. You probably know this, so apply it to the people you befriend, but don't stop there.

Join companies, work groups, and social circles that are made up of people with integrity. And if you own your own business, only hire people with solid character. Include your suppliers, your advertising agency, and your accounting firm on that list. Surround yourself with people of integrity, and you will find it easier to live in a way that is both pleasing to God and good for your fellow man.

"Bad company corrupts good character." Run with a bad crowd, and you begin to live more like pigs! So choose to run with a good crowd. Then you can begin to live a life that builds character.

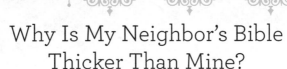

Why Is My Neighbor's Bible Thicker Than Mine?

Every word of God is flawless . . . Do not add to his words, or he will rebuke you and prove you a liar.

Turn with me to 2 Maccabees, chapter 12. You'll find it as the last book in the Old Testament. What? You say you can't find it? That's probably because it's not in your Bible; you can only find 2 Maccabees in the Orthodox and Catholic Bibles. If the two largest groups of Christianity have different books in their Bibles, which Bible is the right one? Here's the story.

During the Protestant Reformation, the Catholic monk Martin Luther called for theological, moral, and biblical reform. Luther called for the church to get back to Scripture alone. Several books called the Apocrypha had been added to the Old Testament. The Reformation sought to return to the original Old Testament. When I asked our neighborhood rabbi about the Apocrypha, he said, "The Jewish people see the books of the Apocrypha as sacred, but not binding, and not on the level of the Bible."

Now you understand why the Protestant Reformers left the books of the Apocrypha out of the Bible we have today. Do not let this alarm you. The Apocrypha may be sacred writings to the Jews, but it is not the holy Word of God. But the thirty-nine books of the Old Testament and twenty-seven books of the New Testament are all the same in the Protestant, Catholic, and Orthodox Bibles. This means the story of Jesus Christ remains identical, universal, and eternal for all.

Is It Tradition, or Is It Biblical?

Then some Pharisees and teachers of the law came to Jesus from Jerusalem and asked, "Why do your disciples break the tradition of the elders?"

Sometimes we have to get outside of our own traditions to notice some of the legalisms we have embraced. During our seminary days, my wife and I were serving as missionaries at a Scottish Baptist church. I soon noticed that there was no invitation at the end of the sermon for people to "walk the aisle" to make a decision to join the church or to accept Christ. I went to the pastor and expressed my concern. "This is not good," I told him. He looked at me with a condescending smile and said, "Well, Bryant, would you show me in the Bible where it says you've got to 'walk the aisle' to become a Christian or join a church?" And then he added, "Why don't you do a little study and see how the Bible teaches us to make a public confession of our faith in Jesus Christ? The only thing you'll see is baptism." He was right.

So often we elevate tradition to the level of the Bible. Tradition can be meaningful, but when we raise it to the level of the Bible, we make it idolatry and ignore the second commandment. Let's be sure that in following Christ, the Bible is our ultimate authority on how to live for Him.

Noise

Give ear and hear my voice, listen and hear my words.

ISAIAH 28:23

Have you ever noticed how noise fills our lives? We wake to music or alarms. We get in the car, and what's the first thing many people do? Slip in a CD or turn on the radio. When we walk in the house or a hotel room, the first thing many of us do is turn on the TV. It seems that with noise, we just don't feel so alone.

In the midst of all of this noise, are you missing the most important voice of all?

God still speaks in a still, small voice. In the busyness and noisiness of our lives, it's easy to miss Him. The only way to hear Him is to make an intentional effort to quiet the noise of our life and spend some time listening, through prayer and reading His Word. You will never get a more important phone call or text message.

Find some time each day to be alone and quiet, and listen to the most important voice of all. It will enrich your life tremendously.

Ark of the Covenant

*The grass withers and the flowers fall, but the
word of our God stands forever.*

ISAIAH 40:8 NIV

To me, the best of the Indiana Jones movies is the first one, *Raiders of the Lost Ark*. Indy is an archaeologist who follows trails and clues, allowing him to snatch the ark of the covenant from, of all people, Nazis. The movie closes with a plain box containing the ark being stacked among thousands of other anonymous boxes in a giant government warehouse, presumably to be lost for a few thousand more years.

Except for the snakes—I do hate snakes—this was a great movie. Unfortunately, its premise is all Hollywood. The ark of the covenant is not lost; it was destroyed thousands of years ago. The Jewish temple that held the ark was destroyed twice: first by the Babylonians in 586 BC and then in AD 70 by the Romans. It is really just dust now.

So, if the ark represented the presence of God to the people of Israel, why would God let it be destroyed? Perhaps God allowed this because He knew that if we had it, with the two tablets of the Ten Commandments inside, we might make it an idol and worship it. But mainly, God allowed it because when we trust Christ as Savior and Lord, we can have the presence of God within us at all times. That presence is called the Holy Spirit.

Finding Jesus is a whole lot better than finding the lost ark.

But Wait, There's More!

"You have heard that the ancients were told, 'You shall not commit murder' and 'Whoever commits murder shall be liable to the court.' But I say to you that everyone who is angry with his brother shall be guilty before the court; and whoever says to his brother, 'You good-for-nothing!' shall be guilty before the supreme court; and whoever says, 'You fool,' shall be guilty enough to go into the fiery hell."

MATTHEW 5:21–22

When reading the Ten Commandments, God seems to be quite clear. For example, He tells us that we shouldn't murder. Most of us breathe a sigh of relief on this one, knowing we've never actually killed anyone. However, Jesus has raised the bar. He explains how God's standards are even higher than man's. In fact, not only is murder a sin, but thinking about it is also!

Jesus tells us that God weighs whether or not our hearts and our thoughts are in line. If we lose our cool with our families, friends, or coworkers and start calling them names, we're in danger of hell because we have broken this commandment on murder! That may seem unfair, but Jesus is clear. God doesn't just judge us by our actions, but by our thoughts and hearts' desires.

Now who among us can pass that test? None of us. Fortunately, Jesus has paid your penalty. Once you turn your life over to Him, He gives you His priceless gift of forgiveness. Jesus' teaching on the Ten Commandments reminds us that we all are in need of a Savior.

Keep Your Eyes on the Goal

[Jesus] said ... "Follow Me."

MATTHEW 4:19

Walking through freshly fallen snow, a father wanted to teach his son a key lesson in life. He said, "Son, I'm going to walk to that tree fifty feet ahead in a perfectly straight line. Then I want you to do the same."

The father walked to the tree. He turned to look at his son, and they both observed the perfectly straight tracks in the snow. Not wanting to fail the test, the son looked at his father and began to walk. He looked down at his steps, wobbled in the snow, and veered to the left. He looked up and corrected his course. He looked down again. He veered to the right and had to correct his course once more.

Arriving at the tree, his tracks told the story of his failure.

His father explained, "Son, as long as you focused on me, your tracks were straight. The moment you took your eyes off me, you got off track. The key is keeping your eyes on the goal."

So it is in life. There is one primary goal, and if it becomes the heart and focus of your life, it will be the key to eternal success. That goal is following Jesus. Keep your eyes on Him, and He will keep you right on track to where you need to go.

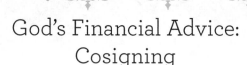

God's Financial Advice: Cosigning

A man lacking in judgment strikes hands in pledge and puts up security for his neighbor.

PROVERBS 17:18 NIV

After winning the Super Bowl, Washington Redskins coach Joe Gibbs had a lot of money to invest. Some friends approached him about an investment that looked like a great opportunity. He didn't have to put up that much; primarily he was just cosigning for the friends. But the economy soon soured, and his friends were broke. The debt fell to him. Although Gibbs was advised to declare bankruptcy, he believed the honorable thing to do was to pay his debts. For more than four years his family lived on basic necessities, using every spare dollar to pay off the debt.[22]

Thus the danger of cosigning. Now, there are times you want to help another and are willing to take the risk. A typical example is helping a grown child buy a new home. But realize the risk and only cosign if you are able and willing to pay the full debt yourself, because that may happen.

We have seen that in the parent-child relationship in churches. When our church built its first facility, we were so new that no bank would make the loan. But our parent church cosigned the note. It was their good faith in us and in kingdom business that motivated their actions. They were willing to pay the note if we failed. Thankfully, we paid it in full.

The Bible gives wise advice in financial matters such as cosigning.

God's Financial Advice: Contentment Versus Want

I've learned by now to be quite content whatever my circumstances. I'm just as happy with little as with much, with much as with little. I've found the recipe for being happy whether full or hungry, hands full or hands empty.

PHILIPPIANS 4:11–12 MSG

Howard Dayton tells of an American company that built a plant in Central America because of the inexpensive labor. Everything went well; they built the plant and hired excellent employees. Then they had their first payday, and everyone was very happy. But a strange thing happened the rest of that week— nobody showed up for work! Management was bewildered and went to the village leader for an explanation. "Well, now we've got all we need. Why should we come back to work?" So management devised a powerful game plan. They sent each employee a four-color mail-order catalog. And all the workers immediately showed back up for work.[23]

We understand that mind-set in American culture. In his excellent book *The Debt Squeeze*, Ron Blue says, "[Banks and retailers know that] merely putting a credit card in a potential user's hand will lead the person to spend 34 percent more [than if they paid cash]."[24] That says a lot about learning to live within our means. A key to this learning is to be content with what you have and not purchasing what you can't afford! Our nation has been learning this the hard way.

Riddled with Guilt

Wash me thoroughly from my iniquity and
cleanse me from my sin. For I know my
transgressions, and my sin is ever before me.

P**SALM** 51:2–3

Are you riddled with guilt?

You need to be free from guilt, for it saps you physically, emotionally, and spiritually. When it comes to guilt, the best way to avoid it is simply to do what is right.

When you don't, you first need to confess your sin to God with a genuine desire to get things right. I promise that when you pursue the forgiveness of God through Jesus Christ, with an attitude of seeking to make things right, it will free you of guilt. He wipes the slate clean.

Second, seek forgiveness from those whom you've wronged. Make restitution.

Third, forgive yourself. This may be the greatest struggle, but when God has forgiven you, you can forgive yourself.

Fourth, don't confuse forgiveness with the removal of consequences. God forgives immediately, but you have to deal with the consequences of your sin.

The good news is, you can be free of guilt when you seek to get things right—God's way.

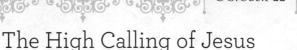

The High Calling of Jesus

"He who has found his life will lose it, and he who has lost his life for My sake will find it."

MATTHEW 10:39

Jesus said, "The only way you really can *find* your life is to be willing to *lose* your life." This statement is one of the paradoxes of meaningful living. What did Jesus mean? How can we find our lives if we lose them? We'd be dead. Now settle down—it's about dying, but not dying physically. *What?*

Think about it this way. How are most people trying to discover their ultimate meaning? Some by achievement; others through education. Many see it through experience; others through relationships. Still others see it through acts of pleasure. Yet the reality of Christ's teaching is a paradox. Until you're willing to lose all of this, let go of it as a source of ultimate meaning, you'll never find yourself. It's about letting go of your priorities, your desires, and your interests to follow Christ's priorities.

So have you made that decision? Are you willing to lose your priorities for Christ's? Yes, it's a paradox, but the only way to really win is to lose your life for Jesus.

There Are No Good Cover-Ups

*If we confess our sins, He is faithful and
righteous to forgive us our sins and to cleanse us
from all unrighteousness.*

1 JOHN 1:9

A great lesson to be learned from scandals is that it's often not the initial act that destroys you; it's the cover-up. David and Bathsheba give a perfect example. First the sin was committed—adultery. Then Bathsheba became pregnant, so David devised a brilliant cover-up. He sent for Uriah, Bathsheba's husband, to be brought home from the battlefield to spend a few days with his wife. David figured that everybody would assume the child was Uriah's. But Uriah didn't cooperate. Since his fellow soldiers were out on the battlefield, he thought it wrong for him to enjoy the pleasures of marriage. So he slept outdoors rather than with his wife.

David's approach to the cover-up wasn't working, so he became more desperate. He ordered that Uriah be killed on the battlefield. Then he quickly married his wife. David was guilty of breaking a whole boatload of commandments: coveting another man's wife, stealing, false witness, adultery, and murder. He stupidly felt his cover-up would work. The only problem was that God knows all. No sin can be covered up from Him.

When you commit a sin, recognize that the jig is up. God knows what happened. Confess your sin, ask forgiveness, and be willing to live with the consequences. God will forgive, but He won't remove the consequences.

Secrets of Fishermen

"Come, follow me," Jesus said,
"and I will make you fishers of men."

MATTHEW 4:19 NIV

Jesus promised His disciples, "I will make you fishers of men." What a wonderful description of their calling. He equated their previous profession with their new role. They would be able to use their knowledge to become experts in this new calling.

What does fishing have to do with leading people to Christ? Consider these skills of good fishermen:

+ *First, they've got the right equipment.* In fishing for men, we have the Bible.
+ *Second, they go where the fish are.* So many Christians live in "holy huddles." All those Bible studies, all that learning how to share your faith, and yet so little time building relationships with nonbelievers.
+ *Third, they know when to use the right bait.* Fish respond differently to different bait, just as people have different interests and needs. You must learn what those needs are and seek to help meet them.
+ *Fourth, they know how to reel them in.* In business, we call this "closing the deal." At some point in your witnessing, you need to call for the decision. The most exciting point in your witness is when that person decides whether or not to follow Jesus. It's a key in becoming a "fisher of men"!

Building a Relationship

Immediately they left their nets and followed Him.

MATTHEW 4:20

Frankly, this verse has always disturbed me. Although it introduces us to two amazing men, Peter and Andrew, whom Jesus transformed from fishermen to fishers of men, I can't get my mind around the scenario in the twenty-first century. Imagine a stranger walking up to you while you are working. You don't know this man, but He says, "Follow Me." And it means giving up all that's familiar in your life to follow Him. Yes, He's dynamic and charismatic. But dropping everything and blindly following Him? I just can't identify with that.

Fortunately, it didn't happen that way. Look at Scripture in light of Scripture. Before this, Andrew and Peter were introduced to Jesus and spent a day listening and talking to Him (John 1:35–42). Then they heard Him preach. They even saw that Jesus knew a whole lot more about fishing than they did (Luke 5:1–11). And they began to be convicted of their sins. Soon after that, Jesus approached them and said, "Follow Me, and I will make you fishers of men." At that point, they were ready to drop everything and follow Jesus (Matthew 4:18–20).

No, they didn't blindly follow Jesus. They had seen and heard enough to believe He was the Man. If you take the time to get to know Jesus through His Word, you will want to follow Him too. If you do, your life will never be the same!

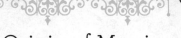

Origin of Marriage

*Because of immoralities, each man is to have his own
wife, and each woman is to have her own husband.*

1 CORINTHIANS 7:2

A hot topic in the news these days is marriage—or should we say a redefinition of marriage? In every culture for thousands of years, marriage has been defined as a lifetime commitment between a man and a woman. The only exception has been polygamy.

Never, though, has marriage been defined as a same-sex union. Now, in the twenty-first century, some so-called enlightened men and women have decided that society and laws should be changed to redefine marriage.

The idea of marriage originated with God when He created man and woman. In its origin, marriage was intended to be between one man and one woman. God's Word gives two reasons for the ideal: companionship and procreation. You can read more about it in Genesis 1–2, the first two chapters of the Bible. Thus began the family as God intended. Has twenty-first-century humanity become so arrogant and selfish that we have suddenly decided we can redefine what God has ordained? I hope not, yet many have. Let's stick with the definition of marriage that's from the Originator of marriage.

Notice: This Is When the World Will End

"This gospel of the kingdom shall be preached in the whole world as a testimony to all the nations, and then the end will come."

MATTHEW 24:14

The speculation has continued for almost two thousand years now . . . when will Christ return? Jesus was clear. No one knows the exact date. But the Bible does give us some guidance. For instance, Jesus tells us that the end will occur after "all the nations" have heard the gospel.

What is the gospel? The gospel is the good news that Christ died for our sins because our sins separated us from God. It is also that Christ rose from the dead to conquer sin and death. So shall we, when we come to receive salvation through faith in Christ.

Jesus also spoke about "nations." The Greek word for *nations* (*ethnos*) does not mean the nations you see on a map. *Ethnos* refers to all the *people groups* on earth. And since all kinds of people groups have not yet been exposed to the gospel, the mission of the church is not yet complete.

But in the twenty-first century, with many modern means of communication and travel, there is the possibility of taking the gospel to every "people group" on earth. At some point, when that mission is accomplished and the church's work is done, the end of this age will come. Christ will return, and finally His will will be done on earth as it is in heaven.

Thanks

As he was going into a village, ten men who had leprosy met him. They stood at a distance and called out in a loud voice, "Jesus, Master, have pity on us!" When he saw them, he said, "Go, show yourselves to the priests." And as they went, they were cleansed. One of them, when he saw he was healed, came back, praising God in a loud voice. He threw himself at Jesus' feet and thanked him. . . . Jesus asked, "Were not all ten cleansed? Where are the other nine?"

LUKE 17:12–17 NIV

One foggy night, many years ago, there was a near tragedy on a large lake. A lot of intoxicated people were on a houseboat when an explosion occurred. It was utter chaos. Fortunately, a resident on the shore saw what was happening. He swam out and directed the panicked people toward the shore. And miraculously, even though many could have drowned, everyone survived.

Later that night, after all the victims and emergency workers had left, the rescuer sat by the fire, talking to a lone reporter. As the interview ended, the reporter asked, "Is there anything else you might like to share about this experience?" The man sat there a moment. Then he looked at the reporter and said, "Yeah. Not one person said thanks. Not one."

One interesting aspect of human nature is that when we find ourselves in a desperate situation, we cry out to God for His help. Even skeptics pray when facing a life-threatening experience.

Then, when God answers and helps us, we often forget to say thanks. Take time to thank God and others. Everyone likes to be thanked—even Jesus.

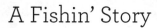

A Fishin' Story

*But when Simon Peter saw that, he fell down at Jesus' feet,
saying, "Go away from me Lord, for I am a sinful man!" For
amazement had seized him and all his companions
because of the catch of fish which they had taken.*

LUKE 5:8–9

On a trip to Israel, I had a chance to see a large first-century fishing boat that was about twenty-six feet long and seven feet wide. Simon Peter had a boat like this one, and Jesus miraculously caused it to be filled with so many fish that when Simon called for his partners to help, the weight of the fish started to make both boats sink! Anybody who's been in the fishing business around the Sea of Galilee knows that this really was some kind of miracle!

Simon Peter responded, "Go away from me Lord, for I am a sinful man!" (Luke 5:8). Jesus had given this fisherman the biggest day of profit in his life. But He'd also shown a power over nature that Peter knew was supernatural. And Peter became convicted of his sin.

Many of you know Jesus is the Messiah and believe He's the Christ. But some of you have never become a Christian because you've never gone through this experience of really seeing Jesus. You haven't seen how great He is. You have not experienced Jesus to the point that you become convicted of your sinfulness. Without this conviction, we don't really understand what it means to be a Christian because we don't understand the meaning of God's grace—undeserved salvation.

This Is the Day; This Is the Time

"For God so loved the world that he gave his one and only Son, that whoever believes in him shall not perish but have eternal life."

JOHN 3:16 NIV

Something is on my mind today, and I feel I must share it with you. My friends, some of you have never made the decision to follow Jesus. I want you to know that everyone who has been reading this daily devotional has been introduced to Jesus. Just by your presence here, just by reading this today, you have been introduced to Jesus. Realize that Jesus has been reaching out to you, long before you've reached out to Him. Jesus is speaking to you at this moment, and it is time for you to respond, regardless of the newness of your acquaintance.

As I mentioned yesterday, many of you know a lot about Jesus. You've come to understand more about Jesus, and yet you've still been hesitant to step out in faith and follow Him as your Savior and Lord. I assure you, He's trustworthy. He's one you want to follow. He knows where He's going. He'll get you to where you need to go—ultimately, heaven. If you've been reluctant to follow Jesus, let today be the day that you step out in faith and decide to follow Him, knowing that Christ has great plans for your life. He sees more potential in you than anybody on this earth does. You don't want to miss out on your eternal destiny. I encourage you—choose to accept the call to follow Jesus. Today.

Laziness Versus Workaholism

Six days you shall labor and do all your work, but the seventh day is a sabbath of the LORD your God.

EXODUS 20:9–10

There are two common problems when it comes to work. One is laziness. We live in a society that sometimes views the irresponsible—those who won't work—as victims. This is insulting to those who are truly unable to work. God's Word is clear: laziness is not good. God wants us to work hard.

At the other extreme is workaholism, and there are four common traits of the workaholic:

+ Tends to be the first person at the office and the last to leave.
+ Tries to please others, and has a tough time saying no.
+ Tends to talk only about work.
+ Feels guilty taking a day off.

Neither workaholism nor laziness is God's intention. The right balance is working hard to please God yet taking time to back away and rest. Take a weekly Sabbath. It is one of God's great ideas for successful living. When we do, we find ourselves refreshed and ready to give our best to our work.

November

They shall eagerly utter the memory of Your abundant goodness and will shout joyfully of Your righteousness.

Psalm 145:7

Legislating Morality

"You shall not murder. You shall not commit adultery.
You shall not steal. You shall not bear false witness
against your neighbor. You shall not covet . . . anything
that belongs to your neighbor."

Exodus 20:13–17

How many times have Christians been told, "You can't legislate morality"? Although it is true that we cannot force anyone to believe in moral principles, we certainly can call for laws to protect the innocent, the weak, and the most basic human rights. For instance, shouldn't there be laws against rape? Or against stealing? Or how about laws against prostitution, narcotics, and child pornography? Of course there should be, and there are, but don't these laws legislate morality?

Understand this: legislatures make laws. That's what they do. And all those laws are based on somebody's view of morality. Laws are passed to try to protect people from being taken advantage of, abused, mistreated, or even killed. So anyone who declares that we can't let Christians influence our moral beliefs is speaking not only bigotry about Christian influence but also stupidity about why all laws are made. All societies base their laws on someone's view of morality. To exclude Christian moral belief is not only naive but closed-minded and prejudiced.

True morality comes from God. We are made in His image, and unlike every other creation, man has a sense of morality. In that light, I ask: can you find a higher sense of morality than Jesus and His Word?

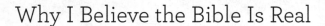

Why I Believe the Bible Is Real

*All Scripture is God-breathed and is useful for
teaching, rebuking, correcting and training in
righteousness, so that the man of God may be
thoroughly equipped for every good work.*

2 TIMOTHY 3:16–17 NIV

Why do I believe so deeply that the Bible is the Word of God?
Let me share with you some of the most meaningful reasons.

- The phrase "Thus saith the Lord" appears more than two
  thousand times in the Old Testament. God was
  speaking!
- The Bible was written more than sixteen hundred years
  ago by about forty different writers, and there is but a
  single theme and author (the Lord). Though at first read
  some things look contradictory, when we accept Christ,
  the Holy Spirit gives us understanding of how it all fits
  together. No group of mortals could possibly produce
  such a book.
- You can study a passage you've known all your life, and
  the Holy Spirit will suddenly give you fresh insight.
  There is an inexhaustible richness in the Scripture that is
  unlike any other book!
- The Bible applies to any race, any tribe, any ethnic
  group, and any age group in any time. Its application is
  universal!

Reason for Living

He who began a good work in you will perfect
it until the day of Christ Jesus.

PHILIPPIANS 1:6

Most everyone is interested in discovering his or her purpose for living—the reason for being born and for existing.

Well, I have good news. God put that desire within you. For as your Creator, He has a purpose and plan for your life. Your role is to discover it and use the gifts, talents, and opportunities that God has given you to make the most of your life. God's ultimate purpose is that everyone would have a personal relationship with Him. And everyone can—through faith in Jesus Christ.

There is more good news. God's Word says in Philippians 1:6, "He who began a good work in you will perfect it until the day of Christ Jesus."

What a promise! Once we put our life and trust in God, He promises us that He'll begin to reveal our life purpose to us. He'll also provide the power needed to see that we get it done. So what are you waiting for? It's time to discover your reason for living and live it out.

Getting Along with Those In-Laws

Your people shall be my people.

RUTH 1:16

Perhaps the relationship people struggle with most is getting along with those in-laws. In-laws are the gift we received in marriage—a gift many want to give back.

Even in healthy in-law relationships there will be tensions and challenges. You and your in-laws both love the same person, and the only reason you're attached is because of that person. That can mean competing interests. In-laws can be made to feel like outlaws. They get to be the brunt of many a tale—especially mothers-in-law—the universal catchall of abusive humor.

Rather than offering advice on the in-law relationship, I offer four stories in Scripture. For a healthy in-law relationship, read about Moses and his father-in-law in Exodus 18, or Ruth and her mother-in-law in the book of Ruth. And if you think you've got it bad, take comfort—it could be a lot worse! Read about Jacob and his father-in-law, beginning in Genesis 29, or David and the all-time worst in-law, King Saul, in 1 Samuel. The good stories inspire us, and the bad stories make us think, *I ain't got it so bad.*

The Disillusionment of Sin

*By this deed you have given occasion to the
enemies of the LORD to blaspheme.*

2 SAMUEL 12:14

David had committed a horrible succession of sins. When Nathan, the prophet, confronted him about them, David finally confessed and sought the Lord's forgiveness. God did forgive him, but the serious consequences remained. Israel's enemies would now be making fun of God. David's actions had been so alien to the Lord's teachings that he was causing God to be ridiculed. "After all," they would say, "if this man of God, who is supposed to be a good man, is your king and he acts like this—committing adultery, murdering a woman's husband, and then marrying the woman—hey! Y'all are no different from us!"

All of us have been around ministries when a spiritual leader has fallen into sin, and we know the disillusionment that occurs within the ministry. But we also know the mocking outside the body of Christ. "He's supposed to be a man of God! He's no different from me or anybody else!" And that is yet another negative consequence for sin in a Christian's life.

Pray for your spiritual leaders. Pray for your government leaders. Pray for those in authority over you because their sins have terrible repercussions for the lives of many. Pray that they will do right and spare us all the disillusionment.

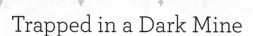

Trapped in a Dark Mine

Jesus said to him, "I am the way, and the truth, and the life; no one comes to the Father but through Me."

JOHN 14:6

In 2010, thirty-three Chilean coal miners were trapped in a small, dark underground area, in what was really nothing more than a large air bubble. For a while, it appeared to be another tragic news story with an inevitable ending. But after sixty-nine days, the world received news that all thirty-three miners had been rescued and brought to the surface through a narrow tube, one miner at a time.

In many ways, that story is a parable of the gospel of Jesus Christ. All of us are trapped by sin at birth. We live in spiritual darkness. The only hope we have of escaping an eternity of death, doom, and darkness is through Jesus Christ. He came down to earth to save us.

What if one of the miners had said, "I really appreciate all those folks have gone through to get us out, but I'm a tough, strong, dedicated miner. You guys can go up through that tube if you want to, but I'm gonna try to make it out on my own." What would you think of the miner who said that? You'd think he was an idiot . . . and he would have been! Unfortunately, that's exactly how many folks respond to the good news of Jesus Christ. They really believe that one way or another, they'll make it to heaven on their own. Yet there is only one way—through Jesus.

No matter how strong, independent, and successful you are, if Christ tells the truth, He is our only hope of salvation. There is only one way out of escaping doom.

The Slippery Slope

Let us examine our ways and test them,
and let us return to the LORD.

LAMENTATIONS 3:40 NIV

Think about the consequences of legalizing gay marriage. What doors have now opened? If marriage is redefined to include same-sex relationships, how in the name of justice can you not allow marriage for other types of relationships? Like polygamy, or marriage between immediate family members. How could anybody object if marriage is redefined to allow any relationship between consenting adults? And in regard to polygamy, doesn't the concept of "equal justice under the law" now require that we accommodate *all* religious beliefs? Because the Koran allows four wives, banning polygamy is certainly anti-Muslim. And in a culture that worships multiculturalism, we sure don't want to be discriminatory.

You are probably thinking, *You're being silly. Nothing like that could ever happen in this country.* Let me ask you a question. In 1960, could you have imagined someone declaring, "Someday same-sex marriages will be legalized"? After all, that had never happened in any nation in history! But there has been a dramatic social change in the past thirty to forty years, with societies embracing so-called tolerance and reversing their traditional moral beliefs. For example, abortions are now routine, and homosexual marriage is now legal in many countries and states. God's Word is clear that this is wrong. It's putting us on a slippery slope toward moral chaos.

Picking Sides

What, then, shall we say in response to this?
If God is for us, who can be against us?

ROMANS 8:31 NIV

People often ask me whom they should vote for. As a citizen, I have my opinions. Yet early in my ministry, I decided it was best that I not endorse candidates. My higher calling is to share Christ with all men—no matter what their political persuasion.

But I do have some thoughts on how you can select candidates to support.

1. Ask, "Are they competent and qualified?" It's great if my doctor and my airline pilot are Christians, but I also want them to be capable of doing their jobs well.
2. Ask yourself where the candidates stand on moral issues the Bible addresses. I love Abe Lincoln's words about choosing the right candidate: "My concern is not whether God is on our side; my greatest concern is, are we on God's side?"
3. Ask yourself, "Are they trustworthy? Do their actions back up their words? Do they have integrity?"
4. Most of all, pray for God's wisdom on how to vote; and if you are a Christian, be a good citizen by voting—always!

True Financial Security

*Tell those rich in this world's wealth to quit being so full
of themselves and so obsessed with money, which is
here today and gone tomorrow. Tell them to go after
God, who piles on all the riches we could ever manage.*

1 Timothy 6:17 msg

If you are wealthy—which God defines as having more than the absolute necessities—don't adopt the hyperspiritual mind-set that material things are bad. That is just not biblical! God wants us to enjoy the wealth He has blessed us with and to use this wealth wisely. But God also reminds us that we should not shift our faith in Him to seeking security through our acquisition of *things*. He wants you to trust that He will continue to meet your future needs. He will continue to give you those blessings. Don't shift your need for security from God's hands to trusting in your financial portfolio, or your bank account, or your accumulation of real estate. All those *things* can be easily lost and offer no real security. The very God who brought you those blessings can take them all away. But He does promise He'll never leave you and will meet all your needs.

Put your trust in a God who will never let you down. He is the only way to have true financial security.

Our Role in the Harvest

*"Therefore beseech the Lord of the harvest to
send out workers into His harvest."*

MATTHEW 9:38

How did the Lord suggest we gather plenty of workers to do His work on earth? He simply told His followers to pray to the Lord of the harvest to send out harvesters to share their faith in Jesus Christ with people who don't know Him personally. Prayer is the starting point.

Now, some of you are thinking, *Thank goodness! I'm off the hook! I just have to pray about it! I don't have to get involved, serve, and take part in the harvest. I'll just pray!* Does Jesus let us off so lightly? Not really. Jesus knows that when we begin to pray for harvesters, the scales will be removed from our eyes. He begins to reveal the world He sees. Then we'll begin to see the people around us as He sees them. The Holy Spirit then convicts us to love them and pray for them to come to know Him. Over time God may use *us* to be the harvesters.

So when you begin to pray for the harvest, beware! God will open your eyes, and you'll be conscious of the needs all around you. He'll transform your heart into the heart of a harvester.

How God Measures a Man

*For God sees not as man sees, for man looks at the outward
appearance, but the LORD looks at the heart.*

1 SAMUEL 16:7

How do you measure the worth of other people? Is it by their wealth, their position, their fame, their looks, their education, or their success?

I don't know how you would answer that question, but I can tell you how God measures the worth of a person. God's Word says, "God sees not as man sees, for man looks at the outward appearance, but the LORD looks at the heart."

The heart speaks of a person's character, courage, and spirit. So often when we measure the worth of a person we just look at the outward appearance, but God looks at the inside.

If that's the case, how does He measure you? If you had a heart exam today, what kind of heart would God find? The good news is this: God has given us a way to have a new heart, and it's found through faith in Jesus Christ.

It's an interesting insight into life that when we begin to have the right heart through Christ, we begin to measure the worth of others God's way.

Your First Priority

God is faithful, through whom you were called into
fellowship with His Son, Jesus Christ our Lord.

1 CORINTHIANS 1:9

Let me clear up a big misunderstanding among many Christians—that when you become a Christian, your main calling is to reach people for Christ. That is *not* the main calling. The main calling when you become a Christian is to follow Jesus. It's a calling to a relationship, to submit your life to Christ and His authority. In that process of following Him, He will teach you what He wants you to do, which is to reach people for Jesus Christ. Don't get it backward! It begins with a focus on the relationship with Christ.

How do we build that relationship? We have to make some decisions:

1. *Decide Jesus is trustworthy.* When you understand what He has done—dying on the cross for us—you will certainly see that He is dependable.
2. *Decide that He knows where He is going and how to get you there.* Yes, He's the only route to heaven.
3. *Decide to leave a life you are familiar with and move into the unknown.* This decision means moving from your comfort zone and being willing to go with Him, wherever He leads.
4. *Decide to stay with Him.* You must remain close to Him.
5. *Decide to stay focused on Him.* And you've got to be willing to go at His pace in fulfilling God's will for your life.

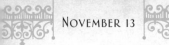

Do You Need a Shepherd?

From Psalm 23 (kjv)

All through the ages, Psalm 23 has been a favorite psalm. Every line is rich with meaning.

The Lord is my shepherd; I shall not want. Trust Christ as your Good Shepherd—He promises to meet our needs.

He maketh me to lie down in green pastures. He gives us rest and spiritual nourishment.

He leadeth me beside the still waters. He calms our troubled souls.

He restoreth my soul. He renews our spirits when we spend time with Him.

He leadeth me in the paths of righteousness for his name's sake. His Word teaches us how to live right.

Yea, though I walk through the valley of the shadow of death, I will fear no evil. He overcomes our fears, even of death.

For thou art with me; thy rod and thy staff they comfort me. He's always with us to discipline and encourage. This makes us feel secure.

Thou preparest a table before me in the presence of mine enemies. He gives us strength with those who aren't for us.

Thou anointest my head with oil; my cup runneth over. He gives us an abundance of blessings.

Surely goodness and mercy shall follow me all the days of my life. Daily, He reminds us of His love and forgiveness.

And I will dwell in the house of the Lord forever. He provides us eternal, abundant life.

Getting the Order Right

Straightening up, Jesus said to her, "Woman, where are [your accusers]? Did no one condemn you?" She said, "No one, Lord." And Jesus said, "I do not condemn you, either. Go. From now on, sin no more."

JOHN 8:10–11

The religious leaders caught a woman in the very act of adultery and brought her before Jesus to see what He would say. She was just a pawn in their desire to discredit Jesus. His response stunned them. Notice the order of Christ's words. Even though she deserved to die according to the law, Jesus said, "I do not condemn you," and then He told her to "sin no more."

Sometimes the church gets this backward. We say, "Look, if you're willing to change your life, *then* you can experience the love of Christ. Change your life first, and then you can be welcomed here." But Jesus is saying, "I've forgiven you; now change your life." When someone realizes that he has literally been saved from the penalty of his sin, his life will never be the same.

Our responsibility is to reach out to those who are broken and in need of a Savior. When someone trusts her life to Christ, her life is made new. A new life means a changed life. The labels are gone. The shame is gone. The guilt is gone. She is a new creation. And in gratitude for this incredible gift, there is an inner desire to change and live in a way that pleases God.

Storms of Life

*"But everyone who hears these words of mine and
does not put them into practice is like a foolish man
who built his house on sand."*

MATTHEW 7:26 NIV

Are you ready for the storms of life? Maybe you're currently in a life storm or have recently endured one. One thing's for sure: storms come to us all. The loss of a job, the death of a spouse, or the doctor's words "You've got cancer" are all storms. When we live life, storms come.

Jesus told a story about two men. One man built his house on the sand. The winds and the rains came, and his house fell in. Another built his house on the rock, and the winds and the rains came, but it withstood the storm. The key difference was in the foundation. The greatest foundation for withstanding the storms of life is the rock of Jesus Christ. A close personal relationship with the Lord builds a solid foundation, and that relationship comes through trusting Him and following Him day by day.

Storms come. Is your foundation secure, built on the rock of Jesus Christ?

The good news is, even if you've been blown away by a storm, it's not too late to start rebuilding on the right foundation.

Visit to the White House

And there is salvation in no one else; for there is no other name under heaven that has been given among men by which we must be saved.

ACTS 4:12

If you were to drive up to the gates of the White House today and tell them you wanted to see the president, do you think they'd let you in? Fat chance for most of us. But let me tell you about a friend of mine who was invited to the White House by President Ford's son when Ford was in office. He said it was amazing.

They came to the White House gates, and guards waved them through. They entered the White House with no one stopping them. They even walked right into the Oval Office unhindered. President Ford stood up and welcomed his son, then looked my friend in the eye and said, "Any friend of my son is welcome here."

That's exactly how it will be getting into heaven. The only way we'll have access is by knowing God's Son. Otherwise, it will be more futile than trying to get into the White House without the right credentials.

Do you know God's Son personally? He really is the key for entrance into heaven.

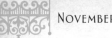

The Busiest Man Who Ever Lived

Immediately Jesus made his disciples get into the boat and go on ahead of him to Bethsaida, while he dismissed the crowd. After leaving them, he went up on a mountainside to pray.

MARK 6:45–46 NIV

He was exhausted, completely worn out from dealing with people and their problems. What He needed was a rest. He got away to spend some time alone with God. When He did, His spirit was renewed and refreshed. When the crowds came, He was able to respond, to care for them and meet their needs.

His name was Jesus Christ, and He was the busiest man who ever lived. He accomplished more than anyone did before or since His time here on earth.

We live in a very fast-paced world with great demands on our time, yet no one has ever been busier than Jesus when He walked on this earth. Why not learn from Him when you're frazzled, exhausted, and burned out. Take some time to be with God. If Jesus needed time alone with God, surely we do as well.

Friends

A friend loves at all times, and a brother
is born for adversity.

PROVERBS 17:17 NIV

What is your definition of true friendship?

Ralph Waldo Emerson said, "Happy is the house that shelters a friend," and, "A friend is a person with whom I may be sincere and before him I may think aloud.... The only way to have a friend is to be one."

Walter Winchell defines a friend as "one who walks in when others walk out."

Someone else has said that a friend is "a man who laughs at your funny stories, even when they ain't so good, and sympathizes with your misfortunes, even when they ain't so bad."

Do you have a friend? Do you know true friendship?

Many, I'm sad to say, would have to answer no. The good news is this: you can have a best friend forever. That friend is Jesus Christ. I encourage you to get to know Him. You'll never be disappointed. He'll always be there with you.

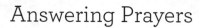

Answering Prayers

He said, "O LORD, . . . now may it be that the girl to whom I say,
'Please let down your jar so that I may drink,' and who
answers, 'Drink, and I will water your camels also'—may she be
the one whom You have appointed for Your servant Isaac."

GENESIS 24:12–14

Abraham sent his servant on an important mission: to find a wife for his son. Once he reached the faraway land, the servant paused at a well to pray, asking God to show him a remarkable sign. Although not quite in the league with a burning bush, the servant's request was, nonetheless, ambitious. He asked that the bride-to-be reveal herself by volunteering to water all of his camels. Perhaps that does not sound like much of a sign to you, but camels were the SUVs of the ancient world. They could go a long time without water, but when they finally did drink, they could gulp about twenty-five gallons at once. Ten camels, 250 gallons of water, that's a lot of trips to the well. It would take a real miracle for a woman to volunteer for such a task!

But suddenly Rebekah walked up while he was still praying. When he asked for a drink, she agreed and added, "I will draw also for your camels until they have finished drinking" (v. 19). Then she filled the camels' tanks. Yet look at what happened next. "Meanwhile, the man was gazing at her in silence, to know whether the LORD had made his journey successful or not" (v. 21).

Doesn't that sound like us? God answers a prayer so clearly, and still we stand back and wonder if it's just a coincidence. If God answers your prayer, get moving. If He doesn't give you the sign you've asked for, perhaps He is saying no or "wait awhile."

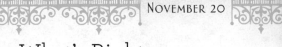

Do What's Right

*You shall do what is right and good
in the sight of the LORD.*

DEUTERONOMY 6:18

Society is caught up in the comparison game, and keeping up with the Joneses seems to be the goal of many. Children compare clothes and curfews. Adults compare cars, vacations, and promotions while smiling and patting each other on the back.

Work and moral ethics may be compromised because "my boss does it" or "the guy at church does it." But you and I both know that doesn't make it right. Too many times we justify our actions because we are comparing ourselves against the wrong measure. God's Word gives us the proper standard; all else will fall short of the goal.

Sometimes life requires us to stand up and be counted. Sometimes we must choose between immediate gratification or denying self. Sometimes we simply must go against the grain because our goal is to please God—not man or even ourselves. In the long run, we will be better people and will be blessed for it. Do what's right.

The Second Coming: Fear or Anticipation?

Just as man is destined to die once, and after that to face judgment, so Christ was sacrificed once to take away the sins of many people; and he will appear a second time, not to bear sin, but to bring salvation to those who are waiting for him.

HEBREWS 9:27–28 NIV

The book of Revelation speaks of some pretty scary images before the return of Jesus Christ. The whole period conjures up scenes of plagues, bowls of wrath, and souls trembling in fear. Rather unsettling, isn't it?

For those who have not accepted Christ, there is a legitimate reason to be fearful of those final days. There's fear that you haven't done enough, because the fact is, you haven't done enough. Unless you have been perfect, you have not done enough. And sure enough, when that time comes and Christ returns, it will be a time of dread and fear because there will be the realization that we deserve the judgment of God.

So why is it that the Christian has no dread of the Rapture? It is because we know that Christ has borne our sins. He has taken upon Himself the judgment we deserve; because of His sacrifice, we will be spared those horrid consequences. Instead of the dread of His return, there is actually a longing for it to happen.

When you think of Christ's second coming, is it with dread or joy? Fear or faith?

The Source of All Blessings for Thanksgiving

Every good gift and every perfect gift is from above,
and cometh down from the Father of lights, with whom
is no variableness, neither shadow of turning.

JAMES 1:17 KJV

In 1674, an Anglican priest wrote a simple song of praise for his students at England's Winchester College. Although the lyrics expressed praise to God for His wonderful blessings, the priest was careful to warn the boys only to sing the hymn in the privacy of their dorm rooms. Why all the subterfuge? At that time the church believed hymns should only include words directly from the Bible. Using your own lyrics was like adding words to Scripture. Blasphemy!

But what beautiful and simple words they were! The hymn shouted its praise to the Source of all our blessings. It announced praise with a joy and passion for all God's glory. Fortunately this hymn, which is today referred to as the Doxology, was soon taken from the shadows and saw its popularity quickly spread. Do you catch the irony here? This hymn, first used in secret, has become the most frequently sung piece of music used in public worship!

Consider singing these joyful words of praise as your Thanksgiving prayer:

Praise God, from whom all blessings flow.
Praise Him, all creatures here below.
Praise Him above, ye heavenly host.
Praise Father, Son, and Holy Ghost! Amen.

Our New Favorite Holiday

Finally, brethren, whatever is true, whatever is honorable,
whatever is right, whatever is pure, whatever is lovely,
whatever is of good repute, if there is any excellence and
if anything worthy of praise, dwell on these things.

PHILIPPIANS 4:8

What is America's favorite holiday? Many will immediately think of Easter, whereas others think of Christmas. Still others might select New Year's Eve. Not even close. Thanksgiving? A favorite, but it's not number one. If you define "favorite" as the day people show the most passion and excitement, many Americans' favorite holiday is Black Friday, the day *after* Thanksgiving. Black Friday gets its name because so much merchandise is sold on that day that retailers literally see their P & L statements move from being in the red to being solidly in the black. But it should be called Black Friday because it exposes the most grotesque, vulgar face of materialism gone wild.

If you want to understand the passion this holiday inspires, watch what happens when stores open their doors at the crack of dawn or earlier. Watch how grown men shove old ladies aside so they can be the first to grab the season's hottest new video game. In New York one year, just a few hours after putting down their Thanksgiving forks, fifty thousand people stood in the rain overnight awaiting the 5:00 a.m. opening of a mall. Fifty thousand people! That's not being smart. It's enslavement.

What's your favorite holiday? Christmas, Easter, Thanksgiving? Those make sense. But Black Friday? Give me a break!

Wanting to Be Rich
Has a Dark Side

*But those who want to get rich fall into temptation and
a snare and many foolish and harmful desires which
plunge men into ruin and destruction.*

1 TIMOTHY 6:9

When a rather selfish TV character was reminded that money doesn't buy happiness, she quickly replied, "Oh, of course it does. That's just something we tell poor people to keep them from rioting." Yet not only does money not buy happiness, but the desire to be rich can also add many complications to your life.

The Bible makes it clear that the desire to be rich brings many new temptations. Like what? It can be the temptation to lie or to steal; to use and even run over other people to get more wealth; or to defraud others to get more wealth. This focus on having more and more money can cause one temptation after another, and we can find ourselves doing things we never thought we'd do. We can make life a mess. When wealth becomes our priority, we forget that what we think we own is actually God's. Victory with money—be it a little or a lot—is using His money in a way that pleases Him.

Wealth earned honestly can be a blessing. It can do a lot of good. But the desire to be rich so we can spend it or hoard it for ourselves can cause us to give in to all sorts of unhealthy temptations. Jesus teaches us to love God—not money. That is the key.

Showing Your Love Through Obedience

"He who has My commandments and keeps them is the one who loves Me; and he who loves Me will be loved by My Father, and I will love him and will disclose Myself to him."

JOHN 14:21

In this verse, is Jesus saying we've got to earn the love of God by being good? Remember, when we study the Word of God, we always want to look at Scripture in light of Scripture. There's no doubt that we are saved by faith alone. But there's also no doubt that the way we prove we are really saved is by how willingly we obey God.

Think about it this way. It's not like God doesn't love bad little boys and girls, because God loves everyone. For instance, as a loving parent, you love your children no matter what they do. If they're bad, you still love them. But when a child consistently obeys you, you appreciate that child even more! Why? Because he or she is saying, "I trust you enough to do what you're asking me to do." Life is better for your children, and for you, when they obey.

It's the same way with God. God loves all of us even when we're bad. But He surely does love it more when we're obedient to Him. Because God knows that when we trust Him, we really do love Him! He appreciates obedience, as any parent would.

Deceit

He is a shield to those who walk in integrity.

PROVERBS 2:7

In the movie *Liar, Liar*, Jim Carrey starred as the profane attorney who was incapable of lying for an entire day after his son made a birthday wish that his dad would stop lying.

Lying has become a pervasive problem. Have you fallen into the habit?

It seems that today's "me-first" mind-set places very little value on honesty and personal integrity. Truth is sacrificed on the altar of self-advancement. At the time, you may think that lying will make your life easier, but one lie almost always requires another and another and another. You have to remember everything you said to keep from confusing your lies.

But when you tell the truth, you don't have to remember what you said. That makes life a lot less complicated!

Which life have you created for yourself?

There's only one way to break the bondage of a lie, and that's with the truth. Seek to live with integrity and honesty, and you'll find a new freedom for living.

How? The truth is found in Jesus Christ. Find Him, and find the truth, the power, and the strength to become a person of integrity.

Bad News/Good News

"The time is fulfilled, and the kingdom of God is at hand; repent and believe in the gospel."

MARK 1:15

The Bible says that Jesus proclaimed the gospel. *Gospel* means "good news"—but there is more. *Gospel* means good news that *follows* bad news. So what's the bad news?

- The bad news is that we're all natural-born sinners. But it gets worse.
- Sin separates us from God. Still, it gets worse.
- If we die separated from God, we'll spend eternity in hell, separated from God. But hold on. It gets even worse.
- The only way to avoid hell by doing good works is by having a life of absolute perfection. Nobody has ever done that—except one. His name is *Jesus*.

Here's where the good news that follows bad news begins:

- God loves us so much that He sent His Son to save us from sin, death, and hell. But it gets better.
- If we admit that our sin has separated us from God and trust Him as our only hope of salvation, we are saved from sin, death, and hell. It gets better still.
- He gives us abundant, eternal life that begins in the here and now the moment we accept salvation through faith.

Now, that's good news that follows mighty bad news!

Tolerance and Diversity

Walk in a manner worthy of the calling with which you have been called, with all humility and gentleness, with patience, showing tolerance for one another in love.

EPHESIANS 4:1–2

If tolerance is the supreme virtue of the politically correct, then isn't there a lot of hypocrisy going on? Why is the tolerance-and-diversity movement so intolerant of biblical Christianity and its values? If diversity is about openness and acceptance of all people, then why do the diversity police seek to force their man-made rules on Christians?

Maybe it is because many people do not understand the true definition of *tolerance*. It means accepting people even if you completely disagree with them and not trying to force them to believe what you believe. Today the definition of *tolerance* has changed to include a requirement to embrace and even affirm values that are immoral because those practicing their self-made values have been discriminated against.

Christianity doesn't try to force anyone to believe in Jesus, but seeks to explain why it is a great way to live and believe. If you are really open-minded and tolerant, I hope you'll consider it. Behind the outward appearances, you'll find the church one of the most diverse groups in the world.

Kindness

But [a] fruit of the spirit is ... kindness.

GALATIANS 5:22

D o you know one character trait that is always appreciated? A biblical proverb tells us: "What is desirable in a man is his kindness" (Proverbs 19:22).

In the movie *The Fugitive*, the character played by Harrison Ford performed several acts of kindness. The fugitive even risked his own life to save the life of a boy who was being neglected in a busy hospital emergency room. The cop obsessed with chasing him began to question whether this fugitive really could have killed his wife. You could just hear the cop thinking, *Cold-blooded killers don't do nice things like this.*

Acts of kindness inspire us, whether it's taking time to help an employee at the office, or defending a person who is being picked on by bullies. The recipients of these acts of kindness are always grateful.

The one person who comes to mind when I think of kindness is Jesus Christ. He shows us that God is kind. And because He is so kind to us, we are to be kind to one another. Especially in a busy world where so many seem to be looking out for number one, acts of kindness are always appreciated.

Here's a Theological Shocker

"Heaven and earth will pass away,
but My words will not pass away."

MATTHEW 24:35

Here is something that may surprise you: heaven—as it is today—is temporary! I know that statement may rattle you, but I'm just quoting Jesus Christ. Listen to what He said in Matthew 24:35: "Heaven and earth will pass away, but My words will not pass away." Christ could not be clearer. Heaven is temporary. Second Peter 3:7 adds insight as to why: "But the heavens and the earth which are now preserved by the same word, are reserved for fire until the day of judgment and perdition of ungodly men" (NKJV).

This does not mean that when you die you don't have eternal life. If you know Christ in this life, you have begun an eternal relationship with Him. And even though heaven, as it is today, is temporary, you do not lose eternal life. Your relationship with Jesus Christ is unending; it can never be lost.

So you may wonder, *How can heaven be temporary?* Well, in Revelation, Christ said that after He returns, the *new* heaven and the *new* earth will be one. So eternal life does not stop when you know Jesus, but heaven as it is now is temporary. As incomprehensibly wonderful as heaven is today, the new heaven will be even greater. Don't miss it!

December

For a child will be born to us, a son will be given to us; and the government will rest on His shoulders; and His name will be called Wonderful Counselor, Mighty God, Eternal Father, Prince of Peace.

Isaiah 9:6

The Most Difficult Question

*Your eyes have seen my unformed substance; and in
Your book were all written the days that were ordained
for me, when as yet there was not one of them.*

PSALM 139:16

As a pastor, there is no more difficult situation than the death of a child. How can I possibly give a satisfactory answer to grieving parents who ask me why?

I know from a human perspective that it is very hard for us to understand when a person dies at an early age. The fact is, none of us knows the number of our days. Only God knows. We live in a fallen world contaminated by sin, and there are all kinds of innocent people who suffer because of that. Not all of us will live that full life of seventy years that Scripture talks about. For some it's a few weeks; for some it's ten years, forty, fifty, even a hundred years. By trusting that God has ordained the number of our days, we can recognize that even when a child goes to heaven—and be absolutely assured that children do go to heaven—we can find comfort in that. Can you imagine heaven without young children? There is an eternal purpose and plan that we are not able to understand completely on this side of heaven, but be assured that God has a perfect plan we will someday understand—in eternity. The key is to trust in God even when it doesn't make sense.

The Incomparable Christ

"All authority has been given to Me
in heaven and on earth."

No person has had more impact on history than Jesus Christ. It is undeniable that He lived and walked in the land of Judea and Israel almost two thousand years ago. But who is He? Colossians 1 tells us:

+ *He is the visible image of the invisible God* (v. 15). He is God in person. You want to know what God is like? Look to Jesus. The fullness of God dwells in Him.
+ *He is the Creator of all creation* (v. 16–17). He holds all creation together. It is His masterpiece. Creation reveals the greatness of God.
+ *He is the head of the church* (v. 18). He is to the church what the head is to the body.
+ *He is the Savior who saves us from our sins* (v. 22). He came to reconcile us with God.

Once you know who He is, you have a choice—a decision to make. It's the biggest one ever—to trust Him as your Savior and Lord or to reject Him. Who is Jesus? The Bible is clear, but the important thing for you is, do you believe it?

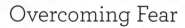
Overcoming Fear

*Immediately He spoke with them and said to them,
"Take courage; it is I, do not be afraid."*

MARK 6:50

To learn courage you have to know fear. Isaac Stern, the great violinist, observing a nine-year-old playing the violin amazingly well, once said, "You can't really tell how an artist will be until the teen years, for that is when fear comes in. Then and only then can you see if the person has courage. You can't learn courage until you know fear." Fear can paralyze us. Finding the courage to overcome it is a real key to successful living.

One day, Jesus' disciples were caught at sea in a storm. They were afraid they wouldn't make it. Jesus walked out to them and said, "Take courage; it is I, do not be afraid."

That's the key to finding courage in the face of fear. It comes through faith in Jesus Christ. Fear and faith do not mix—they're like oil and water. You see, when faith kicks in, fear moves out; and when faith disappears, fear moves in like a tidal wave. The key to finding the courage to overcome fear is faith in Jesus.

The Creator and His Creatures

I will be a Father to Him, and He shall be a Son to Me.

HEBREWS 1:5

One day, a bird became caught in our chimney and flew into our house. I tried desperately to get it out the door, but it didn't get the message. After a while, totally frustrated, I had the ridiculous thought, *If I could become a bird for a few seconds and talk its language, I could show it how to be free.* Then I remembered that God did just that.

The Creator of the universe became one of His own creatures—a man—to communicate perfectly with humankind. Jesus took on a human body and personality, with all its limitations, so you and I could understand how to be free from captivity to sin and have a relationship with God.

This is really what Christmas is all about. God chose to reveal Himself to us in the form of a baby, Jesus Christ. When we get to know the God who loves us so much that He would humble Himself to become a man, then Christmas always has a sense of wonder.

Appreciation

*In everything give thanks; for this is God's
will for you in Christ Jesus.*

1 THESSALONIANS 5:18

Have you ever given a gift or done a favor for someone who didn't express appreciation? It's not much fun and certainly doesn't inspire you to give to that person again. But if we're honest, we all have to admit that we've failed to say thank you at some point.

Think about the people in service positions we encounter daily. Do you thank the folks at the dry cleaners when your shirts are ready when promised? How about saying thanks to the person behind the counter in the fast-food restaurant? Do you express appreciation to the people in your office who answer the phone or process the mail?

All of us like to be appreciated, to hear "thank you" for things we've done well. Why not start today by saying thanks to the people who make your day run more smoothly? While you're at it, don't forget to thank God for all His blessings in your life.

Saying thank you is always appreciated. It sure makes the day a bit brighter.

The Millstone

"Whoever causes one of these little ones who believe to stumble, it would be better for him if, with a heavy millstone hung around his neck, he had been cast into the sea."

MARK 9:42

A millstone was a heavy stone used for grinding grain. It was so heavy a man couldn't pick it up; a donkey would have to pull it. So imagine the depth of Jesus' feelings when He said that it would be better for someone to be cast into the sea with a millstone around his neck than to cause a little one to stumble. If you want to get Christ riled up, then mistreat or mislead a child.

It's also interesting that Jesus talked about little ones not only as children but also as ones who believe, regardless of age. In other words, He was warning any adult who would take advantage of a child in Christ and misguide his or her belief in God.

But also note that "little ones" is more properly translated as "humble ones." Now, that could be an adult who is mentally disabled or physically limited. It could be that Jesus was even referring to new believers who are overjoyed about coming to salvation in Christ and then are misled by a teacher who guides them astray by misinterpreting God's Word. Whomever it is that Jesus was referring to, He was quite clear. For these evil people, an agonizing death is preferable to leading the innocent into sin.

Is Heaven All We Hope For?

The heavens are telling of the glory of God; and their expanse is declaring the work of His hands.

PSALM 19:1

Is heaven all we hope for? Dr. R. G. Lee, one of the twentieth century's greatest preachers, was on his deathbed in a coma when suddenly his eyes opened and he exclaimed to his daughter, "I see heaven." She said, "Tell me about it," to which Rev. Lee replied, "Oh, my sermons never did it justice. I see your mother. I see Jesus. It's so beautiful." One of the past century's greatest preachers couldn't do it justice. Human language is simply inadequate to describe it.

I remember standing at the edge of the Grand Canyon, and for a moment, I stood in awe at the grandeur of the sight. I walk on a quiet beach, and I'm in awe of God's creation. But as magnificent as these are, they are nothing compared to heaven.

Imagine being in the presence of the King of the universe and all who follow Him. What a sight that will be! It will be greater than we can hope or imagine. So don't miss out. The key for getting there is knowing Jesus Christ as your Savior and Lord.

Questioning Your Faith

"Blessed are those who have not seen;
and yet have believed."

Do you sometimes worry about your faith because you find yourself questioning some events in the Scriptures? Let's be honest; seas parting, a fish swallowing a grown man, the turning of water into wine, Jesus walking on water . . . sometimes biblical events can test your capacity for belief. But realize that you are in some pretty good company. Take the claim of the virgin birth. Joseph and Mary could relate!

How did Mary respond when told she was going to birth the Son of God? After the initial shock, she immediately began to question the angel: "How can this be, since I am a virgin?" That angel must have given her a mighty convincing answer, because where Mary initially doubted, she then believed.

But when Mary told Joseph, he didn't buy it for a minute. He knew he wasn't the daddy and immediately made plans to dump her. Once again, it took an angel to convince him that Mary was telling the truth. Joseph doubted, but then believed the word of God through the angel.

So if you find yourself feeling guilty for harboring occasional doubts, relax. You are in good company. There is no sin in doubting. Doubts only become sin when we begin to believe them as fact. We have the written, historical Word of God. So next time you're struggling with doubts, share them with God and ask for His help in working through them.

Nothing Is Impossible

"For nothing is impossible with God."

LUKE 1:37 NIV

Jesus born of a virgin? Many sophisticated minds classify such claims as preposterous. It's classified right alongside other legends and myths. The virgin birth may seem like a tabloid headline: "Teenage Virgin Claims God Is the Father." As we discussed in yesterday's devotion, a virgin birth, like many other supernatural Bible events, does make a good story, but it is often impossible for a rational person to accept.

But realize that if you choose not to believe in the virgin birth, you're going to miss out on the true nature of Jesus Christ. If Jesus had not been born of a virgin, the only conclusion you can draw is that he was just a man—a good man, but just a man. If you reject the virgin birth, you have chosen to believe in a mighty small God. But our God resurrected a man from the dead, so what's the big deal about a virgin birth?

Think about what it means if you do accept the virgin birth. It means you believe what God's Word says: "Nothing is impossible with God." Right now, you may be facing some real trials and struggles in your life and see no possible way to deal with those issues. When you believe in the virgin birth, you can realize that nothing is impossible with God! There is no problem, there is no hardship, there is no difficulty that is too tough for God.

The virgin birth is important to understanding Jesus, and it's important that we face impossible challenges since it reminds us that we have a great and mighty God.

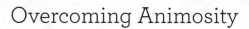

Overcoming Animosity

Never pay back evil for evil to anyone. Respect what is right in the sight of all men. If possible, so far as it depends on you, be at peace with all men.

ROMANS 12:17–18

When Adolph Coors IV was a teenager, a ranch hand murdered his father. For years, this horrible event so unraveled Coors that the bitterness shaped his life. Even his marriage fell victim to it. He was still struggling with it when he came to know Christ.

Two years later, his vision of "serving self through power and personal possessions" had been replaced by "telling God's love story to others." As a result, Adolph went to meet Joseph Corbett, his father's murderer, at the Colorado State Penitentiary. But Mr. Corbett would not see him. In place of a face-to-face meeting, Adolph wrote him a letter asking for his forgiveness "for the hatred that I had been harboring for seventeen years. I told him I had forgiven him. As I walked from the prison, I felt God's love and I was a free man." [25]

Almost immediately, Coors's life began to be transformed. Even his struggling marriage began to be reconciled. God began to bless their lives.

When bitterness takes root, we need the forgiveness of God and the power of God to forgive. This supernatural ability can come through the power of Jesus Christ working in your life.

Christmas Greetings from the Griswalds

*When Jesus spoke again to the people, he said, "I am
the light of the world. Whoever follows me will never
walk in darkness, but will have the light of life."*

JOHN 8:12 NIV

During Christmas season, Anne and I often ride through
nearby neighborhoods, enjoying the Christmas lights. Every
so often we'll come across a truly extravagant display covering the
house and yard and trees, and Anne will say, "Now, that really is
over-the-top there!" And I'll say, "Yeah, bless their hearts." (That's
a Southern gentleman's way of saying, "You know, it really is pitiful, isn't it?") But whatever the case, I've got good news for you
if you're one of those who has all those lights. You see, lights are
an important symbol of the meaning of Christmas. Jesus entered
this world to be the Light in the darkness, and God created the
original light show. After all, the angels appeared to the shepherds,
and whenever angels appear, they often have this dazzling array of
light around them. And then there was the star over Bethlehem
that the wise men were drawn to. What a light!

So the next time you go driving around looking at the lights
of Christmas, remember the coming of Jesus, "the Light of the
world."

God's Clock

With the Lord one day is as a thousand years,
and a thousand years as one day.

2 PETER 3:8 ESV

Have you ever thought about how God doesn't see time as you and I do? The Bible tells us that to God, one day is as a thousand years and a thousand years are as one day. He sees the past, present, and future all at once, for He is over time. That blows my mind. We are so finite. We begin; we end. God always was, is, and will be. Isn't that amazing?

When we get to heaven, there will be no clocks, no calendars—just unlimited time. That unsettles me. Clocks and calendars give order to my life. A place with no time just boggles my mind. But we'll never be tired, and that will be great! Even though God is over time, at the perfect time He became one of us, as a baby boy. He invaded history right on time—BC/AD, it was the zero hour—to show us Himself and save us from sin and offer us eternal life with Him, timeless life. Isn't that amazing? Won't you take time this Christmas to say, "Thank You, God"?

Mary's Response

And Mary said, "Behold, the bondslave of the Lord;
may it be done to me according to your word."

LUKE 1:38

Picture the scene: an angel had just informed Mary that she, a virgin, would become pregnant and would carry the Son of God. Not the sort of news a woman hears every day and certainly not the kind of news a woman in first-century Israel would welcome. She knew she would soon face the wrath and scorn of her family, friends, and society in general—not to mention the man to whom she was engaged!

She could have run away. She could have had an abortion. Or, like many unmarried pregnant women in that time, Mary could have taken her own life. But how did Mary respond? She chose a different path. What she said was, "I am willing to be a voluntary slave of the Lord. I am willing to be a servant of God. What God has said, may it come true!" What a woman! What a true profession of faith! She was truly the greatest woman who ever lived. Nothing any woman has ever done or will do is more important than what Mary did.

When you think of the Child she gave birth to—who He is and what He came to do—will you choose to follow the example of Mary and believe what God's Word says about her Son? You will never truly experience Christmas until you do.

Use It or Lose It

[Scripture gives] you the wisdom that leads to salvation through faith which is in Christ Jesus.

2 Timothy 3:15

I have friends who are learning to speak Spanish. They are struggling with different sounds, different sentence structure, and different words. Acquiring a new skill takes practice and patience. You have heard the cliché: "Use it or lose it." My friends realize that they have to use the few Spanish words they know or they quickly forget them. We must use what we know, or we don't retain knowledge.

This principle applies in the spiritual dimension as well. Faith in God is like a muscle. The more you use it, the stronger it becomes. The manual for getting this muscle in shape is the Bible, and the personal trainer is the Holy Spirit. If you submit yourself to Christ and His leadership and His guidance, you will discover how to use the faith muscle each and every day. It's either use it or lose it.

I hope that you will choose to use it. You will be amazed at how your faith will grow day by day.

Scrooge or Christian This Christmas?

But the fruit of the Spirit is love, joy, peace, patience, kindness, goodness, faithfulness, gentleness and self-control. Against such things there is no law.

GALATIANS 5:22–23 NIV

Scrooge is making a comeback this Christmas, reappearing in many hearts. So, are you more like Scrooge or like a Christian? Let's do some comparison illustrations:

1. Scrooge is stingy and hoards all he can. A Christian is as generous as heaven, which gave up God's Son.
2. Scrooge fears he'll lose it all. A Christian trusts in the Lord for all.
3. Scrooge is haughty to the poor. A Christian loves the poor and helps those in need.
4. Scrooge worships at the Church of Dow Jones while claiming belief in God. A Christian worships the Lord while professing to be a sinner saved by grace.
5. Scrooge resents joy in bad economic times. A Christian feels joy for the good news of Jesus' birth.
6. Scrooge feels entitled to all he's earned. A Christian feels thankful for what he has.
7. Scrooge says, "Bah! Humbug!" to Christmas. A Christian says, "Merry Christmas" because the Savior is born.

Are you a Scrooge or a Christian? What would God say?

The Unearned Gift

*As it is written: "There is no one righteous,
not even one.... For all have sinned and
fall short of the glory of God."*

ROMANS 3:10, 23 NIV

You can't earn your way into heaven. Just can't do it. There is just too much sin in our lives to ever be offset by any good works we may perform. No matter how hard you try, the ledger can never be balanced. The only way to heaven is through the acceptance of Jesus Christ as your Lord *and* Savior. Salvation is a gift we accept or reject; there are no other choices.

For the Christian, I picture it this way. We're standing before the throne of Jesus Christ. All of our deeds for this life are brought out. It's very evident that we deserve hell, because unless we're perfect, we certainly deserve eternal separation from our Creator. But then Christ steps down from that throne of judgment and stands beside us. He takes His robe of righteousness and puts it on us. And He says, "It's obvious you're guilty. Clearly, you deserve hell. But I have paid the penalty, I have taken the judgment you deserve upon Myself on the cross, and you have accepted this gift. May you live forever in the joy and gratitude of what I have done for you!"

And what a celebration of gratitude and praising of the Lord that will be.

Have you received, in faith, the unearned gift? The Christmas season is a good time to receive this gift and pass it on to others.

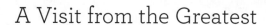

A Visit from the Greatest

*So the Word became human and made his home
among us. He was full of unfailing love and
faithfulness. And we have seen his glory, the glory
of the Father's one and only Son.*

John 1:14 NLT

Get the picture: It's a quiet day on the driving range. Two teens are hitting golf balls, trying to figure out the game. Suddenly, the world's number one player comes up and offers to give them a few tips on how to play.

What would you do if you were one of those guys? You would probably be issuing high fives, excitedly trying to convince your friends that the greatest player in the world had just humbled himself to spend time showing you the secrets of the game. It would be an awesome experience!

But do you understand that the story of Christmas is millions of times more awesome than this? For even though these teens might be in awe of that great player reaching out to them, the one true God of the Universe did something far more important. Jesus Christ became a man and dwelled among us, the ultimate expression of humility. And then He showed His love for us by coming to be our Savior and showing us how to play the game of life.

Having a great player show you how to hit golf balls would be a once-in-a-lifetime experience. But Jesus coming to earth as a baby? Now that is a story for the ages.

The Light of the World?

"You are the light of the world. A city on a hill cannot be hidden."

MATTHEW 5:14 NIV

Was Jesus contradicting Himself? In John 8:12, Jesus said, "'I am the Light of the world.'" And then, in Matthew 5:14, He said, "You are the light of the world." How can that be? Well, think about it this way. Let's say you are hiking on a clear night under a beautiful full moon. You're able to walk on those trails without a flashlight because the moon is so bright. But is it really? No, the moon actually produces no light on its own; it merely reflects light generated by the sun.

Do you see it? Jesus said that the Christian is the light of the world because when we accept Christ, His light dwells within us—others see His light through us. Have you ever noticed that unique sparkle in the eye of that Christ-centered life? Have you ever seen the deadness in the eyes of people who live far from God and get hardened over time? The eye is the window of the soul. It reveals what's there, what's inside. Well, Jesus said, "You are the light of the world," because when you receive Christ, His Spirit, His Light, dwells within you. You really are the "light of the world" whenever others see that reflection of the Son in you.

So Christian, let that Light shine!

The Real Story of Christmas

She will give birth to a son, and you are to give him the name Jesus, because he will save his people from their sins.

MATTHEW 1:21 NIV

I once heard a talk show host declare on one of his shows, "Let me share with you my story of Christmas. To me, Christmas is not about the birth of the baby. It is about what that baby grew up to become, how He decided to live His life and the choices and the sacrifices He made in the end. To me, Christmas points to the redemption, the redeeming power of that man." And I said to myself, "He is really getting it—the redemption of Christ." But then he followed by saying, "It's about starting over." And I said, "Uh-oh!" He went on to suggest that his listeners use the season to start over, wipe their slates clean, and become "who you really are"!

Talk show hosts like to say outrageous things, but the story of Christmas is not about starting over. Yes, the Christmas story is about God's love and grace and the humility and servanthood of the little baby who was born. That baby grew up to be a man, and He came to redeem for our heavenly Father what is rightfully His in the first place—our lives. He came to pay the greatest price for our redemption—His life, dying for our sins on the cross. The story of Christmas doesn't stop at the manger. It continues throughout the perfect, sinless life and the cross and the resurrection of the only Son of God. The story of Christmas is that the Father desires for every single one of us to be redeemed. Not to start over but to become whom God created us to be. Christ came to save us from whom we really are by transforming us into whom God wants us to be. That's the real story of Christmas!

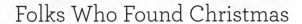
Folks Who Found Christmas

*He who comes to God must believe that He is and that
He is a rewarder of those who seek Him.*

HEBREWS 11:6

It's easy to miss the real meaning of Christmas, but the story of Christmas tells us who found it.

- *The shepherds.* They were social nobodies—yet God sent them a supernatural birth announcement through the angels. They believed God's word, and they searched in faith to find Jesus, and they did. They found Christmas.
- *The wise men,* pagans from another culture. They studied the stars for insight. God spoke to them where they were, and they stepped out on faith to follow a star that appeared in the sky, thinking it meant the birth of a special king, and they found Christmas—when they found Jesus.

The shepherds found Christmas because they believed the word of God. The wise men found Christmas because they sought Jesus. Find Jesus as Savior and Lord, and you'll find Christmas—*guaranteed*!

Folks Who Missed Christmas

*"Seeing they do not see, and while hearing they
do not hear, nor do they understand."*

MATTHEW 13:13

Christmas comes, Christmas goes. But many miss out on the real meaning of Christmas. It's always been that way, and the first Christmas reminds us of those who missed Christmas.

- *The innkeeper.* He was so busy. A full hotel . . . so many customer needs. No time or place in his inn for Jesus at Christmas.
- *The religious leaders.* When the wise men came inquiring about the birth of a kingly Messiah, the religious leaders told Herod that God's Word said He would come from Bethlehem. Yet they were so focused on staying close to worldly power that they didn't take God's Word seriously, and they missed Jesus at Christmas.
- *Herod.* He tried to eliminate Christmas before it got off the ground, and people are still seeking to use political power to do that today.

Will you miss Christmas as well? If you find Jesus personally through faith, you will never miss Christmas again.

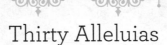

Thirty Alleluias

All day long we praise our God.
We give thanks to you forever.

PSALM 44:8 GW

The children's choir had just rehearsed a song they were performing that night. Although the song was technically correct, their performance was flat when it should have been joyous. The director tapped her baton. "Boys and girls, this song has only one word, *alleluia*. It means 'Praise the Lord.' But we sing that word thirty times." She continued, "Now, the way I figure it, getting a good grade on a test is worth one alleluia. Being allowed to have your best friend spend the night is worth a couple of alleluias. And let's say that getting that hot new video game is worth three alleluias." They all nodded their agreement. "But I want each of you to take a moment and imagine this. What is worth *thirty* alleluias to you?"

Like random fireflies, their faces lit up as each child imagined that one thing that would generate their thirty alleluias. After a few minutes the director said, "Now, tonight, when it comes time to sing this song, I want you to recall what really calls for thirty alleluias."

Some of the children understood. Some weren't so sure. But nothing deserves thirty alleluias like knowing that "Jesus loves me."

Jesus loves me! This I know,
For the Bible tells me so.
Little ones to Him belong;
They are weak, but He is strong.

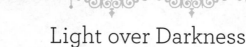

Light over Darkness

The Light shines in the darkness, and the darkness did not comprehend it.

JOHN 1:5

The candle-lighting service is a beautiful moment in our church's Christmas Eve celebration. When all the lights are out, we light a single candle, and that one candle overcomes all the darkness of the entire room. It's a wonderful demonstration that darkness cannot overpower light. Well, it's the same with spiritual darkness and the spiritual light of Jesus Christ. His Light will overpower the darkness.

There have been times in history when it seemed as though the spiritual darkness was overpowering the spiritual light. For instance, in the twentieth century, Marxism had great momentum. First, the Soviet revolution; then the Communist revolution in China; then Cuba, Eastern Europe, and Southeast Asia soon followed suit. It seemed as if the darkness of atheism was overpowering the light within the church. But by the end of the century, the Soviet Union was no more. Eastern Europe became the birthplace of many fledgling democracies. And not only that, do you realize that there may be more Christians in China than in the USA? Even though it sometimes seems as though darkness wins for a time, it never permanently overpowers the Light.

Of course, the greatest example of that is the cross. On Friday, it appeared that the devil had won. Darkness and evil had triumphed. But on Sunday, the Light was turned on, never to be snuffed out again. For in the end, the Light of Jesus always overpowers the darkness.

O Holy Night!

*And the angel said unto them, Fear not: for, behold, I
bring you good tidings of great joy, which shall be to all
people. For unto you is born this day in the city of David
a Saviour, which is Christ the Lord.*

LUKE 2:10–11 KJV

Every Christmas Eve service, the members of our church are blessed to hear our worship pastor sing "O Holy Night." This has become such a tradition at our church that the thought of a Christmas Eve service without it is, well, hard to imagine!

"O Holy Night" was set to music by Adolphe Adam in 1847 to the lyrics of a French poem written by Placide Cappeau, a wine merchant and poet. Cappeau had been asked to write a Christmas poem by a parish priest.[26]

The music is so beautiful that we sometimes fail to notice the perfection of the lyrics. May these lyrics help you contemplate the wonder and blessing of Jesus' birth.

O holy night! The stars are brightly shining,
It is the night of our dear Savior's birth.
Long lay the world in sin and error pining,
Till He appear'd and the soul felt its worth.
A thrill of hope the weary world rejoices,
For yonder breaks a new and glorious morn.
Fall on your knees! Oh, hear the angels' voices!
O night divine, O night when Christ was born;
O night divine, O night, O night divine.

Merry Christmas!

No Crib for a Bed

*And she gave birth to her first son. Because there were
no rooms left in the inn, she wrapped the baby with
pieces of cloth and laid him in a feeding trough.*

LUKE 2:7 NCV

Read it again. This is the New Century Version's rendering of one of the most familiar pieces of scripture in the Bible. What's that? Not quite the way you recall the story? You ask, "What happened to the soft, swaddling clothes and the quaint little manger?" It's easy for us to sanitize the reality of the situation, and thereby remove some of the irony. The fact is, the Savior of the human race, the King of kings and Lord of lords, was wrapped in rags and set to rest in an icky trough that was used to feed pigs and cows.

Why would a mother allow this for her child? Well, she had no choice because there was no room for them anywhere else. Perhaps a better question would be, why would our Father permit His Child to be treated in this manner? Well, in addition to prophecy being fulfilled, maybe God also knew that His Child had to experience humanity. He needed to know what it was like to be homeless, helpless, and in poverty. Later, He needed to understand hunger, the deaths of loved ones, persecution, and even His own death. Jesus needed to experience humankind—as He came to die for humankind.

And that, my friends, is the real, unvarnished Christmas story.

The Gift to the Wise Men

When they saw the star, they were overjoyed. On coming to the house, they saw the child with his mother Mary, and they bowed down and worshiped him. Then they opened their treasures and presented him with gifts of gold and of incense and of myrrh.

MATTHEW 2:10–11 NIV

When we think of the wise men who visited Jesus, we normally picture the gifts they brought. But if you look closer, you will realize that the real story of the wise men is not just what they gave, but what they received. Look at what happened after they acknowledged the star that would lead them to Jesus: Matthew wrote, "When they saw the star, they were overjoyed!" You don't have to be a Bible scholar to get it. They were filled with joy and emotion because they were going to do what all of us are created to do—meet the King of all kings. All they could do was submit to Jesus and worship their newfound King.

If you've never encountered Christ, the good news is that, today, He waits for you. He desires to give you a life of deep joy and satisfaction . . . with a big bonus: an eternity with Him. That's the good news of Christmas.

And if you do know Christ, rejoice that every day you have the privilege of worshipping the King. And one day we will join the wise men and that everlasting throng that will worship Him forever as we see Him, the King of kings and Lord of all!

Discouragement over Money

*I know what it is to be in need, and I know what it is
to have plenty. I have learned the secret of being
content in any and every situation, whether well fed
or hungry, whether living in plenty or in want. I can
do everything through him who gives me strength.*

PHILIPPIANS 4:12–13 NIV

Several years ago, after Christmas, I began to sort through the
bills. What a sobering experience. First I paid the MasterCard
bill and then my quarterly estimated state and federal taxes.
This was followed by out-of-state college tuition—a 17 percent
increase that year. (At that point I had that mental picture of a
giant vacuum cleaner in the sky, sucking up all the money we had.)
Then I checked on our retirement account, noting it had, for the
third year in a row, dropped double digits. I began to have this
sinking feeling. I was really discouraged.

Then it was as if the Lord said, *Haven't you paid all your bills?
Haven't I met all of your needs? Haven't I* always *met all of your
needs? What makes you think that after all these years of so-called
spiritual maturity, I'm no longer going to meet your needs?*

That was very convicting. Then the Lord said to my heart,
*Bryant, it never was yours in the first place. And whether you're riding
high for one year and down in the dumps the next,* that's My decision. *It has always been My decision. It has never been yours. I'm just
interested in your managing what I entrust to you to the best of your
ability. Trust Me with the rest.*

Thanks, God. I needed that!

Symphony

*For You are my rock and my fortress ... You
will lead me and guide me.*

PSALM 31:3

What is the most important position in the symphony orchestra? Some would say it's the violinist, because the violins often carry the melody. Others would argue for the musician who plays their favorite instrument. The fact is that the conductor has the most important role of all. Without him, the players would easily go their own way, and disharmony and chaos would result. A master conductor leads the symphony to make great music. Without a good conductor, there is no music—only noise.

I have good news for you when it comes to living life successfully. God has provided a Master Conductor. His name is Jesus Christ. When all in His church submit in faith to His leadership, He provides perfect direction and guidance for our lives. He shows us how to work well with other people.

Why not allow the Master Conductor to guide your life? Instead of discord and disharmony, He'll help you hit the right notes every single time!

Life's Certainties

In reply Jesus declared, "I tell you the truth, no one can see the kingdom of God unless he is born again."

JOHN 3:3 NIV

In November 1789, Benjamin Franklin wrote these words: "In this world, nothing can be said to be certain except death and taxes." We realize one of those certainties each year as we face the deadline for filing taxes. And someday we will all face that other certainty, because for every life, there is death. In fact, the stats on death are 100 percent. Even Jesus had to face death.

Although wise Ben correctly identified those two certainties, there is a third one he failed to mention. No one has ever received the gift of eternal life *after* they died. Not one! If you have not received eternal life in this life, then when you die, it is too late for you to receive it. God made it easy for us. He sent His Son, Jesus, to die on a wooden cross for our sins. Then, three days later, He rose victorious from the grave, in order that we might receive eternal life in this life.

We have no control over two certainties of life—death and taxes. But there's a third certainty we have complete control over. If you have not accepted this gift today, what are you waiting for?

Another year without eternal life is another wasted year.

How Sweet the Sound!

Then King David went in and sat before the LORD, and he said: "Who am I, O LORD God, and what is my family, that you have brought me this far? And as if this were not enough in your sight, O God, you have spoken about the future of the house of your servant. You have looked on me as though I were the most exalted of men, O LORD God."

1 CHRONICLES 17:16–17 NIV

Is any hymn more beloved than "Amazing Grace"? The lyrics do seem to sum up a Christian's journey of redemption, the divine grace of God, and the promise of eternal life. With its simply stated definition of *eternity*—"When we've been there ten thousand years . . . We've no less days to sing God's praise than when we've first begun"—it is no wonder that it is sung at many funerals. Understanding how the hymn came to be written deepens the meaning of the words. An Anglican priest, John Newton, used the hymn to reflect on his earlier service as captain of a slave ship. He was haunted by the evil of those deeds but was amazed that God would provide such grace despite his wretched past. Note the passion in his words:

Amazing grace, how sweet the sound that saved a wretch like me!
I once was lost, but now am found, was blind, but now I see. . . .
'Tis grace has brought me safe thus far, and grace will lead me home.

Know that if God gives grace to a man with this depth of sin, He can certainly forgive your past and open the gates of heaven to you for eternity. Why don't you trust in His grace today?

Are You In or Out?

"He who is not with Me is against Me."

LUKE 11:23

Church pews often fill up whenever there's been a great crisis. Shattering earthquakes, devastating hurricanes, evil terrorist attacks . . . they all prompt many to seek comfort and protection from their Creator. But realize this: you will be grossly disappointed if your motivation for coming back to God is to escape danger. God does not promise that we'll escape danger or even death. Whether it's a terrorist attack or a heart attack, whether it's a plane crash or a car crash, we will all face death.

Instead, come to the Lord with a spirit of repentance that says, "Lord, I realize how much of my life I've ignored Your will and focused on my own self-interests. God, I now come to You with a repentant spirit. I want to call on the forgiveness and salvation of Christ. I know it's a dangerous world we live in, but, Lord, I want to get things right with You from here on out. I want to do things Your way through the salvation of Christ and the teachings of Scripture."

Being ready for the hereafter is the best way to live for today. You will never be disappointed if you will take advantage of this opportune time to get right with God. He not only extends forgiveness but will give you the promise of abundant, eternal life with Him now and forever.

So what's it going to be? On this final day of the year, are you with God or not? You're either in or you're out.

Acknowledgments

Jack Countryman, founder of Thomas Nelson's gift division, and his wife, Marsha, for casting the vision and encouraging me to move forward with writing this book.

Laura Minchew, vice president and publisher of specialty books at Thomas Nelson, for her assistance in setting the project in motion.

Lisa Stilwell and Michelle Burke, Thomas Nelson editors, for their expertise in selecting and fine-tuning these devotionals.

The congregation of Johnson Ferry Baptist Church in Marietta, Georgia, for encouraging and strengthening me with their prayers. Many of these devotionals were gleaned from sermons I've preached as their senior pastor.

Jim Murphy, executive director of Right from the Heart Ministries, for his capable leadership in overseeing the operations of our ever-expanding ministry.

Mary Stephens, media director of Right from the Heart Ministries, for her creativity and invaluable assistance in typing, compiling, and editing these thoughts.

Marty and Joan Young, for their special support and encouragement.

Danette Ramsey and Barbara Leake, for their behind-the-scenes help in making this book become a reality.

My executive assistant, Olivia Mahon, who tirelessly keeps any ministry project I have going on track and on time.

My wife, Anne, the joy of my life and my confidante, adviser, and very best friend, who always offers insightful and helpful feedback.

Most of all, for God the Father who loves me; God the Son who saved me; and the Holy Spirit who teaches me how to understand God's Word and apply it to everyday life.

Notes

1. James S. Hewett, ed., *Illustrations Unlimited* (Carol Stream, IL: Tyndale, 1988), 99.
2. Mark Kelly, "LifeWay Research: Unchurched Americans Turned Off by Church, Open to Christians," LifeWay Research Web site, http://www.lifeway.com/article/?id=166950.
3. Cathy Lynn Grossman, "Survey: Non-Attendees Find Faith Outside Church," *USA Today*, January 9, 2008, http://www.usatoday.com/news/religion/2008-01-09-unchurched-survey_N.htm.
4. Harold Kushner, *When Bad Things Happen to Good People* (New York: Avon, 1981), 6.
5. William Bennett, "Does America Have a Future?" Hillsdale College, *Imprimis*, December 1998, http://www.hillsdale.edu/news/imprimis/archive/issue.asp?year=1998&month=12.
6. Meredith Ford, "What Women Really Want. Put Simply, It's Chocolate," *Marietta Daily Journal*, May 19, 2005.
7. Adapted from *The Andy Griffith Show*, season 3, episode 66, "Mr. McBeevee," aired October 1, 1962.
8. Dominique Enright, ed., *The Wicked Wit of Winston Churchill* (London: Michael O'Mara Books, 2001).
9. Alfred H. Ackley, "He Lives!" in *Celebration Hymnal* (Nashville: Word Entertainment, 1997), 368.
10. Stephen Hawking, *A Brief History of Time* (New York: Bantam, 1998), 191.
11. "Statistics/Opinion Polls," *Georgia Right to Life*, accessed March 1, 2011, http://www.grtl.org/statsandpolls.asp.

12. "Facts on Induced Abortion Worldwide," *Guttmacher Institute*, February 2011, accessed March 1, 2011, http://www.guttmacher.org/pubs/fb_IAW.html.

13. Norman L. Geisler, "Reasons for Our Hope—Why We Can Trust the Bible," *Decision Magazine*, Billy Graham Evangelistic Association (July–August 2006).

14. Edmund Morris, *Dutch: A Memoir of Ronald Reagan* (New York: Random House, 1999; repr. New York: Modern, 2000), 430.

15. James Patterson and Peter Kim, *The Day America Told the Truth: What People Really Believe About What Really Matters*, 1st ed. (Upper Saddle River, NJ: Prentice Hall, 1991), 199.

16. Jeanna Bryner, "Money Can Buy Happiness—If You Give It Away," *MSNBC.com*, March 20, 2008, http://www.msnbc.msn.com/id/23729084/ns/health-behavior.

17. Tom Elliff, "Kingdom Families," *SBC Life* (June/July 2004).

18. Bob Buford, *Half Time: Changing Your Game Plan from Success to Significance* (Grand Rapids: Zondervan, 1994).

19. Cathy Lynn Grossman, "Gay Episcopal Bishop Says, 'Holy Spirit Led Us,'" *USA Today*, October 21, 2004, http://www.usatoday.com/news/nation/2004-10-21-bishop_x.htm.

20. James Dobson, *Dr. Dobson Answers Your Questions* (Wheaton, IL: Tyndale, 1982), 345.

21. George Orwell, *Animal Farm*, with an introduction by Julian Symons (New York: Everyman's Library, 1993), 93.

22. Joe Gibbs, *Racing to Win* (Sisters, OR: Multnomah Books, 2003).

23. Howard Dayton, *Your Money Counts* (Carol Stream, IL: Tyndale), 46–47.

24. Ron Blue, *The Debt Squeeze* (Pomona, CA: Focus on the Family Publishing, 1989), 95.

25. Harvey A. Hook, *The Power of an Ordinary Life: Discovering the Extraordinary Possibilities Within (Transforming the World One Day at a Time)* (Carol Stream, IL: Tyndale, 2007), 96.

26. Ace Collins, *Stories Behind the Best-Loved Songs of Christmas* (Grand Rapids: Zondervan, 2001), 132–138.